GW00579417

Terror in Ireland
1916–1923

*In memory of Peter David Hart,
born 11 November 1963,
died 22 July 2010.*

Terror in Ireland
1916–1923

edited by David Fitzpatrick

Trinity History Workshop

THE LILLIPUT PRESS
DUBLIN

First published 2012 by
THE LILLIPUT PRESS
62–63 Sitric Road, Arbour Hill,
Dublin 7, Ireland
www.lilliputpress.ie

Copyright © The Lilliput Press and individual contributors, 2012

All rights reserved. No part of this publication may
be reproduced in any form or by any means
without the prior permission of the publisher.

A CIP record for this title is available
from The British Library.

1 3 5 7 9 10 8 6 4 2

ISBN 978 1 84351 199 1

Set in 10 on 13.5 pt Sabon by Marsha Swan
Printed in Spain by GraphyCems, Villatuerta, Navarra

Contents

Illustrations

Abbreviations

BMH	Bureau of Military History
CC	Chief Constable
CI	County Inspector
CID	Criminal Investigation Department
CILI	Court of Inquiry in Lieu of Inquest
CMO	Courts Martial Officer
CO	Colonial Office
CS	Chief of Staff
DD	DÉ, *Parliamentary Debates: Official Report*
DÉ	Dáil Éireann
DED	District Electoral Division
DMP	Dublin Metropolitan Police
CO	Colonial Office
DORA(R)	Defence of the Realm Acts (Regulations)
FJ	*Freeman's Journal*
GOC	General Officer Commanding
GSO(1)	General Staff Officer (1st Grade)
HC(P)	House of Commons (Papers)
HL	House of Lords
HO	Home Office
ICA	Irish Citizen Army
IG	Inspector General
II	*Irish Independent*
IRA(B)	Irish Republican Army (Brotherhood)
IT	*The Irish Times*
IWM	Imperial War Museum, London
LHC	Liddell Hart Centre, King's College, London

MAD	Military Archives, Dublin
MCR	Monthly Confidential Report
MO	Medical Officer
MP	Member of Parliament
MS(S)	Manuscript(s)
NAD	National Archives, Dublin
NAL	National Archives, London
NLI	National Library of Ireland, Dublin
OC	Officer Commanding
OMN	O'Malley Notebooks, UCDA
OS	Ordnance Survey
PD	*The Parliamentary Debates: Official Report*
RDC	Rural District Council
RIC	Royal Irish Constabulary
RTÉ	Radio Telefís Éireann
RUC	Royal Ulster Constabulary
TC	Town Commissioner
TCD	Trinity College, Dublin
TD	Teachta Dáil
Thom's	*Thom's Official Directory*
UCD(A)	University College, Dublin (Archives)
UDC	Urban District Council
UVF	Ulster Volunteer Force
WS	Witness Statement, BMH

1. Introduction

David Fitzpatrick

I

Revolutionary terror is a topic of never-failing public interest, periodically revived by horrific news of contemporary attacks on civilians by revolutionaries or by oppressive régimes. In Ireland, the desire to analyse and interpret terrorism in the revolutionary period has been heightened by later conflicts in Northern Ireland, still not fully resolved. Did the British government organize, or collude in, a campaign of counter-revolutionary terror conducted by 'murder squads' or an 'Anti-Sinn Féin Society'? Did the IRA, or maverick groups within it, select certain groups of civilians as 'targets' for terrorism, and, if so, why? How did the new government manage to apply coercion during the Civil War on an unprecedented scale, without following the example of its predecessor by losing legitimacy and popular support? To what extent did civilians endorse or subvert the various campaigns of terror that demanded their loyalty and claimed to act on their behalf?

Since its creation in 1986, the Trinity History Workshop has published four volumes of essays by undergraduate and graduate students (past and present) and staff associated with Trinity College, Dublin. These books continue to be widely read and cited, partly because they addressed topics in modern Irish history which had been neglected by academic historians. I myself edited *Ireland and the First World War* (1986, reissued with The Lilliput Press, 1988) and *Revolution? Ireland, 1917–1923* (1990); David Dickson edited *The Gorgeous Mask: Dublin, 1700–1850* (1987) and *The Hidden Dublin: The Social and Sanitary Conditions of Dublin's Working Classes in 1845 Described by Thomas Willis* (2002). The

purpose of this book is to present fresh findings by historians, associated with Trinity College, who have worked on aspects of terror
and its victims. As befits a Workshop, most chapters have been
substantially modified as a result of seminar and class discussions,
not to mention editorial interference in matters of style and presen-
tation. The outcome is a truly collaborative work of scholarship, in
which students distinctly hold their own in the company of professional historians.

Versions of eight chapters were delivered to the Workshop's
inaugural seminar in November 2010; three chapters were dis-
tilled from undergraduate research essays; and two were specially
commissioned from postgraduate students with relevant interests.
Thomas Earls FitzGerald, Michael Murphy and Ross O'Mahony
are Sophister students at Trinity College who took a course on 'Revolution and Civil War in Ireland' in 2010–11. Brian Hughes is a
doctoral student at Trinity College; Eve Morrison, Gerard Noonan
and Justin Dolan Stover have all been doctored since the inaugura-
tion of the Workshop. Jane Leonard, who contributed three chapters to earlier Workshop volumes, is the author of several studies
of conflict and commemoration in twentieth-century Ireland. Brian
Hanley and Fearghal McGarry, both holders of doctorates from
Trinity College and authors of several books on modern Ireland,
teach history in the University of Liverpool and the Queen's University of Belfast. Anne Dolan, Eunan O'Halpin and the editor all
teach at Trinity College and have published extensively in the field.

For financial assistance in organizing the seminar and publication, the Workshop is deeply grateful to the TCD Association and
Trust, the Arts and Social Sciences Benefactions Fund, and David
Ditchburn on behalf of the Department of History. We are also
indebted to Antony Farrell and Fiona Dunne of The Lilliput Press
for exempting us from some of the chores, rewarding yet tedious,
associated with publication. The Workshop has come a long way
since 1986, when its exclusively undergraduate contributors developed auxiliary skills as designers, photographers, typesetters,
printers, paper-folders, fund-raisers, marketeers and distributors.

II

The current Workshop was inspired by the early and lamented death in July 2010 of Peter Hart, a contributor to *Revolution?* who went on to hold a Canada Council chair in Irish history at the Memorial University of Newfoundland, St John. Having studied at the Queen's University in Kingston, Ontario and then Yale, he spent four productive years at Trinity College before being doctored in 1992. As a research student, he was remarkably self-assured and self-sufficient, a supervisor's dream, slow to deliver drafts until a deluge of polished, eloquent chapters surged forth in the final months. His thesis had the rare distinction of being accepted exactly as it stood, and was subsequently published as *The I.R.A. and Its Enemies: Violence and Community in Cork, 1916–23* (1998). Despite serious illness during the decade before his death at the age of forty-six, he maintained a steady flow of publications, conference papers and spirited dialogue with those who challenged his findings. His provocative and well-documented thesis-book and essays on *The I.R.A. at War, 1916–1923* (2003), followed by *Mick: The Real Michael Collins* (2005), touched many raw nerves in Ireland and continue to arouse controversy. I remember him still as a brilliant boy, audacious yet unruffled.

In my view, he was a model for historians invading contentious territory: more interested in the dynamics of violence than its morality; lacking any clear political convictions beyond a preference for peace; lucid, sceptical, mild-mannered and unpretentious in his prose and debating style; adept at deploying sensational material to provoke discussion rather than to bully his readers; skilful in sifting and interpreting primary sources, if occasionally careless in citing them; influential in arousing academic and popular interest in the topics that he tackled. Hart's fair-minded and compassionate scholarship was recognized in 1999 when his first book was awarded the Ewart-Biggs Memorial Prize. This remarkable work set the agenda for several recent studies by concentrating on Cork, the county most affected by revolutionary violence. In a contentious analysis of Tom Barry's assertion that the execution of soldiers at Kilmichael in November 1920 was justified by their 'false surrender', Hart argued that Barry had invented the episode in order to disguise his own dishonorable conduct as a commandant. The reliability of Barry's account and Hart's critique are assessed by Eve Morrison, in a chapter based on witness statements for the Bureau of Military History and other oral testimony not previously made public.

The I.R.A. and Its Enemies also revealed that over 200 civilians in the county were killed by the IRA, of whom 36% were Protestants, five times the Protestant proportion in Cork's population. Though these victims were usually identified as 'spies' or 'informers', Hart argued that many were selected as 'soft targets' on the basis of flimsy intelligence. Republican terrorism intensified in late 1920 and early 1921, in a 'tit-for-tat' cycle of reprisals and punishments for which uncontrolled Crown forces were at least equally culpable. But the fact that such killings peaked in early 1922, during the Truce period, suggested vengeance against various detested groups, now that the country was virtually unpoliced. Republican suspicions, all too often, were based on categorical assumptions about the unpatriotic disposition and corruptibility of groups such as declared 'loyalists', Freemasons, Orangemen, ex-servicemen, military deserters, ex-policemen, those associated in any way with the Crown forces or administration, and, most contentiously, Protestants. The execution of alleged 'spies' and 'informers', and the extent to which they were victims of sectarianism, are issues further explored in Thomas Earls FitzGerald's chapter on West Cork in early 1921.

In essays such as 'The Protestant Experience of Revolution', first published in 1996 and reissued in *The I.R.A. at War*, Hart went further. He suggested that killings, raids, and arson were the tip of an iceberg of social exclusion and personal harassment amounting to 'what might be termed "ethnic cleansing"' (p. 237). This analysis called into question the morality and sincerity of the republican movement, which strenuously disavowed sectarianism and defined the enemy as Britain and her Irish garrison. Hart's findings outraged readers for whom the integrity of the revolutionaries of 1916–21 was an article of faith. Even many who deplored and despised the actions of the IRA's purported successors in Northern Ireland believed, or wished to believe, that the revolutionaries retained and acted on the high principles and motives attributed to the men and women of 1916. More sceptical analysts also judged the revolutionaries leniently by comparison with modern terrorists. Their revolution was much briefer than the Northern 'Troubles', they were less well armed and less ruthlessly efficient, the illegitimacy of their 'British' adversary was more demonstrable, and they enjoyed much broader public support (or at least acquiescence).

Whether for political, sentimental or historical reasons, Hart's hypotheses of 'ethnic cleansing' and republican duplicity have provoked a steady stream of academic criticism and also counter-'revisionist' polemic, often ugly and personally offensive. Any slip in Hart's footnotes is construed by some bloggers and letter-writers as deliberate falsification in pursuit of a preconceived revisionist agenda. Such enthusiasts may be reassured that there is no need for an intellectual guerrilla campaign against counter-insurgents masquerading as academic historians. This book is not an apologia for revisionism or for Peter Hart, but an attempt to restore balance and decorum to a debate of crucial importance to modern Irish history. Terror, more than most topics, is best discussed calmly and dispassionately.

III

First, some working definitions. *Terror*, apart from being a state of mind, may be defined as a conscious attempt to create an acute fear of violence against the person or property, which may affect individuals, groups or the population at large. *Terrorists* are those who perpetrate any form of terror, for any purpose. *Terrorism* implies a sustained and systematic attempt to generate terror. To make sense of terror, it is necessary to break down the concept according to its origins, rationale, practitioners, targets, forms and consequences.

Terror as practised in revolutionary Ireland had multiple and cosmopolitan origins. Within Ireland itself, characteristic techniques and rituals had evolved over centuries of agrarian, sectarian and republican agitation. Strong echoes of past Ribbon, Orange, and Fenian campaigns were audible in the Irish troubles from 1916 to 1923. But Irish revolutionaries also drew on the growing terrorist repertoire of communism, anti-colonialism and feminism, forming productive international alliances of convenience in the United States and Europe. The unusual severity of state terror after the 1916 rebellion, though exploiting 'coercion acts' introduced to quash nineteenth-century challenges, was largely a product of the subordination of political to military imperatives during the Great War. The governments of the new Irish states reapplied many of the coercive measures and methods devised by Lloyd George's administration, sometimes with even greater ruthlessness. The forms of revolutionary and counter-insurgent terror were therefore the outcome of a long and complex process of experiment and imitation.

Terror may constitute a deliberate strategy to isolate adversaries from their own communities, to provoke counter-terror from adversaries in order to reinforce popular support for the terrorists, or to threaten and marginalize 'deviants' within the community that the terrorists claim to represent. In other cases, its rationale is simply revenge, giving rise to the cycles of 'tit-for-tat terror' that so interested Hart. Terror may also signify indiscriminate violence occasioned by fear of unknown adversaries, frustration at one's inability to identify the enemy, or anarchic delight in destruction when normal inhibitions are lifted. A central issue for those confronting terror is to determine how far it is strategically planned and centrally directed, and how far it is irrational, uncontrolled and localized. Strategic terror invites a strategic response from adversaries, which may be more or less effective; irrational terror can only be counteracted, if at all, by the exercise of internal discipline within the responsible groups. For historians trying to assess the effectiveness of guerrilla warfare and counter-insurgency, the distinction between strategic and irrational terror is crucial.

As Brian Hanley's chapter points out, responsibility for terror in twentieth-century Ireland has been shared by many groups, including republicans, social radicals, loyalists and agents of the state. Within each group, terror has been propagated not merely by armed activists but by the politicians, propagandists and unarmed supporters who contribute to the desired climate of fear. In moral or legal terms, it might be argued that those practising violence are more culpable than those abetting violence, or that state-directed terror is more legitimate than that undertaken against the state or between unofficial groups. Others might maintain that any action tending to further Irish independence, however distasteful, is justified by the intended outcome. Historians, however, should take care to banish such moral judgments from academic analysis, whose primary function is to explain what occurred by assessing events from the perspectives of victim, perpetrator and onlooker alike.

The range of targets or victims of terror is even broader than that of its perpetrators. In its simplest and least effective variant, terrorism is an informal version of a traditional war, being primarily directed against identified adversaries, who may not, however, be armed or uniformed. As demonstrated in Jane Leonard's forensic biographical study of those attacked by the IRA on Bloody Sunday morning, terror directed against unarmed or off-duty targets, often misidentified as intelligence agents, was a recurrent and bloody ingredient of terror in revolutionary Ireland. Terror restricted to enemy combatants seldom prevails in civil conflicts, since opposing forces quickly raise a defensive shield that renders the targeted groups less accessible and, in some cases, virtually invulnerable. Hence the range of targets is often extended to embrace relatives and associates of identified adversaries, as Brian Hughes and Justin Dolan Stover show in their chapters on violence affecting policemen and prison officers. An even softer target is the 'collaborator' accused of sheltering, sustaining or supplying information to adversaries. As obvious 'enemies' move out of range, the terrorist is tempted to punish not only authenticated collaborators, 'spies' and 'informers', but also members of suspect sub-groups who might be disposed to act as collaborators. This form of terrorism, though ostensibly directed against the state or rival groups, typically concentrates on 'deviants' and 'traitors' within one's own camp.

The most far-reaching form of terrorism, however, is that directed against entire communities accused of sustaining adversaries. This may embody a self-conscious strategy for isolating enemy terrorists from their own communities (as with 'official reprisals'); or panic attacks motivated by revenge or frustration (as with many 'unofficial reprisals'); or sectarian conflict, intended to promote the common interest of one community at the expense of another (as with the so-called 'pogroms' and counter-terror that tore Belfast apart between 1920 and 1922). According to Gerard Noonan's chapter, revenge for state-directed violence in Ireland lay behind most republican terrorism in Britain, such as incendiary attacks on warehouses and farm buildings. The logic and consequences of unofficial reprisals are analysed in two chapters on the 'Sack of Balbriggan' in September 1920. Ross O'Mahony shows how one night of reprisals transformed a relatively peaceful district into the scene of 'tit-for-tat terror' spanning several months; while the editor identifies those compensated for malicious injuries and constructs a collective profile of victims utterly unlike that of revolutionary activists. Like the increasing focus of republican terror on deviants and traitors within the 'nation', reprisals against local communities were a sure sign of failure (military, political and moral). The more elusive the enemy, the less discriminate terrorist attacks became, so tending to discredit the perpetrators and to weaken popular support for their cause.

Terror in revolutionary Ireland was instilled by a variety of means, many of which are illustrated in Anne Dolan's chapter. These included violent attacks on individuals or their property; indiscriminate attacks on crowds, 'suspicious' strangers, public buildings or transport; 'boycotts', exemplary punishments, abuse or humiliation; threats of violence calculated to inspire fear; and displays of power designed to awe and intimidate both enemies and recalcitrants. The task of cataloguing and counting the cost of revolutionary terror has scarcely begun, but Eunan O'Halpin's report on *The Dead of the Irish Revolution* summarizes the most ambitious attempt so far to categorize all fatalities resultant from political violence between 1916 and 1921. Though fatalities are better documented than any other manifestations of terror, untapped sources such as compensation records also invite systematic studies of the broader impact of terrorism on Irish life.

Over the revolutionary period, the practice of terrorism was radically altered, as all protagonists discarded their initial inhibitions, devised new tactics to cope with increasingly effective opposition, and expressed their growing frustration in ever more ruthless brutality. The code of honour and fair play observed by the rebels of 1916, as portrayed in Fearghal McGarry's chapter, rapidly disintegrated as the 'War of Independence' degenerated into a morass of ambushes and assassinations in the year preceding the Truce. Likewise, the admittedly crass and coercive attempts to restore 'law

and order' between 1916 and 1919 soon seemed benign, by comparison with the campaign of reprisals against civilians conducted
by paramilitary police in 1920. The Civil War caused further muta-
tion, as anti-Treaty 'Irregulars' attempted to maintain guerrilla
resistance in the absence of widespread popular support, while the
new government applied state terror through systematic executions
on a scale never attempted by the old régime. These issues are raised
in Michael Murphy's chapter on the unexpectedly vicious Civil War
in Kildare, a county where the economic importance of the British
military presence had discouraged vigorous prosecution of the War
of Independence. Otherwise, most contributors concentrate on the
Anglo–Irish struggle rather than the civil conflicts that ravaged both
Southern and Northern Ireland in its aftermath.

   Though this book cannot claim to encompass the entire terrain
of its title, it deploys documentary evidence, often recently released,
to confront major unsettled questions about the legacy of terror.
What effects did the practice of terror have on the morale and mentality of its targets, and also of its perpetrators? What was its broader
impact on the families, friends and descendants of the protagonists?
How important were terrorist acts and threats in further alienating
the Irish from the English, and Irish Protestants from Irish Catholics? To what extent, and in what sense, was terrorism effective?
Did any protagonist gain from the use of terror between 1916 and
1923? On the whole, the contributors offer a bleak assessment of
the origins, practice and consequences of revolutionary terror. Hov-
ering in the background is another question, requiring a broader
political analysis outside the scope of this book. Could a mutually
acceptable Irish settlement have been achieved without the widespread use of terror? If so, how much was lost as the result of an
unpredictable chain of events, instigated by the perverse determination of a few hundred rebels to challenge the British government of
Ireland in 1916? What, then, was the ultimate cost of terror?

2. Terror in Twentieth-Century Ireland
Brian Hanley

The use of the term 'terror' in relation to political violence, in Ireland and elsewhere, is problematic. Its derivative 'terrorist' is generally seen as pejorative and is rarely, if ever, accepted by those to whom it is applied. Many would reject D. J. Whittaker's contention that what he calls 'social "facilitation"' leads to tolerance for 'terrorism':

> This concept refers to social habits and historical traditions that sanction the use of violence against the government, making it morally and politically justifiable ... Social myths, traditions, and habits permit the development of terrorism as an established political custom. An excellent example of such a tradition is the case of Ireland, where the tradition of physical force dates from the eighteenth century, and the legend of Michael Collins in 1919–21 still inspires and partially excuses the much less discriminate and less effective terrorism of the contemporary Provisional IRA.[1]

By contrast, Sinn Féin's Gerry Kelly has suggested that 'a Palestinian, a US Congressman, a British soldier or an Irishman will have different views on what a just war is. There is no one definition of a just war, or of terrorism.' Gerry Adams has stated that, for him, terrorism involves the 'deliberate targeting of civilians. In my view the IRA has never deliberately targeted civilians.'[2] Many who honour the memory of Michael Collins or Edward Carson would likewise deny that 'terror' was part of the strategy behind the campaigns that brought the two Irish states into being. It is worth noting that historians are not immune to viewing this subject from their own political standpoints.

The *Oxford English Dictionary* offers a number of definitions of terror: 'the state of being terrified or greatly frightened; intense fear, fright, or dread; ... a state of things in which the general community live in dread of death or outrage; ... a policy intended to strike with terror those against whom it is adopted; the employment of methods of intimidation; the fact of terrorizing or condition of being terrorized.'³ Any act of violence, even if directed at specific targets, can lead to feelings of terror, so defined. There are many examples of this in the Irish context. A recurrent aspect of twentieth-century violence in Ireland was forcing people from their homes or workplaces, threatening them with future violence or otherwise making their lives intolerable. Such violence often had an inter-communal or sectarian aspect, as with the expulsion of Belfast Catholics and dissident Protestants from their workplaces in 1912 and 1920, or the wider attacks on northern nationalists between 1920 and 1922. Further riots and disorder forcing major population movements occurred in Belfast in July 1935, August 1969 and August 1971.

As Richard English observes, a number of other definitions of terrorism have suggested that it is primarily violence directed against non-combatants. Thus Kydd and Walter, in *The Strategies of Terrorism*, define it as 'the use of violence against civilians by non-state actors to attain political goals'. The US State Department describes terrorism as 'premeditated, politically motivated violence perpetrated against noncombatant targets by subnational groups or clandestine agents, usually intended to influence an audience'. Conor Gearty maintains that 'violence is unequivocally terrorist when it is politically motivated and carried out by sub-state groups; when its victims are chosen at random; and when the purpose behind the violence is to communicate the message to a wider audience'.⁴ Under these definitions, neither the Kilmichael ambush of November 1920 nor the preceding assassinations of military and intelligence personnel on Bloody Sunday were terrorist acts. In both cases the targets of the IRA were military or state actors, not civilians or non-combatants.

The emphasis in these definitions on 'sub-state groups' is clearly problematic, as states can, and do, engage in similar forms of terrorism. 'The Terror' was a term originally applied to 'Government by intimidation' in Robespierre's France (1793–4). Likewise, the British state in Ireland, and both Irish states after 1921, were prepared to utilize terror tactics. In 1920–2, Crown forces were involved in forcing people from their homes, destroying property and intimidating and killing citizens. Well-known examples include the reprisals in Banbridge, Dromore and Lisburn and the burning of Cork City centre in 1920.[5]

Describing such actions of the British state in the revolutionary era as 'terrorist' is not problematic for Irish nationalists. More controversial has been the suggestion that the IRA in that era carried out actions that might be defined as sectarian terror, an argument that inspired much of the debate on Peter Hart's *The I.R.A. and Its Enemies*. Hart examined the impact on West Cork's Protestant population of a number of shootings in April 1922, documenting the fear that these killings produced and the flight that they helped provoke. Along with his allegations about the conduct of the IRA during the Kilmichael ambush, Hart's interpretation touched a raw nerve. His work was enthusiastically endorsed by polemicists and self-publicists, eager to utilize his research for their own purposes. This further muddied the waters, as battle lines were drawn not just on the basis of what was said, but what was presumed to have been said.[6] Though an early republican reviewer had stated that Hart's work (along with that of Joost Augusteijn and David Fitzpatrick) 'would add to anybody's understanding of the reasons behind many of the military strategies implemented during the revolutionary period', the debate degenerated into a tussle between those who felt duty-bound to defend the honour of the IRA, and those who wished to denounce them.[7] Hart's use of the term 'ethnic cleansing' to describe the events in West Cork certainly did not clarify the issue.[8] As he himself later admitted, there was 'no ethnic cleansing in the Irish revolution (though the attacks on Catholics in Belfast came close) but there was ethnically targeted violence'. Hart also conceded that 'Unionist organizations embraced or acquiesced in sectarianism in a way nationalist ones – to their credit – did not'.[9]

The killings in West Cork had already been documented by republican activist Jim Lane, almost forty years ago:

> In April 1922, at the time of the Truce, a pogrom every bit as vicious as any one in Belfast, took place in West Cork. Following

the shooting dead of an IRA officer by a Protestant, armed men visited Protestant homes in the districts surrounding Bandon, and on one day alone nine Protestants were shot dead. A young boy of 18 years was shot in his home in Clonakilty, a married man with a young family was shot in Dunmanway, as well as two old men in their 70s and 80s. Elsewhere, in Ballineen, Enniskeane, and Castletown–Kenneigh the story was similar, a knock at the door at dead of night and the men of the house were taken out and shot before their families. By the weekend Protestants poured out of West Cork, taking the Rosslare boat to Britain. The week was finished off with the shooting of an old Protestant, aged over 70 years and crippled with arthritis.

Lane made clear that what differentiated that Cork case from killings of Catholics in Belfast was that, unlike the unionist government, Sinn Féin immediately condemned the killings and republicans moved to prevent any more.[10] In the south, at least, these killings were exceptional, though the IRA's retaliation at Altnaveigh, for B-Special violence in the South Armagh area during 1922, was also designed to instil terror.[11]

Many were genuinely shocked and upset by the idea that the 'old' IRA might have engaged in a sectarian slaughter that played a part in forcing people from their homes and indeed from Ireland. In some cases this reflected a long-standing desire among supporters of constitutional nationalism to draw a sharp distinction between the 'old' IRA and the modern version. As a nephew of the 'Big Fella' argued passionately in 1996, Michael Collins had 'kept the fight to the fighting areas, whereas the IRA has committed countless acts on violence on civilians in the past 25 years. That sort of violence did not happen in Collins's time.' This was a view endorsed by many enthused by Neil Jordan's movie of the same year, with one young cinema-goer claiming that 'everybody knows the modern IRA are some of the most highly-trained terrorists in the world. The film shows that in 1920 they were only boys, most of them.'[12] That such views were sincerely held was not surprising, given that they were endorsed by some historians. Speaking at Béal na mBláth in August 1982, John A. Murphy had argued that the 'urban terrorist violence of the last 12 years ... had no counterpart in the events of 60 years ago, at least not on the Irish side'. Then, he argued, the republicans

had possessed 'a popular vote, a popular mandate, the popular will
– this is what crucially distinguishes the IRA of Collins's day from
today's gunmen and bombers'. While accepting that many of those
killed by the IRA had been Irish policemen, Murphy asserted that
'the enemy fought by Michael Collins was undoubtedly the British
Crown and its imperial servants', who were 'devoid of popular
support in the greater part of Ireland.' He contrasted this with the
Provisional IRA, 'a self-appointed group' without a 'mandate' who
wished to 'terrorise the whole Unionist community'. Collins in contrast, Murphy claimed, had 'ruled out the coercion of the Unionists
in the north-east'.[13]

Partly in response to claims such as Murphy's, many of the more
brutal (and, for nationalists, unpalatable) aspects of the IRA campaign had been documented in *The Good Old IRA*, published by
the Sinn Féin Publicity Department in 1985. Its aim was to answer
critics of the Provisional IRA who drew a distinction between the
war waged by Collins and that being carried out by the Provi-
sionals. This pamphlet included details of the shooting as alleged
informers of dozens of ex-soldiers, cases where civilians (including
women and children) were killed in cross-fire, and many killings of
unarmed police and military. It did not claim to be:

> a definitive list of IRA operations in the 1919–21 period. Indeed,
> the majority of attacks on RIC men, Black and Tans and regular sol-
> diers are not included. Nor is the death of every civilian recorded.
> This list is morbid enough and is intended to illustrate a number
> of important points to confront those hypocritical revisionists who
> winsomely refer to the 'Old IRA' whilst deriding their more effec-
> tive and, arguably, less bloody successors.

Furthermore: 'Even if these operations are shocking revelations
to those who have a romantic notion of the past then the risk of
their disillusionment is worth the price of finally exposing the
hypocrisy of those in the establishment who rest self-righteously
on the rewards of those who in yesteryear's freedom struggle made
the supreme sacrifice.' Confronting criticism that the Provisional
campaign was being waged against fellow Irishmen, the pamphlet
argued that 'the reality is that in any colonial war native agents and
informers, be they of the same or opposite race, religion, colour or

creed, were struck down for being agents and informers. The same is true today.' Far from claiming that the armed struggle had then possessed a democratic mandate, *The Good Old IRA* asserted that 'nobody was asked to vote for war' in December 1918 and implied that constitutional nationalists had been intimidated from standing against Sinn Féin in 1921, leaving republicans 'not so much elected as selected '. As for freedom of the press and other niceties, it noted that Collins had once ordered the destruction of printing machinery at the *Irish Independent* at gunpoint.[14] It was stirringly 'revisionist' stuff and would have been roundly denounced, if from the pen of someone critical of the IRA, old or new.

Much debate arose from Hart's assertion that the IRA had killed Auxiliaries at Kilmichael after their surrender. Some of the criticism concerned Hart's sources, but some reflected either a 'misplaced belief that the IRA upheld codes of chivalry' or the assumption that Tom Barry would not have lied about such an occurrence.[15] Recent work by John O 'Callaghan shows that of the eleven policeman killed at Dromkeen, Co. Limerick, in February 1921, at least two were killed after their surrender. The Dromkeen ambush was second only to Kilmichael in the number of Crown forces killed. It is note-worthy that the key figure involved in the Dromkeen shootings was a veteran of the wartime British army, and that the IRA commander had given orders before the ambush to 'kill them without pity, without mercy'.[16]

The use of terror by the new Irish state to maintain itself during the Civil War had, for some, more justification. Tom Garvin has argued that the Free State's policy of executions demoralized the anti-Treatyites and played an important role in their defeat. He quotes a claim by Tom Ryan, a National army officer in Tipperary, that 'after the first executions, the morale of the Irregulars cracked. The rank-and-file deserted from the columns, particuarly the Tru-cileers. ... The Irregulars were boastful after arrest right up to the executions. ... Some Irregulars [were] convinced no Irishman would sign [an] execution order.' Ryan also stated that, in response to a threat by anti-Treatyite Dinny Lacey to kill five brothers of National army officers if IRA prisoner Liam Deasy were executed, he sent a message warning Lacey that 'should you ... carry out your threat to execute the five prisoners now held, inside twenty-four hours of execution confirmation – every male member of the Lacey family in South Tipperary will be wiped out'.[17] Though Ryan's threat was not carried out, the impression given is that Lacey was sufficently worried not to act on his own threat.

Similarly, the unofficial killing of members of the anti-Treaty IRA, sometimes after abduction and usually carried out by officers of the CID, is deemed by Eunan O'Halpin to have had an impact on the IRA's operations in Dublin. He suggests that the CID 'succeeded in its task of suppressing small-scale republican activities in the Dublin area, not by the sophistication and efficiency of its intelligence work ... but by the more direct method of striking terror into its opponents'.[18] For some, there is a certain red-blooded attraction in the idea of the fledgling state, under siege from an irresponsible 'public band', adopting harsh but ultimately successful measures to ensure its survival.

It is worth noting however, that the anti-Treaty IRA's decision to target politicians came *after* the first executions of their volunteers had taken place. Erskine Childers and several young IRA men had already been shot before the IRA responded to repression with assasination. Unofficial killings of anti-Treatyites, including teenagers, had been taking place since August. Thus Liam Lynch, the Chief of Staff, could argue in early November 1922 that 'we (have) honourably stood by the rules of war. We have met the enemy in open warfare, pitting our weak arm against his strong one and our armed forces against the resources of the British Empire. We have not adopted against him the same tactics adopted against the British.' While 'our prisoners have been tortured and murdered in the most devilish fashion', the anti-Treatyites had tried to fight a conventional war.[19] That was to change, but it is worth considering how this turn was influenced by the use of both legal and extra-legal killing by the government.

The effectiveness of the executions policy is also open to question. Philip McConway has astutely noted that many executions took place in areas where the IRA was relatively weak such as Kildare (where seven men were shot in December 1922), yet there were no executions in areas such as Sligo where the IRA was extremely active. In fact, the executions policy may have stiffened republican resistance and further radicalized the IRA; it certainly contributed to long-lasting bitterness.[20] This was the case in Kerry, where both executions and the killing of prisoners carried out in the spring of 1923 helped sustain an anti-Treaty tradition. During the 1930s, gardaí regarded the behaviour of the National army as being a key factor in the persistence of support for the IRA in Kerry. Noting the large crowds (including relatives of men killed in the Civil War) who attended a republican demonstration in January 1935, a local officer had 'no doubt but that the Division was ruthlessly treated in the past and acts committed which will long live as a bitter memory to a big section of the youth – generous allowance must accordingly be made'.[21] Less than a decade later, Military Intelligence accounted for residual republican support in Kerry by explaining that while many of those prepared to aid the IRA 'cared little' about republican policy, 'some tragedy in the Tan or Civil War period' was 'very vivid in their minds'.[22]

In Dublin, it may be argued that the CID's 'dirty war' simply added over twenty martyrs to the movement's Roll of Honour, rather than terrorizing the IRA. Most of the killings may have been acts of vengeance for Michael Collins and other dead comrades, and devoid of political rationale. One republican prisoner beaten in custody in Portobello barracks remembered how his captors 'threatened to murder me, beat me about the head and body with revolvers, stuck the muzzle of same down my ears and mouth', while all the time asking 'are you glad Mick is dead? Are you glad that Mick (bang) is dead?'[23] It has been suggested that the killing of Noel Lemass in July 1923 was in retaliation for an ambush in June 1922 in which two army officers died.[24] The fact that many of the worst offenders were former members of Collins's 'Squad' points to wider questions about the role of 'élite' units in wartime, suggesting that their image as reluctant teenage warriors (reinforced by Jordan's film, *Michael Collins*) cannot survive scrutiny.[25] For some, such as the republican propagandist Frank Gallagher, the experience of war eventually led to rejection of the logic of militarism:

> I know there are different views of how to best further the establishment of an Irish Republic. Some believe one of the ways is stealing up to an old man's door, calling him out, shooting him

down and running away. ... I have been through that kind of thing in the past, and know where it leads. Those who came to worship the gun before 1921 were the first to surrender to Britain at the treaty time. And they afterwards became those who committed the most terrible outrages on captured Republicans.[26]

Though the anti-Treaty IRA burned over 200 'big houses' belonging to unionists and killed some supporters of the Free State while raiding their homes, there was little widespread killing of uninvolved civilians during the Civil War.[27] Yet other forms of terror characterized the widespread class conflicts of the period. In 1920, the Irish Farmers' Union had contemplated forming a 'Farmers' Freedom Force' or 'White Guard' to combat workers' militias such as the 'Red Guards'.[28] In 1922, as strikes and occupations were brought to an end at gunpoint, the Labour movement warned both factions of the IRA against copying 'the worst methods of British imperialism' and engaging in 'sheer imitation of the militarism of the British, French, German, American and other armies'.[29] By 1923, the National army was intervening on the side of employers and farmers in industrial disputes.[30]

The dynamic behind the actions of British state forces in Ireland between 1916–21 remains more obscure than the strategies of the IRA.[31] There has been relatively little modern published work on the Black and Tans or Auxiliaries.[32] Padraig Óg Ó Ruairc's listing of members of these forces recruited in Clare, with their previous occupations, offers a pointer towards future research.[33] Ann Matthews and Robert Lynch have suggested some ways in which violence was directed specifically against women in this period.[34] The preconceptions and mentalities of those who directed British Intelligence in Ireland have been well illustrated by Paul McMahon, while John Borgonovo's study of Cork City has illuminated aspects of the Intelligence war at local level.[35] We know even less about loyalists, who were central to much of the violence in Ulster between 1920 and 1922.[36] Recently, Tim Wilson's examination of Owen McMahon and his sons has shown what a powerful message was conveyed by killing a successful businessman, Home Ruler and director of Glentoran Football Club, in a mixed residential area that had seen relatively little trouble. The killers, if not acting on behalf of the state, were certainly members of its police forces.[37] But there is still much to be revealed about the rôle of loyalist paramilitaries in that era, whether or not they acted in collusion with the Crown forces. We also know very little about their shadowy successors such as the Ulster Protestant League of the 1930s.[38]

Few would deny that much of the violence that occurred after 1969 was 'terrorist' in nature. It is worth noting that that while the IRA of the 1950s were strongly influenced by events in Palestine and Cyprus, they did not adopt the tactics of either Jewish or Greek Cypriot insurgents.[39] There was republican praise for the Irgun who 'belted the British out of Palestine', but not emulation of their tactics, such as the bombing of the King David Hotel in which ninety-one people died.[40] Between 1955 and 1958, EOKA in Cyprus killed over 100 civilians and targeted off-duty British soldiers and policemen in bomb attacks on resturants and bars.[41] Yet the IRA of the 1950s attempted to fight their campaign with very different tactics, and (with one exception) did not target off-duty police or B-Specials. In 1965, Cathal Goulding urged IRA volunteers to 'read of Cuba, of Algeria, of Cyprus'; but his organization increasingly limited its use of force to industrial and agrarian disputes, while not abandoning it as the ultimate tool for revolution.[42]

There was certainly an early and marked shift in the tactics of the Provisional IRA by comparison with those of the 1956–62 campaign. In August 1970 two RUC constables were blown up in Crossmaglen and later that year two local criminals were shot dead in Ballymurphy.[43] Republicans were well aware that some of these actions might not be considered acceptable forms of military action. Hence none was claimed by the Provisonal IRA at the time. Even more shocking was the killing of three young, off-duty, Scottish soldiers in March 1971. The character of these killings, whose victims were 'unarmed and lured', was acknowledged by republicans to involve a step too far for most nationalists. As one leading IRA activist (Martin Meehan) later remarked, 'it was not the type of job Patrick Pearse would have done'.[44] Again, there was no admission of responsiblity. But in the context of increasing confrontation between nationalists and the British army, and the killing of unarmed civilians by soldiers, attitudes soon changed.

The Provisional IRA's urban bombing campaign, beginning in 1970, had a military and economic rationale. In May 1972, this was expounded in *Republican News*, which proclaimed that a new weapon was winning the war:

> The IRA's new car bomb ... first appeared in early March. Prior to the introduction of this bomb four or five armed men placed low powered bombs which only destroyed a single shop or building. Quite obviously the chances of being caught by the enemy were great. It is quite true to say that with this old type bomb the IRA destroyed the centre of Belfast. Nevertheless this bomb was rarely used in small towns for the obvious reason that men on foot doing this type of job would have no chance of escape. Consequently apart from Belfast, Derry and Newry there was little or no IRA bombing in any other town. Since March however nearly all major towns in Northern Ireland have been badly hit by the new car bomb. It is not clear whether Lisburn or Shipquay Street Derry was the first target of this bomb early in March. The Lisburn bomb destroyed eighty shops and the Derry bomb destroyed an entire street ... then it was the turn of Banbridge, Bangor, Carrick-fergus, Enniskillen and of course the centre of Belfast.[45]

There was little indication that the Provisional IRA either understood or cared about the human impact of these bombs, which during 1972 killed and injured hundreds and made normal life impossible for thousands.

Yet the biggest death toll in a bombing to that date had actually been the result of loyalist action. In December 1971, McGurk's bar in Belfast's North Queen Street had been bombed by the UVF. Fifteen people were killed and dozens injured. All were civilians. Yet this bombing never matched the notoriety of 'Bloody Friday' in the following year – though more people died – and for many years the authorities maintained that it was the result of an IRA operation, leading to speculation that the bomb had been prepared in McGurk's itself.[46] The loyalist view of their activities in those years was that 'a strategy of counter-terrorism was both called for and adopted'.[47] It should be recalled, however, that loyalist killings commenced in 1966, four years before the onset of the Provisional IRA's campaign. It is also noteworthy that 'the UVF had within its ranks volunteers who as former British soldiers in Cyprus, Borneo and

Malaya, knew the limitations of conventional forces in combating terrorism. They had been involved in carrying out covert counter-terrorist measures, including "dirty tricks".'[48]

Other loyalist bombings were equally significant. The bombs in Dublin in December 1972, which killed two people, coincided with the debate on the Offences against the State Bill and were audible in the chamber of the Dáil. In the following days, 'tension, bomb scares and rumours swept Dublin'.[49] Few doubt that the bombs directly affected the vote on this Bill. The attacks were highly successful in generating fear and influencing politics. They were part of a series of bomb attacks in Donegal, Cavan, Monaghan, Louth and Dublin between 1971 and 1975. The worst were, of course, the Dublin and Monaghan bombings of May 1974, which left thirty-three dead, the largest toll until the Omagh bomb in 1998. In terms of responsibility, Seán Donlon of the Department of Foreign Affairs was sure there was 'close collaboration between elements of the RUC and members of loyalist paramilitary organisations'. The consequences of such collusion being uncovered were spelt out by Justin Keating: 'If there was a revelation of co-operation between British state terrorists and Northern unionist terrorists, the country would have become practically ungovernable. The outrage and reaction here would have been so powerful as to make it ungovernable.'[50] But while the bombs seem to have terrified southerners, they did not lead to an appreciable rise in support for republicanism. What is notable is how little scholarly work has appeared on the bombs south of the border.[51]

Loyalist violence has sometimes been judged less harshly than that of republicans. Mainstream figures such as Sammy Wilson of the Democratic Unionist Party could assert that the 'majority of Loyalist violence has been reactive'.[52] John Taylor, when an Official Unionist MEP, even suggested that if loyalist paramilitaries were to be active then their efforts should be 'directed to targets within the Republic of Ireland'.[53] After the IRA ceasefire of 1994, Taylor argued that:

> The Loyalist paramilitaries achieved something which perhaps the security forces could never have achieved, and that was they were a significant contribution to the IRA finally accepting that they

couldn't win. ... Sometimes people don't like to face this reality
and some people say you shouldn't say it, but I always think it's
important to say what is correct – that the Loyalist paramilitaries,
in their illegal activity, actually began to overtake the IRA as the
major paramiltary organization and terrorist organization in
Northern Ireland. Indeed in the year before the ceasefire by the
IRA the Loyalist paramilitaries killed more people than the IRA. So
I think this got a message over to the IRA that no longer were they
going to be the one and only terrorist organization. There was a
comparable one now on the Loyalist side which was actually being
more effective.[54]

This is the same logic by which some republicans claim that the
Kingsmill massacre of January 1976 brought an end to loyalist
attacks on Catholics in South Armagh for many years.[55]

The view of loyalist violence as reactive was shared by John
Bruton:

I think the campaign of violence initiated by the IRA, firstly
against the security forces then gradually spreading out to affect
all of the Protestants has led to counter-terror on the part of the
Protestants. ... if the IRA stopped it wouldn't be long before the
Loyalist counter-terror would also stop and in that sense I think
the IRA is the primary cause – not the sole cause but the primary
cause – of violence.[56]

This blind spot with regard to loyalism has led Garret FitzGerald to
suggest that unionist opposition to the Anglo-Irish Agreement 'did
not involve lethal violence'.[57] In fact, opposition to the Agreement
resulted in formation of the Ulster Resistance organization, in which
the Democratic Unionist Party was involved, and the importation
of South African arms. Between 1986 and 1994, loyalist paramilitaries killed 265 people.[58] Their victims included republican activists but also members of their families; the majority were civilians,
killed in attacks on pubs, workplaces and homes. Any balanced
discussion of terror in twentieth-century Ireland must identify all
of its origins and agencies, not just those which confirm our own
opinions and prejudices.

NOTES

1. David J. Whittaker (ed.), *The Terrorism Reader* (London 2003; 1st edn 2001), p. 15.

2. Anthony McIntyre, 'Calling a spade a shovel', *The Blanket*, 28 Nov. 2001.

3. *The Oxford English Dictionary* (Oxford 1989 edn), vol. 17, pp. 820–1.

4. Richard English, *Terrorism: How to Respond* (Oxford 2009), pp. 3–4.

5. Pearse Lawlor, *The Burnings, 1920* (Cork 2009); Gerry White and Brendan O'Shea, *The Burning of Cork* (Cork 2006); James S. Donnelly, Jr., ' "Unofficial" British reprisals and IRA provocations, 1919–20: the cases of three Cork towns', *Éire-Ireland*, 45, nos. 1–2 (2010), 152–97.

6. Eoghan Harris, *Sunday Independent*, 25 June 2010; Kevin Myers, *Irish Independent*, 3 Aug. 2010.

7. Aengus Ó Snodaigh, *An Phoblacht / Republican News*, 20 Aug. 1998.

8. 'The Protestant experience of revolution in Southern Ireland' in Peter Hart, *The I.R.A. at War, 1916–1923* (Oxford 2003), pp. 223–40.

9. 'Hart to heart', *History Ireland*, 13, no. 2 (Mar.–Apr. 2005), 48–51.

10. Jim Lane, *On the IRA: Belfast Brigade Area* (Cork 1972), p. 6.

11. Robert Lynch, 'Explaining the Altnaveigh massacre, June 1922', *Éire-Ireland*, 45, nos. 3–4 (2010), 184–210.

12. *IT*, 9 Nov. 1996.

13. *IT*, 23 Aug. 1982.

14. Sinn Féin Publicity Department, *The Good Old IRA: Tan War Operations* (Dublin 1985), pp. 3, 1, 4, 7.

15. John Regan, review of *Tom Barry: IRA Freedom Fighter* by Meda Ryan, *History*, 91, no. 301 (2006), 163–4; RTÉ, *Leargas* documentary on Kilmichael, 28 Nov. 2000 ('Tom Barry wasn't capable of lying').

16. John O'Callaghan, *Revolutionary Limerick: The Republican Campaign for Independence in Limerick, 1913–1921* (Dublin 2010) pp. 139–41.

17. Tom Garvin, *1922 – The Birth of Irish Democracy* (Dublin 1996), pp. viii, 119.

18. Eunan O'Halpin, *Defending Ireland: The Irish State and Its Enemies since 1922* (Oxford 1999), p. 13.

19. CS to OCs of all areas, 'General activities', 4 Nov. 1922, UCDA, Twomey Papers, P69/02 (61–2).

20. Philip McConway to author, 1 Dec. 2010.

21. Chief Superintendent's report, 10 Jan. 1935, NAD, Jus 8/201.

22. G2 Intelligence report, 26 Feb. 1942, MAD, G2/X/0058.

23. David O'Donoghue, *The Devil's Deal: The IRA, Nazi Germany and the Double Life of Jim O'Donovan* (Dublin 2010), pp. 70–1.

24. C. H. Bretherton, *The Real Ireland* (London 1925) p. 77; *Irish Independent,* 29 June 1922.

25. Anne Dolan, 'Killing and Bloody Sunday, November 1920', *Historical Journal,* 49 (2006), 789–810; idem, 'Ending revolution in a "sportsmanlike manner": the milestone of revolution, 1919–23' in Thomas E. Hachey (ed.), *Turning Points in Twentieth-Century Irish History* (Dublin 2011), pp. 21–38.

26. Frank Gallagher to Joseph McGarrity, 25 June 1938: NLI, MS 17,544 (1).

27. John Dorney, *The Story of the Irish Civil War, 1922–1923* (Dublin 2010), p. 47.

28. David Fitzpatrick, *Politics and Irish Life, 1913–1921: Provincial Experience of War and Revolution* (Cork 1998; 1st edn 1977), pp. 224–5; Emmet O'Connor, *A Labour History of Waterford* (Waterford 1989), pp. 161–71; Paul Bew, 'Sinn Féin, agrarian radicalism and the War of Independence, 1919–1921' in D. G. Boyce (ed.), *The Revolution in Ireland, 1879–1923* (London 1988), pp. 217–34; *Voice of Labour,* 10 Dec. 1921.

29. *Voice of Labour,* 15 Apr. 1922; *Workers' Republic,* 16 June 1923.

30. O'Halpin, *Defending Ireland,* p. 33.

31. Donnelly, 'British Reprisals'.

32. Richard Bennett, *The Black and Tans* (Kent 2001; 1st edn 1959).

33. Padraig Óg Ó Ruairc, *Blood on the Banner: The Republican Struggle in Clare, 1913–1923* (Cork 2009), pp. 332–4.

34. Ann Matthews, *Renegades: Irish Republican Women, 1900–1922* (Cork 2010), pp. 266–82; Lynch, 'Altnaveigh massacre'.

35. Paul McMahon, *British Spies and Irish Rebels: British Intelligence and Ireland, 1916–1945* (Woodbridge, Suffolk 2008); John Borgonovo, *Spies, Informers and the 'Anti-Sinn Féin Society': The Intelligence War in Cork City, 1920–1921* (Dublin 2007).

36. Timothy Bowman, *Carson's Army: The Ulster Volunteer Force, 1910–22* (Manchester 2007).

37. Tim Wilson, ' "The most terrible assasination that has yet stained the name of Belfast": the McMahon murders in context', *Irish Historical Studies,* 37, no.145 (2010), 83–106.

38. Ronnie Munck and Bill Rolston, *Belfast in the Thirties: An Oral History* (Belfast 1987), pp. 40–1.

39. *United Irishman,* July 1956.

40. *An t-Óglac,* May 1965. Jewish militants were also influenced by the IRA: David Cesarani, *Major Farran's Hat: Murder, Scandal and Britain's War Against Jewish Terrorism, 1945–1948* (London 2009), p. 15.

41. Dónal Donnelly, *Prisoner 1082: Escape from Crumlin Road, Europe's Alcatraz* (Cork 2010), p. 100; John Newsinger, *British Counter-Insurgency: From Palestine to Northern Ireland* (London 2002), pp. 84–106.

42. *An t-Óglac*, May 1965.

43. Ciarán de Baróid, *Ballymurphy and the Irish War* (London 1990) pp. xv–xvi.

44. Anthony McIntyre, 'Modern Irish republicanism and the Belfast Agreement: chickens coming home to roost, or turkeys celebrating Christmas?' in Richard Wilford (ed.), *Aspects of the Belfast Agreement* (Oxford 2001), pp. 202–22.

45. *Republican News*, 14 May 1972.

46. Susan McKay, *Bear In Mind These Dead* (London 2008), pp. 25–30; *IT*, 22 Feb. 2011.

47. Progressive Unionist Party, *Principles of Loyalism* (Belfast 2002).

48. Colin Crawford, *Defenders or Criminals? Loyalist Prisoners and Criminalisation* (Belfast 1999), p. 9.

49. *IT*, 4 Dec. 1972.

50. Oireachtas, *Final Report on the Report of the Independent Commmission of Inquiry into the Dublin and Monaghan Bombings* (Dublin 2004), pp. 34–5.

51. J. Bowyer Bell, *In Dubious Battle: The Dublin and Monaghan Bombings, 1972–1974* (Dublin 1996).

52. *Hot Press*, 22 Sept. 1993.

53. *IT*, 31 Aug. 1979.

54. Peter Taylor, *Loyalists: Ulster's Protestant Paramilitaries* (London 1999), p. 234.

55. Toby Harnden, '*Bandit Country': The IRA and South Armagh* (London 1999), pp. 185–90.

56. *Hot Press*, Christmas edn, 1991.

57. *IT*, 13 Nov. 2010.

58. David McKittrick et al., *Lost Lives: The Stories of the Men, Women and Children Who Died as a Result of the Northern Ireland Troubles* (Edinburgh 1999), p. 1476.

3. 'The shadow of a great fear': Terror and Revolutionary Ireland

Anne Dolan

In January 1934, Doris Hunt tried to steal a handbag in Dickins and Jones in Regent Street. She was a poor thief: the handbag bulged beneath her overcoat and the police were called to take her from the shop. At the London County Sessions she was sentenced to six months in jail, six months because she had been caught in this way before: she pilfered small things even though she always had the money to pay. At the time of her arrest she had more than £1000 invested, had more than £80 to spend as she pleased. By March she found herself before the Court of Criminal Appeal. After one month in prison, Dr Watson, the prison medical examiner, made a case for her release. In his view she was not fit to answer for her petty crimes. Doris Hunt was twenty-three years old in March 1934, but she had what Watson described as the mind of a child – a child of nine or ten, a mind fixed in time by what the judge called 'a shock of an appalling character'.[1] When Doris Hunt was nine or ten she had watched her father die.

On 26 June 1921 Doris Hunt was having tea in the parlour of the Mayfair hotel in Baggot Street, Dublin, with her father and mother and two of their friends. Four (or six or eight) men came into the parlour and shot her father, William Hunt, three times.[2] He was shot in the chest. He was turned over on the ground and shot twice more in the back to make sure he was dead. 'You are dead D.I. Hunt' was all that witnesses remembered one of those four or six or eight men saying before they fired.[3] Doris Hunt was injured by one of the bullets that struck her father; she had tried to run to him as he fell.[4] The court of inquiry heard that there were bullet marks all over the parlour of the Mayfair hotel, and bullets embedded in the walls, in the floor, and in the window frames. The other patrons were terrified by what they saw, terrified enough by the thought of a similar fate to remember nothing when the time came to stand before that court of inquiry. In the confusion no one could be sure how many men had entered the parlour, or how many had continued to fire until their revolvers were empty. Hunt's wife, Alice, could only say that they were all 'lads', maybe seventeen to twenty years old, all dressed in old dark grey suits. She recalled no faces, no features, just one face maybe covered by a mask. She remembered one man's torn sock, recalling the details around the edges as if fear and confusion had taken over everything in between.[5]

Both mother and daughter were compensated for their loss, being awarded almost £3000 for the death of husband and father,[6] but no compensation could prevent the 'sad case' that came before the courts in the spring of 1934. When the Court of Criminal Appeal considered what Doris Hunt had seen in the Mayfair hotel thirteen years earlier, 'every one admitted that the experience had arrested and affected her development', and she was released immediately into her mother's care. In 1934, Doris Hunt was just a small headline (the 'girl who saw her father killed'), a 'sad' postscript to terror and revolution in Ireland.[7]

The straight line that the Court of Criminal Appeal seemed content to draw between events in June 1921 and January 1934 is certainly not as seamless as it would appear. Many reasons might have been given for Doris Hunt's difficulties; many other misfortunes might explain her actions in 1934. She might be the Doris Hunt who ran away from home when she was fifteen, who took a four-year-old child and went missing for two days in the spring of 1927.[8] Age and place suggest she was, and this might explain the pilfering and the stealing just as much as the nature of her father's death. Alternatively, she is just one of many possible 'sad', not very significant, cases that might be found if the consequences of violence in Ireland can be traced to their bitterest ends. The small headlines just make her easier to find.

Terror and revolution may likewise have left their mark on the family of Nicholas Prendergast or Canon T. J. Magner, both killed

by Auxiliaries in December 1920;[9] and on the family of Hannah
Keegan, shot at the age of twelve because it seemed acceptable in
Dublin in March 1921 to fire in the streets regardless of the passing
crowds.[10] It might also be found in the Loughnane family, who kept
photographs of their dead brother's bodies, which proved the Auxiliaries had tried to burn the evidence of death.[11] Terror also left
contemporary traces in descriptions of those taken in the night, in
the screams and struggles of wives and elderly fathers and squealing
children. It was present at the time of death in the long-drawn-out
hours waiting for victims to come home, voiced in the shouts or
cries or shots that confirmed they were gone, felt in the hours or
days spent waiting for a body to be found, or once it was found,
waiting for identification. It lingered, long after the death of a 'spy',
for those labelled as the wife or father or child of the 'spy' as clearly
as if the label on the body was tied around each of their own necks,
isolated by a community that had no wish to be visited by the same
fate. The example of Doris Hunt is not intended to suggest that the
terror experienced by victims of the IRA was qualitatively different
from that affecting victims of the Crown forces. Instead, such cases
suggest that terror lives long beyond the terrorism done, that more
questions might be asked of the nature of terror itself.

    Dwelling even superficially on these human consequences sug-
gests the need for an entirely different chronology of terror. It has
long been assumed that terror left its mark on the two Irish states,
that the nature of their beginnings made them revert more readily
than they might to the use of emergency legislation to contain the
threat of renewed terror. It is, perhaps, only beginning to be possible
to consider terror's broader, more personal consequences. The Military Service Pension applications, when fully released, may explain
more. The files of the Irish Grants Committee are indicative not
simply of financial loss but also the kinds of fear and distress that
saw many people leave Ireland throughout the 1920s, long after
'terrorism' had stopped. Terror was also present in the journey
many made across the border with small bundles of worldly belongings that testified to the urgency of the flight. And though greed may
have inflated many pension applications and compensation claims
from all sides, though outpourings about the loss of crops or the

destruction of a shop front may sound hollow beside a more sober assessment of the loss of a father or husband or wife or child, traces of terror may be detected in every type of testimony.

Terror's reach must be allowed to extend to the perpetrators of terror as well as its victims. There are admittedly different human costs to be counted, but they need to be counted nonetheless, and those costs and consequences can be heard in a number of participants' evidence. One IRA veteran, Matty MacDonald, remembered that 'Charlie Dalton was very nervous. We went to the Capitol [Theatre] to ease his mind ... Charlie Dalton couldn't sleep the night of Bloody Sunday. He thought he could hear the gurgling of the officers' blood and he kept awake all night until we told him a tap was running somewhere.'[12] Liam Tobin was said to have had a nervous breakdown before Bloody Sunday in November 1920.[13] He had become, according to David Neligan, 'gaunt, cynical, with tragic eyes, he looked like a man who had seen the inside of hell'.[14] Others hid it in drink. When he was released after the Truce, Eamon Broy was 'disagreeably surprised to see many fine and highly strung young Irish Volunteers, who had been teetotallers when I last met them, drinking whiskey neat. It was bound to have a bad effect on them especially after the long struggle they had endured.'[15] Harry Colley admitted 'there was heavy drinking in Dublin. Charlie Dalton never drank till the truce. Reaction from strain.'[16] Bernard Byrne spoke of men who 'became nerve cases as a result of their work'.[17] Indeed, the often erratic shooting, the shots to parts of the body where a wound would never kill, maybe tell as much about the nervous, often shaking, hands that fired the weapons as they do of the marksman's maybe limited skills, as they do of the struggle or the intimacy of the fight.

Some opponents of the IRA left similar accounts. On 21 November 1920 Captain A. C. C. Farmer found his room-mate, Temporary Cadet Henry Spenle, 'half lying in the bed with a revolver in his right hand and a bullet wound through his head'. Farmer had been living with Spenle for just two weeks. He thought him nervous, depressed; in high spirits one moment, in despair the next. Spenle had served in the Royal Air Force during the War; it was known in Dublin that he had 'crashed badly', that he sometimes relived that crash, in what one witness called 'spasms', which always ended with strange, unsettling laughter. Despite this, witnesses were adamant that Spenle had never talked of taking his own life. Perhaps they were trying to protect the dead man's reputation; perhaps a fortnight's acquaintance had been insufficient to induce Spenle to confide that he could no longer bear to be alive. While the court of inquiry pronounced 'suicide whilst of unsound mind', Farmer felt that 'the happenings of the morning which [Spenle] had been discussing' had 'preyed on his mind'; that he was frightened to his death, frightened by what the IRA had done in Dublin that very morning, that the rumours and exaggerations and the news of fourteen dead men, shot in their flats, boarding houses and hotel rooms, some in front of their own wives and children, had been just too much for Spenle to take.[18] Like Doris Hunt, Spenle is, of course, an extreme example. There may have been countless reasons why he chose Bloody Sunday 1920 to die, but his comrades certainly believed the terror of that morning had caused him to act.

Rumours of terror generated further terror. In army circles, it was said that the IRA had the means and the will to spread typhus, that poisoned sweets and cigarettes were being dispensed, that even the most innocent of apparent kindnesses could not be trusted.[19] The sheer ubiquity of actual terrorism lent credence to such rumours. RIC men were shot inside churches; gunmen faded in and out of crowds. Then there were the sudden ambushes, the shots from behind walls, the mutilated bodies of Auxiliary Cadets at Kilmichael, the murdered, the assassinated, the bodies left labelled as spies, all encouraging unease about where the next threat might come from. Captain Douglas Wimberley of the Cameron Highlanders was not alone in admitting that he slept with a loaded pistol under his pillow. That he continued to do so for several months after he had left Ireland is more revealing still.[20] Many accounts reflect how unsettled many of the Crown forces were by the violence they encountered in Ireland. As a visiting journalist was told: 'Straightforward fighting is our job, but this sort of thing! … Why, fighting the IRA is fighting assassins. It's low, cowardly cunning they excel at. I tell you I'd sooner do another two-and-a-half years in France than the same length of time here … Yes, it's a rum kind of war.'[21] Captain J. S. Wilkinson of the

Sherwood Foresters wrote: 'All in all I far preferred the War to civil duties in Ireland. In war one does know roughly where the enemy is, but in the conditions in Ireland in those times one never knew.'[22]

The tension this seemed to breed in many was clear. Some recorded travelling in trains with a revolver in each pocket, while whole areas were issued with orders that forbade civilians to walk in the streets with their hands in their pockets. Men's leave was restricted, making them more restless still; classes in guerrilla warfare were introduced, officers were ordered to practise firing their revolvers. Such precautions only heightened the fear further still.[23] E. M. Ransford of the Suffolk Regiment came to Ireland after Mesopotamia and India. He complained that there was no 'frontier', that the possible dangers kept the men confined to barracks and left them little or no opportunity for training or recreation, that there were problems of indiscipline, poor health and even poorer morale. He shot himself in the foot and narrowly escaped a court martial because he could prove that it was an accident, but he noticed a lot of what he called 'self-inflicted injuries', and that the men seemed prepared to do anything to get home.[24] Brevet Lieutenant-Colonel E. Craig-Brown of the Cameron Highlanders wrote home that 'there has been a very marked increase in the number of cases of drunkenness since we left Aldershot'.[25] The same officer remarked that 'the troops that wrecked Fermoy ... put themselves on the level of the Bosches'.[26] Captain H. C. N. Trollope of the Suffolk Regiment admitted that 'due to the Irish war the state of the Army was so low that it was not considered reasonable to do any training by battalions, barring one or two static battalion schemes.'[27] For Lieutenant F. A. S. Clarke of the Essex Regiment it was simpler still: 'I did not like myself in Ireland. I don't think anybody else did either.'[28]

While Clarke may not have liked himself in Ireland, there were participants on both sides who appeared to take a kind of pleasure in terror. Vinnie Byrne admitted 'it was the joy of my life when I was handed a .45 revolver and six rounds', recorded how he liked 'plugging' British soldiers.[29] For Ernie O'Malley his Webley had become 'as indispensable as a fountain pen'; with his Parabellum he felt 'a great warmth in my body and a rich joy as I filled my magazine'.[30] After firing his first shot, Todd Andrews was left in 'a state bordering

on ecstasy'.[31] Evelyn Lindsay Young, a British officer in Bandon, rev-
elled in the details of how he tortured prisoners, claiming to show
them corpses to try and frighten them to confess.[32] In some senses
it was left to others to feel disquiet on their behalf. Todd Andrews
was outraged at the behaviour of Joe Dolan and the men from the
squad on Bloody Sunday morning, even accusing them of behaving
like Black and Tans.[33] Though Pat McCrea was proud that he had
driven a car for one of the killings that day, his wife, who had been
under the impression that he had been fishing, put him out of the
house when he joked about how plentiful the morning's catch had
been. He could not see what had made her so concerned.[34]

The consequences of terror can also be reckoned at a further
remove. The temptation to focus on only the most active participants in revolution overlooks the part the aider or the abettor or
even the unwitting play. The maid who had given Charles Dalton
the information needed to kill three men in Pembroke Street on
Bloody Sunday came crying to him shortly afterwards, when she
realized what she had done or, at least, contributed to. She protested
that 'I thought you only meant to kidnap them', sought solace from
a priest, and admitted guiltily that 'I was so upset I did not leave the
house for days. You see, I felt I had had a hand in it, and I couldn't
bear my thoughts.'[35] When small pieces of information, when
rumours and whispers were passed from spy to soldier, from postal
worker to IRA man, when letters were opened and secrets known,
how many others felt that they 'couldn't bear' their thoughts when
the deed was finally done? Alternatively, how many others gloried
in the small part played in their own type of fight? To understand
terror does more account need to be taken of women like Margaret
Browne, who happily carried Tom Cullen's gun 'knowing that he
might well have to kill someone', that she was 'more distressed by
his frequenting prostitutes than by his carrying out executions'?[36]
Do the fetchers and the carriers, those who fed and concealed, those
who whispered information, those who helped one side or the other,
need to play a more vocal part if the nature of the revolution's terror
is to be more fully understood?

Terror's definition also needs to include the opportunist, take
account of the advantage taken of chaos and disorder, calculate the

land stolen, the cattle driven, the small local slights that the cover of terror turned into a fight for freedom. Account has to be taken of those who boycotted out of enthusiasm or intimidation, those who penned short threatening letters and ran no risk of getting caught, and those who did all or some of these or other things out of malice or misdirection or because it seemed that the safest thing to do was to take a side. More problematic are those who turned a blind eye, who did not help when help was pleaded for, who ran in the opposite direction when shots were fired, or who could not remember names or faces when questioned in court. It is all too easy to cry coward from almost a century's remove. The doctor who admitted that he refused to treat a dying man 'on the grounds of personal fear' was only being honest.[37]

The defiant also have to be allowed for, people who doggedly adhered to their side, refused to take a side, or won or lost small wars against local tyrannies. Because of that defiance they are relatively easy to trace in the records of their opponents. The indifferent and the unaffected are more elusive; they get lost in this kind of contemporary report, by an Auxiliary Cadet attached to Basil Clarke's Public Information Bureau:

> Over the whole of Ireland there hangs the shadow of a great fear. Whilst Sinn Fein carries on its guerilla warfare against the Crown Forces, and the Crown Forces conduct their policy of reprisals against Sinn Fein, ordinary civilians, whose only wish is to be allowed to live in peace and attend to their own affairs, walk in terror of their lives. No man knows how soon he may be called upon to give an account of his movements or a statement of his politics to secret agents of Sinn Fein or of the Crown. He may be arrested on suspicion. Too intent a glance from a stranger is enough to make him feel uncomfortable for the rest of the day. Everyone suffers from nerves, and the women of Ireland, after the manner of womankind, suffer untold agonies of apprehension for the safety of their men.[38]

Everyone did not 'suffer from nerves' or endure 'agonies of apprehension'. Within pages of sensational reports newspapers still proclaimed life passing with some of its normal regularity, advertisements suggest that trade continued, that fashions changed, that 'The Kid'

played at the cinema and was for many, just what it claimed, '6 reels
of joy'. The indifferent, the apathetic, the unperturbed are possibly
the measure against which terror makes sense yet form still the most
unconsidered part of revolution. Even within revolution, even for
those said to be embroiled in the terror, the normal remains more
pressing than it might seem. Major C. H. Foulkes of the Royal Engineers, stationed in Dublin in 1921 and responsible for Irish military
propaganda, fuelling the intensity of terror with his own reports,
kept a diary recounting the shows he went to, the films he saw, the
dinners he had in decent hotels.[39] Terror was not part of his chronicle of Dublin life. Similarly, Major-General Strickland, commander
of the embattled 6th Division in Cork, used his diaries to record
not only acts of violence but planting chrysanthemums, playing
tennis after tea, and taking 'infants to cinema'.[40] F. O. Cave, with
the Rifle Brigade in Londonderry, kept a record of days spent taking
pot shots at different kinds of birds, at pigeons and woodcocks,
at wild swans and ducks, though his sporting life was periodically
interrupted by round-ups, interrogations and mornings 'spent intel-
ligencing' between Londonderry and Donegal.[41] For every Douglas
Wimberley, sleeping with a revolver under his pillow, there was also
a J. V. Faviell, guarding the Glen of Imaal, shooting rabbits and
having 'tremendous fun'.[42] For every Charles Dalton, nervous and
unable to sleep, there was the more typical IRA volunteer having a
quiet, safe and small kind of war.

   Terror was clearly defined differently in different places, and certainly the measure of terror in Wicklow or Kildare operated on a
quite a different register to that at work in Cork or Dublin or Belfast
or Tipperary. The very definition of an 'outrage' could be qualitatively
different both between and within counties. The trenching of a road
or burning of hay, though constituting an 'outrage' in some places,
would be ignored in others where shooting or ambushing prevailed.
Likewise, what constituted an act of terror in 1920 was almost commonplace by June 1921. Many types of terror persisted during the
Truce, not simply in the form of extreme violence as in the Bandon
valley.[43] Many communities were unsure of how long they needed to
fête the fighters, and remained anxious about the tyrannies of young
men with guns who showed no desire to settle 'back at his plough'.[44]

Though measures of death and violence clearly plot out the geography of violence during the revolution, it would be dangerous to assume that the experience of terror could be plotted on to the same map. The threat or expectation of violence could be as terrifying as violence itself. The threatening letter received in one townland was read by the same eyes that read reports of shots fired through a window somewhere else, or of dead bodies labelled as spies. The capacity of a letter to terrify intensified with every one of these deaths. The towns that heard tenders and lorries coming after curfew had read enough about the burning of Cork to imagine the same taking place in their own midst; any stray shot could suggest a massacre. In many respects it did not need to be a very violent revolution for terror to take its effect. Terror has to be imagined more than experienced, and terror and violence and revolution were experienced most readily and most easily through the press, through propaganda, through the descriptions that fuelled a sense of something to fear. If every townland could conceive of itself as the next Balbriggan, if every city could think of itself as the next Cork, then fear of the threat was as potent as the threat itself.

Similarly, if British soldiers preferred the war in France to the hole-and-corner fight they found in Ireland, they must have been terrorized by what they imagined far more than what they fought. In the words of a fictitious 'loyalist': 'Our men don't know friends from enemies, there are no rules of warfare, consequently they take justice into their own hands.'[45] The sense that no one could be trusted, that every pram might hide weapons, that a man with his hands in his pockets was readying his revolver and not just reaching for his keys or his handkerchief, could heighten the fears of Crown forces uncertain of their rôle and remit in Ireland. Bernard Montgomery declared that 'I think I regarded all civilians as "Shinners", and I never had any dealings with any of them.'[46] Rumour and misconception could cast every civilian as a 'Shinner', just as they could turn every soldier or policeman into a raging, rampaging, drunken Black and Tan. There was enough truth in it somewhere to sustain or fuel the fear, and terror thrived in the thought of terrorism itself.

Terrorism and counter-terrorism are meant to terrify. That has to be their ultimate point – to terrify their opponent into submission or concession. Whether terror or terrorist is understood in a pejorative light is the stuff of political debate and not at issue here. Terror and counter-terror instead need to be understood and interrogated on their own very practical terms. To take William Hunt's death, for example, shooting him in a hotel parlour in front of his wife and child made a certain kind of practical sense. It knowingly or unknowingly took for granted the fear of the frightened wife and child, counting on their presence as the very thing that made Hunt vulnerable and easier to kill. The very things that made it terrifying – the man being off duty, with his family, the fact that he was turned over and shot again to make sure that he was dead – reveal the essence of the kind of guerrilla war that was fought with few resources and limited opportunities and was maybe all the more callous for that. In the same way curfew had its logic, martial law had its logic, reprisals had their logic – and that logic was to terrify.

There is scope, of course, to measure or consider terror in so many other ways throughout the revolution. Terror was a type of discipline for some within the IRA. In the Monaghan IRA killing was sometimes used to keep 'our weak ones right'.[47] In Tralee, one Volunteer caught discussing 'IRA matters in the presence of strangers' was ordered to kill because it implicated him, it meant that he could never tell, or talk so freely anymore.[48] The terror behind had to be greater than the terror of going forward, just as for any other army. It was alleged that John Buckley was shot because he had stopped attending night operations with the Solohead IRA. Diverted by a new wife, he paid the price of his disloyalty to the IRA; he was a lesson to the others to keep their minds firmly on their duties.[49] But this is just another way to broaden the definition of terror. Certainly, account for it in the erection of barriers at Downing Street, and record the number of bodyguards Lloyd George was obliged to have. Of course, count it in the assassinations, the dead bodies, in the burned out houses, in the reprisals; examine it as an integral part of guerrilla war, part of its very essence or intention; but admit the possibilities of other measures, other chronologies, other geographies of terror, as well. In as many ways, admit the terror of the terrorist and the terrified just the same.

NOTES

1. *The Times*, 6 Mar. 1934.

2. His companion Enfield White was also shot in the back and in the face and survived the attack: *IT*, 27 June 1921, 4 Feb. 1922.

3. CILI, 27 June 1921, NAL, WO 35/152. In fact, William Hunt was not a District Inspector in the RIC but a Temporary Cadet in its Auxiliary Division.

4. *The Times*, 6 Mar. 1934.

5. CILI, 27 June 1921, WO 35/152.

6. Alice Hunt was awarded £1200 and Doris £1500: *IT*, 26 Jan. 1922, *Weekly IT*, 4 Feb. 1922.

7. *The Times*, 6 Mar. 1934.

8. *Ibid.* 6 Apr. 1927.

9. Prendergast, a Catholic ex-officer and hotelier, married with two children, had taught in St Colman's College, Fermoy. Taken from a bar, he was beaten and thrown into the Blackwater: CILI, 7 Jan. 1921, WO 35/157b. Canon Magner witnessed an attack on Timothy Crowley in Dunmanway and was shot dead by Temporary Cadet Harte: CILI, 17 Dec. 1920, WO 35/155b.

10. Hannah Keegan was shot in an attack on Denis Lenihan in Dublin: CILI, 26 Mar. 1921, WO 35/152.

11. Harry and Patrick Loughnane were involved in the ambush that caused the death of Constable Timothy Horan. Arrested by Auxiliaries, an attempt was made to burn and bury their bodies. When the stony ground near Ardrahan, Co. Galway, proved too unyielding, the bodies were dumped. The two men were found on 4 Dec. 1920, eight days after they had been taken from their home: CILI, 18 Dec. 1920, WO 35/153a.

12. Matty MacDonald, OMN, UCDA, p17b/105(79).

13. Charles Dalton, OMN, p17b/122(22).

14. David Neligan, *The Spy in the Castle* (London 1968), p. 71.

15. Eamon Broy, MAD, BMH, WS 1280.

16. Harry Colley, OMN, p17b/97(5).

17. WS 631.

18. CILI, 23 Nov. 1920, WO 35/159b.

19. NAL, CO 904/168; LHC, C. S. Foulkes Papers.

20. IWM, PP/MCR/182.

21. Wilfrid Ewart, *A Journey in Ireland, 1921* (Dublin 2008; 1st edn 1922), pp. 69–70.

22. IWM, 88/56/1.

23. H. C. N. Trollope, IWM, PP/MCR/212; Lt.-Gen. A. E. Percival, 'Guerrilla warfare in Ireland', IWM, P18; Lt.-Gen. Sir Hugh Jeudwine, 'History of the 5th Div. in Ireland', IWM, 72/82/2.

38 ANNE DOLAN

24. IWM, 80/29/1.

25. IWM, Con Shelf (92/23/2).

26. *Idem.*

27. IWM, PP/MCR/212.

28. LHC, 1/6 1968.

29. Quoted in Calton Younger, *Ireland's Civil War* (New York 1969), pp. 114–15.

30. Ernie O'Malley, *On Another Man's Wound* (Dublin 1990; 1st edn 1936), pp. 203, 181.

31. C. S. Andrews, *Dublin Made Me* (Dublin 1979), p. 164.

32. 'Under the shadow of darkness – Ireland', LHC, GB99.

33. Andrews, *Dublin Made Me*, p. 153.

34. Pat McCrea, WS 413.

35. Charles Dalton, *With the Dublin Brigade, 1917–1921* (London 1929), pp. 116–17.

36. The prostitutes were 'frequented', so it was claimed, 'in quest of "intelligence" ': Máire Cruise O'Brien, *The Same Age as the State* (Dublin 2003), p. 56.

37. CILI (William Good), 29 Mar. 1921, WO 35/149b.

38. Ernest S. Dowdall, 'Ireland under the new terror: what it means to live under martial law', *The London Magazine* (date unknown): clipping in CO 904/168.

39. Diary, 1921, LHC, Foulkes Papers, 2/20.

40. Diary, 25, 26, 22 Apr. 1921, IWM, General Sir Peter Strickland Papers, P363.

41. Diary, 11 Feb. 1921, IWM, Col. F. O. Cave Papers, DS/MISC/84.

42. Brig. J. V. Faviell, Memoir, IWM, 82/24/1.

43. Peter Hart, *The I.R.A. and Its Enemies: Violence and Community in Cork, 1916–1923* (Oxford 1998), esp. pp. 273–92.

44. Tom Carragher to Revd Peadar Livingstone, 29 Dec. 1965, Monaghan County Museum, Marron Collection, 1986: 6C14–15.

45. Joice M. Nankivell and Sydney Loch, *Ireland in Travail* (London 1922), p. 127.

46. Montgomery to Percival, 14 Oct. 1923, IWM, Percival Collection, P18 4/1.

47. Patrick Corrigan to Revd Peadar Livingstone, 27 Dec. 1965, Marron Collection, 6D1–10.

48. John O'Riordan, WS 1117.

49. CILI, 30 June 1921, WO 35/147a. According to Tadhg Crowe, however, Buckley was killed by policemen dressed in civilian clothes: WS 1658.

4. Violence and the Easter Rising

Fearghal McGarry

I

Accounts of the violence of Easter 1916 have primarily focused on the strategy and rationale of the rebels, and (to a smaller extent) the Crown forces, rather than asking how this violence occurred. Attention has centred on the motivations and objectives of the organizers. Was the Rising an attempt to overthrow British rule or merely a symbolic gesture: a *coup d'état* or 'blood sacrifice'?[1] Much has been written about its leaders, most notably Patrick Pearse who, in death, became the public face of the Rising. The romantic ideals of the cultural nationalist intellectuals on the military council, particularly their belief in the rôle of sacrificial bloodshed in national regeneration, are seen as forming part of a broader European militarism espoused by 'the generation of 1914'.[2] We know less about the more pragmatic motivations of the Fenian organizers, Tom Clarke and Seán MacDermott, who committed themselves to insurrection at a time when Pearse was a recent, and not very influential, recruit to the Irish Republican Brotherhood.[3] We know least of all about the attitudes of rank-and-file Volunteers.

This essay focuses on how 'ordinary' rebels perceived, experienced and remembered the violence of 1916, rather than the strategy and rationale of the rebellion (of which they had little knowledge). It begins by surveying historiographical responses to the violence of the Rising. It then assesses what the recently released witness statements of the Bureau of Military History add to our understanding of the violence of 1916. What forms of violence were used? How were they shaped by moral and cultural assumptions about the acceptable use of violence? Who was targeted, and who

was not? How were people killed? What constraints were imposed
on the use of violence? And what did the rebels wish to demonstrate
by the forms of violence that they used, and the ways in which they
remembered them?

II

From the outset, the violence of the rebels divided Irish opinion.
Was it cowardly or chivalrous, appalling or admirable, heroic or
criminal? Although James Stephens observed that most Dubliners
were reluctant to express publicly any opinion on this during Easter
week, many who subsequently did so were predictably disparaging.[4]
Unionist and English observers who, due to their social background,
accounted for most of the eye-witness accounts published in the
aftermath of the Rising, often depicted the rebels' violence as irrational, indiscriminate and unconventional. 'There was absolutely
no safety anywhere from the snipers', the wife of the secretary of
the GPO claimed in a letter to her family: 'man, woman or child,
nothing came amiss to them. It was dastardly fighting, if it could
be called fighting at all.'[5] The rebels were criticized, by civilians and
soldiers alike, for the manner in which they fought. At St Stephen's
Green, two feisty 'ladies of the Vigilance Committee' denounced the
rebels as 'skunks and cowards' for hiding behind the park's shrub-
bery rather than fighting 'in the open like men'.[6]

Irish Party politicians were outspoken in their denunciation
of the rebels: John Redmond described them as traitors inspired
more by hatred of Home Rule than of England. Some reactions,
however, were less predictable, reflecting emotional as much as
political responses to the mounting executions. In a passionate,
controversial speech at Westminster on 11 May, John Dillon struck
a radically different note from his leader. Insisting that they had
fought 'a clean fight, a brave fight', he expressed his pride in the
rebels whose 'conduct', however 'misguided', was 'beyond reproach
as fighting men'.[7] Despite urging the execution of its leaders, the
unionist *Irish Times*'s first leading article after the Rising betrayed
a hint of ambivalence. Although declaring that 'Innocent civilians
have been murdered in cold blood', in what it described as a 'criminal adventure', it conceded 'a certain desperate courage to many

of the wretched men who to-day are in their graves'.[8] English press opinion also fluctuated in the aftermath. On 29 April, *The Times* commended aspects of the Rising, including the fact that the rebels had paid for some goods commandeered from local businesses. However, the tone had changed a week later with reports of rebel atrocities appearing under headlines such as 'The Butchery of Civilians' and 'Callous Rebels'.[9] Within nationalist Ireland, a shift in the opposite direction could be discerned in press coverage of the Rising over the weeks and months that followed.

The treatment of rebel violence in the historiography of the Rising has been characterized by similar fluctuations. The first account of the rebellion by a professional historian appeared in 1923. Written by Walter Alison Phillips, Lecky Professor of Modern History at TCD, *The Revolution in Ireland, 1906–1923* remained the only study of the Rising by a professional historian for over four decades.[10] A reactionary unionist, Phillips' account was unsurprisingly critical and, notwithstanding his access to the records of the Chief Secretary and Royal Irish Constabulary, often misleading. The term 'terror' was used by Phillips, whose account emphasized the indiscriminate nature of rebel violence:

> The first attack on the Castle had been signalised by the brutal murder of an unarmed policeman, and the same ruthlessness characterised the proceedings of the rebels elsewhere. Everyone in uniform was marked out for death, and among the victims were not only unarmed officers and police, but army doctors, wounded soldiers in hospital uniform, and elderly members of the Veterans' Corps, five of whom were fatally and many seriously wounded by a volley poured into their defenceless ranks, without warning, by Sinn Feiners in ambush in Haddington Road. In Stephen's Green a carter was shot in cold blood for protesting against the requisitioning of his cart to add to a barricade.

Phillips did not place all of the responsibility for the 'butchery' of Easter week on the organizers. Rather, in a manner reminiscent of Protestant and unionist accounts of the Gaelic and republican uprisings of 1641 and 1798, the 'young idealists' who were 'the nominal leaders of the rebellion' were blamed for unleashing 'forces which they were unable to control'. The army, in contrast, was credited with suppressing the Rising without 'undue destruction of life and property'.[11]

By the 1950s, following several decades of independence, such critical perspectives had been replaced by a no less partisan nationalist historiography (much of it written by veterans of the Rising), which emphasized the piety, chivalry and self-sacrifice of the rebels. These accounts highlighted British atrocities, while sanitizing the rebels' actions.[12] It was not until the 1960s that professional historians began to tackle the Rising. The publication in 1961 of a memorandum written shortly before the Rising by Eoin MacNeill, rejecting armed rebellion on moral and practical grounds, demonstrated how the justification for violence would become central to the emergence of the 'revisionist' controversy.[13] The subsequent outbreak of the conflict in Northern Ireland intensified and complicated this historiographical debate. There were obvious challenges for historians in addressing such issues as the legitimacy of the Rising's élitist violence given the Provisional IRA's appropriation of this tradition to legitimate its own struggle.

By the time of the (distinctly muted) seventy-fifth anniversary, which coincided with a particularly grim spate of violence in the North, it was clear that historiographical (and, to some extent, political and public) attitudes to the Rising had been significantly revised, with greater emphasis on 'the conspiratorial, undemocratic, and destructive nature of the rebellion'.[14] David Fitzpatrick's account of the rebellion provides one example of this more critical approach:

> The planning and conduct of the Rising provided chilling confirmation that military victory was not its primary objective. ... By raising their tricolour in the centre of the main shopping area and close to Dublin's north-side slums, the rebels ensured massive human and material losses once their position was attacked. It is difficult to avoid the inference that the republican strategists were intent upon provoking maximum bloodshed, destruction, and coercion, in the hope of resuscitating Irish Anglophobia and clawing back popular support for their discredited militant programme.[15]

In this reversal of the traditional nationalist narrative, it was the ordinary people of Dublin who were sacrificed for the nation, the

principal achievement of the rebels was the destruction of Home
Rule rather than winning Irish freedom.

By the ninetieth anniversary, the pendulum had swung towards
a more sympathetic interpretation of the Rising. Due to the end
of the long war in the North and the economic boom in the
South, it occurred within a radically different context from previous commemorations: the Irish Republic, it then appeared, was
finally a success. The violence of the Rising continued to provoke
controversy but public, political and historiographical attitudes
had shifted in a more approving (or less critical) direction. Com-
menting on the government's controversial decision to reinstate a
military parade to mark the event, for example, the prominent historian Diarmaid Ferriter declared: 'The post-revisionists won the
argument – the commemoration was about what happened, not
about what some people believe should have happened or fervently
wished did not happen.'[16] Accusing 'the revisionists' of 'living in
the past', the conclusion of a scholarly volume published to mark
the commemoration celebrated the triumph of the 'valuable, noble
and enduring' elements of the Irish republican tradition over 'the
rhetorical assaults it had endured for over three decades'.[17]

Regardless of whether one agrees with such views, it seems
evident that historiographical and, more clearly, political and
public attitudes to the Easter Rising since the late 1960s have been
influenced by contemporary republican violence. This is not to say
that the 'Troubles' were responsible for 'revisionism', or to reject
the interpretations advanced by historians during this period; but
it seems reasonable to suggest that the polarized politics of the
period influenced how such accounts were framed by historians and
deployed in public debate.

III

Like any source, the records of the Bureau of Military History must
be treated with caution. Recorded by military investigators working
on behalf of the Irish government during the 1940s and 1950s,
its 1773 witness statements were influenced by the interviewees'
(and interviewers') subjectivity, subsequently acquired knowledge,
imperfect memories and political bias (not least as a result of the

Irish Civil War). Inevitably, they tend to cast the rebels' motivations and actions in a more favourable light than other sources. Nonetheless, this vast archive of first-hand testimony provides new insights into the rebels' experiences of violence during Easter week.

One unexpected feature of these accounts concerns how few rebels engaged in combat. After the débâcle at Mount Street, when the British army's direct assault on several well-positioned rebel outposts resulted in almost half of all military casualties during the Rising, the military pursued a more cautious and effective strategy of cordoning off rebel garrisons, while subjecting the GPO to artillery bombardment. With the exception of a handful of locations – such as part of the South Dublin Union and some of the streets north of the Four Courts – few rebel outposts were engaged by British soldiers at close quarters. 'During the whole of my time in the Four Courts,' George O'Flanagan recalled, 'I never saw a single man of ours killed or wounded.'[18] During the first half of the week, self-inflicted wounds (caused by rebels accidentally shooting themselves or their comrades) and attacks by hostile civilians posed a greater danger to the rebels than did the Crown forces. In the GPO, where the largest rebel contingent was located, only nine men were killed in action, most of these (often self-inflicted) deaths occurring during the chaotic retreat on Friday. Like many Volunteers, Kevin McCabe spent Easter week at his GPO outpost 'waiting for something to happen. We did practically no shooting as there was no target.'[19]

Much of the fighting that did occur consisted of long-range sniping duels. Advancing through streets where they could be fired on from almost any angle, British soldiers found street-fighting a novel and disconcerting experience. John Regan, a police officer on wartime secondment to the 3rd battalion, Royal Irish Rifles, described the difficulties posed by snipers: 'Some we got on the roofs of houses, but those who fired from inside a room, over a blanket stretched across it and through a window from which the glass had been removed were nearly impossible to spot.'[20] In such circumstances, it was sometimes not clear why individuals were shot or by whom: crossing the Ha'penny Bridge, for example, James Kavanagh 'saw two people, a man and woman, fall shot dead at the corner of Liffey Street and Bachelor's Walk. I don't know where the shots came from.'[21]

In contrast to the War of Independence, the violence of the Rising was largely impersonal, devoid of intimacy or hatred: combatants were killed at a distance, their identity unknown to their assailants.[22] This must have made killing easier. After the initial shock, many found that firing a rifle, or even killing, became routine, even exhilarating. Under fire for the first time, Jimmy Grace recalled trembling 'from hand to foot in a panic of fear and it was only when I was able to reply to the fire that I overcame the fear'.[23] Lieutenant Jameson, an officer in the Leinster Regiment, 'felt horrid' after shooting his first rebel. But, although he had to suppress an instinctive urge to 'apologise and help' his first victim, he 'very soon got over that and was very annoyed when I missed anybody'.[24] Although the leaders debated the ethics of the Rising in the GPO, few rebels express regret about their use of violence in the witness statements. As in all conflicts, some found it satisfying or pleasurable.[25] Con O'Donovan, one of the few rebels to describe the experience of killing, did so in positive, if ambiguous, terms:

> We were really suffering from the strain of looking for a soldier to fire at, and I remember well the callous and, shall I say, brutal pleasure I felt when I 'picked off' one who was crossing Grattan Bridge, although he dodged from side to side, and kept his head low most of the time. Another who fell to one of our group was too easy a mark. He walked out of Chancery Street in full kit. ... Here was a soldier, armed and probably looking for a chance to fire on us. One bullet did it, and then the marksman raised his hat, and said, 'He's dead, or dying now, anyhow. May the Lord have mercy on him.'[26]

Some rebels expressed sympathy for their victims: remembering the 'shocking losses' at Mount Street, Tom Walsh conceded that they 'were brave men and, I must say, clean fighters'.[27] But few indicated much squeamishness about what was done. Despite the horrific scale of the casualties at Mount Street, where over 230 soldiers were wounded or killed in a single afternoon, the tiny number of Volunteers responsible were thrilled by their success. Moments before he was killed, a euphoric Paddy Doyle exclaimed: 'Boys, isn't this a great day for Ireland?'[28] Observing the carnage – one witness claimed 'the place was literally swimming with blood' – James Walsh felt he 'had accounted for the whole British army in Ireland. What a thought! What joy! What a day!'[29]

Such positive responses may have been influenced by the nature of the violence that unfolded as the rebels, barricaded within fortified positions, cut down wave after wave of soldiers as they charged towards Mount Street Bridge to the sound of their officers' whistles. William Christian recalled the sight of 'hundreds and hundreds of them – stretching right across the road ... We opened fire and men fell like ninepins.'[30] The violence, taking the form of mass slaughter from a distance rather than face-to-face killing, lacked intimacy. Walsh described the plight of the soldiers in detached terms:

> Those who managed to get by '25' ran towards the bridge and took cover anywhere they could find it, on house steps, behind trees, and even in the channels of the roadway. We kept on blazing away at those in the channels, and after a time as they were killed, the next fellow moved up and passed the man killed in front of him. This gave one the impression of a giant human khaki-coloured caterpillar.[31]

And, in contrast to the War of Independence, the battle (subsequently celebrated as 'the Irish Thermopylae') conformed to conventional, even heroic, notions of combat: uniformed men, fixed positions, an enemy superior in firepower and numbers. The rebels even observed the 'rules of war', permitting informal truces to allow doctors and nurses to clear the dead and dying from the road.

Rebel accounts of the battle of Ashbourne, the only other substantial rebel victory (when a force of over forty Fingal Battalion Volunteers out-fought a larger contingent of Royal Irish Constabulary, killing eight and wounding fifteen) indicate a similar pride in their military achievements. While demonstrating no desire to kill policemen during the raids that occurred earlier that week, the Volunteers welcomed the opportunity of a set-piece battle that accorded with chivalrous conceptions of warfare. A civilian observer described their mood after the battle: 'They were very excited and were cheering, as men would after a football match.'[32] 'The boys were in great form,' one Volunteer remembered.[33] One difference, however, between the battles at Mount Street and Ashbourne was the more intimate nature of the violence of the latter, which had concluded with a bayonet charge and close-quarters combat. Joseph Lawless described what ensued:

> Hearing the movement of my father towards him, he [District Inspector Harry Smyth] fired at him on the instant, and his bullet, missing my father, penetrated [John] Crinnigan's heart, killing him instantly. My father's shot at the same time hit Smyth on the fore-head and smashed his skull. He still lay as he fell – as I came along – feet on bank and head near the edge of the roadside, and, although his brain matter spattered the grass beside him, he yet lived, his breath coming in great gasps at long intervals, and the muscles of his face relaxed ... I neither lamented nor rejoiced in his passing.[34]

Whereas conventional battles are recalled by rebels in an unabashed or even celebratory tone, accounts of less conventional (or justifiable) violence are often circumspect, hedged with doubt, or evasive. The witness statements, though revealing so many minutiae of Easter week, do not include a single description of the death of Constable Michael Lahiff. Often attributed to Countess Markievicz, the killing of Lahiff at St Stephen's Green – he was one of six unarmed DMP men shot (two of them fatally) on Easter Monday – probably occurred within view of numerous rebels. The death of Charles McGee, an unarmed 23-year-old constable killed in disputed but unheroic circumstances at Castlebellingham, was described by Volunteers of the Louth Battalion in vague, contradictory or regretful terms, in contrast to the celebratory accounts of the battle of Ashbourne.[35] The Louth and Fingal Volunteers had very different experiences of the Rising. Both columns (of similar size) spent Easter week roaming through the countryside in a desultory fashion, arresting soldiers, raiding post offices and capturing police stations, but increasingly frustrated by the unwillingness of Crown forces to engage them in battle. It was only the decision of the RIC (resented by some of its members) to attack the Fingal Volunteers that resulted in the heroic outcome at Ashbourne. In contrast, shadowed by a large contingent of policemen who refused to engage them in battle, the Louth Volunteers were denied an opportunity to take their place in the history books. Rather than targeting all in uniform as Phillips and others alleged, the rebels demonstrated restraint, usually killing only those who attacked them.

Despite such efforts to 'play by the rules', the rebels were widely accused of responsibility for a variety of atrocities including the shooting of civilians, unarmed policemen and unarmed soldiers; the use of expanding (or dum-dum) bullets; the use of prisoners as human shields; and the abuse of prisoners. Unsurprisingly, the witness statements provide little evidence to substantiate these charges, with many rebels noting the constraints imposed by their officers. 'Wilful damage was as severely eschewed as indiscriminate shooting,' Desmond Ryan claimed: 'Orders were given that prisoners were to be treated courteously. No firing was to take place except under orders or to repel attack.'[36] But it does seem that the rebels sought to live up to these standards. Policemen and unarmed soldiers were not systematically targeted, and Volunteers clearly spurned many opportunities to shoot men in uniform. Fr Michael Curran, Archbishop Byrne's secretary, recalled his surprise at how a group of DMP constables stood around Nelson's Pillar throughout Monday afternoon, while the rebels in the GPO fired past them at British soldiers. He was struck also by the rebels' restraint in avoiding easy targets, including a drunken soldier who stood in front of the GPO 'eating something, in an act of bravado'.[37] Fr John Flanagan observed how uniformed soldiers on leave stood around Sackville Street, watching the fighting with friends and family, apparently unconcerned that they might be targeted.[38] One Volunteer described how a detective casually leaned over his barricade to ask him 'how long we thought we could hold out'. 'I told Pearse about this,' he recalled, 'and asked if we could shot him. He said "No, let him go".'[39]

The witness statements provide little evidence to sustain charges of widespread or casual rebel atrocities. The Volunteers did use expanding bullets, but this may be attributed to shortage of ammunition rather than malice. Large numbers of prisoners were taken, sometimes on questionable grounds, but they were generally treated well. Many – like Laurence Kettle (who spent Easter week building barricades with library books in the Royal College of Surgeons), or the stoical Tommies who staffed the GPO's kitchen, or the Indian army doctor who treated its wounded – voluntarily, even cheerfully, assisted the rebels. Despite being shot and almost bayoneted when he drove into a rebel road-block, Lord Dunsany was unstinting in his praise of his treatment by the rebels.[40]

Nor was it true that prisoners in the GPO were used as a human shield or left 'to die like rats' in a cellar full of bombs. These claims, originating from the same dubious source (2nd Lieutenant A. D. Chalmers of the Royal Artillery), so outraged Diarmuid Lynch that he participated in his court martial purely to refute them.[41] Joe Good's account confirms that prisoners were treated as reasonably as could be expected during the chaos of the evacuation:

> Our military prisoners whom we had captured during the week appeared terrified, as was only natural in the confusion. I suggested to ['The'] O'Rahilly that they be let go and take their chance of escaping. It looked to me as if we were trapped. O'Rahilly misunderstood me at first, thinking I wanted to exploit the prisoners in some way and he almost struck me. Then he saw my point and apologized.[42]

The refusal of many prisoners (including policemen) to identify their captors after the surrender suggests that they were satisfied with their treatment (even if fear rather than gratitude may have influenced some). Some, like Lord Dunsany, even helped rebels to escape after the surrender.

Perhaps the most controversial charge against the rebels concerns the killing of members of the Volunteer Training Corps outside Beggar's Bush barracks on Easter Monday. Four or five of these men were killed (accounts vary), but it is questionable whether this can described as 'the casual murder' of 'unarmed reservists'.[43] Some, if not all, of these men appear to have been armed (although most, or possibly all of them, had not been issued with ammunition), and they were returning, under orders, to a military barracks to assist in its defence.

If the witness statements tend to exonerate the rebels from responsibility for callous behaviour, some caveats must be noted. Civilians, unarmed policemen and unarmed soldiers were intentionally shot by rebels. The first victim of the Rising (Constable James O'Brien) was unarmed, as were other men, women and at least one child deliberately shot by rebels. Looters were killed, as were civilians who appeared suspicious, hostile or merely unco-operative. Many witness statements describe the furious response of working-class Dubliners to the rebels in parts of inner-city Dublin. Matt Walton, for example, was shaken when one of his comrades shot a woman who made to strike him: 'I just remember seeing her face and head disappear as she went down like a sack. That was my baptism of fire and I remember my knees going out from under me. I would have sold my mother and father and the Pope just to get out of that bloody place.'[44]

Members of the Irish Citizen Army, in particular, were involved in dubious killings around St Stephen's Green. By his own account, Frank Robbins was prevented from shooting civilians, policemen and unarmed soldiers by his officer.[45] In his witness statement Jim O'Shea recalled 'constantly using my rifle, firing down Dawson Street at any movement of cars', firing on an unarmed policeman, attempting to bayonet an abusive woman, and shooting an unarmed (and probably inebriated) British soldier who had harangued him from the railings of St Stephen's Green.[46] The ICA's relative ruthless-ness may have stemmed from bitter memories of the 1913 lock-out. Asked how they should treat the police, James Connolly told his men: 'Remember how they treated you in 1913.'[47] Patrick Kelly, a Volunteer, was initially angered when his officer prevented him from shooting an unarmed policeman outside Broadstone station: 'I remarked that I was unarmed in 1913.'[48]

In addition, much of the moral responsibility for the civilian deaths of Easter week, an inevitable consequence of the decision to base the insurrection within the densely populated inner city, lies with the military council. This decision, whatever its tactical ratio-nale, conflicted with the rebels' perception of themselves as a con-ventional force fighting by conventional means. Some 2600 people were wounded during the Rising, while civilians accounted for over half of the rebellion's 450 fatalities. The rebels occupied convents, hospitals and homes, bringing death and destruction to the inno-cent. It is difficult, for example, to understand why it was considered acceptable to occupy the South Dublin Union, the largest work-house in Ireland with over 3000 sick or destitute inmates. However, the rebels' reaction to the pitiful plight of civilians when they finally witnessed it at first hand, following their evacuation from the GPO to Moore Street, suggests an abysmal lack of foresight rather than a cynical intention to wreak havoc on Dublin's civilians.

Although there is little evidence to support claims of poor discipline or brutality by rebels, the evidence against the British army is stronger. Curiously, one of the rebels' most common complaints against British soldiers concerned their 'filthy language'.[49] But there were also numerous accounts of drunkenness, looting and brutality. John Regan, a Royal Irish Regiment officer, was shocked by the heavy drinking by officers and privates that he witnessed in Dublin Castle.[50] In his witness statement, Constable Patrick Bermingham described how he arrested a British soldier 'who was very much intoxicated, firing indiscriminately in the air and at windows and doors'.[51] Robert Barton, a British army officer (who developed republican sympathies), claimed that the War Office was concerned by the scale of looting by soldiers in Dublin, 'an offence for which they would have been shot if they were in France'.[52] Many witness statements describe how the rebels were routinely robbed by soldiers after their surrender.

It seems likely that it was the military, rather than rebels, that accounted for most civilian fatalities. This was partly a consequence of its use of artillery and heavy machine guns, as well as its crude tactics. Soldiers were instructed to methodically crush all resistance: 'the head of the columns will in no case advance beyond any house from which fire has been opened, until the inhabitants of such house have been destroyed or captured'. Brigadier-General Lowe further directed that 'every man in any such house whether bearing arms or not may be considered as a rebel'.[53] In areas where the military encountered stiff resistance, such as North King Street where fourteen soldiers were killed and another thirty-three wounded in a 28-hour battle for control of 150 yards, the troops appeared to have regarded any remaining residents as legitimate targets.[54]

There were other practical reasons that explain why the military accounted for much of the more questionable violence of the Rising. Being few, poorly armed and increasingly confined to their garrisons, the rebels were in little position to inflict much harm. While most soldiers behaved professionally, there were vastly more of them (20,000 had flooded into the capital by the end of the week) and they were heavily armed, mobile, and dispersed over a greater area. Many were young, inexperienced and inefficient. Captain Gerrard described the men under his command as 'untrained, undersized products of the English slums. ... The young Sherwoods that I had with me had never fired a service rifle before.'[55]

The confusion and frustration of street-fighting also contributed to civilian deaths. Soldiers were often unable to distinguish between civilians and the many rebels who did not wear uniforms. Captain Gerrard related how one of his sentries shot two girls: 'I said, "What on earth did you do that for?" He said, "I thought they were rebels. I was told they were dressed in all classes of attire." At a range of about 200 yards I saw two girls – about twenty – lying dead.' John Regan observed that the English troops he fought alongside 'had a gruelling time coming into Dublin and did not know friend from foe. They regarded, not unreasonably, everyone they saw as an enemy, and fired at anything that moved.'[56] General Sir John Maxwell, the British GOC, was remarkably candid about this aspect of the fighting in one press interview:

> These rebels wore no uniform, and the man who was shooting at a soldier one minute might, for all he knew, be walking quietly beside him in the street at another. ... Nearly everything had to be left to the troops on the spot ... how were the soldiers to discriminate? They saw their comrades killed beside them by hidden and treacherous assailants, and it is even possible that under the horrors of this peculiar attack some of them 'saw red'. That is the inevitable consequence of a rebellion of this kind.[57]

His comments highlighted a revealing gulf between the rebels' perception of their own conduct and the military view of the illegitimate nature of rebel violence.

Less understandably, as Maxwell strongly hinted, military discipline collapsed entirely on some occasions. One chilling witness statement recounts how George Duggan, the manager of the Provincial Bank on College Green, came close to being murdered by a drunken sergeant, until he was able to prove to a junior officer that several of his sons had enlisted in the British army (two had lost their lives at Gallipoli).[58] Others suggest that rebels were killed after surrendering: accounts by Dick Balfe, Jimmy Grace, Dan McCarthy and Patrick Colgan describe how each was spared only by the intervention of British officers. The two most notorious atrocities of Easter week were committed by the military. Captain J. C. Bowen-Colthurst was responsible not only for the death of Francis Sheehy Skeffington, a prominent Dublin pacifist, but also the more obscure deaths of Thomas Dickson, Patrick MacIntyre and a teenage boy whom he killed during an earlier rampage through Portobello. The revelation that the army was also responsible for killing fifteen civilians on a short stretch of North King Street added to nationalist outrage after the Rising, both because of the manner in which the deaths occurred (as a result of a systematic military operation rather than in the heat of the battle) and the attempt to cover them up.

IV

Though obvious, the difficulty in justifying much of the state violence that occurred during Easter week has sometimes been neglected in 'revisionist' historiography. Academic historians have tended to analyse republican violence in forensic detail, while devoting less attention to that perpetrated by the Crown forces. This is partly due to the greater availability of sources for republican violence, but it also reflects the broader political and historiographical context in which the scholarly analysis of revolutionary violence has emerged since the 1970s, as well as the wider public debates generated by this research. Much of the controversy prompted by Peter Hart's groundbreaking research on guerrilla warfare in Cork, for example, stems from an ideological conflict about the legitimacy of physical-force republicanism rather than scholarly interest in who did what. Also, because the British state violence of the revolutionary period (such as that of the 'Black and Tans') has few defenders, critical analysis of it generates little controversy, whereas accounts of republican violence retain the power to provoke furious debate.

What do these accounts of violence tell us about the Easter Rising (as opposed to its historiography)? That the rebels' idealism contributed to their high standards of discipline and restrained use of violence seems evident, but the reasons for what some would assert as a kind of moral superiority should be contextualized. As the military council regarded the Rising as – above all – an act of propaganda, one intended to win Irish and international support for their cause, a 'clean fight' was imperative. The Proclamation urged the rebels not to dishonour their cause 'by cowardice, inhumanity or rapine'. 'The valour, self-sacrifice and discipline of Irish men and women,' Patrick Pearse declared during the Rising, would 'win for our country a glorious place among the nations.'[59] The essentially symbolic purpose of the violence of the Rising also helps to explain its peculiarly defeatist strategy.

The rebels' belief that they were engaged in a legitimate form of warfare – crucial for their self-perception as a chivalrous force – accounted for their enthusiasm for the trappings of militarism. Striving to present the Rising as a conventional and legitimate act of violence, they wore uniforms, mimicked formal army structures and titles, and proclaimed themselves a lawful authority. Officers in the GPO assigned themselves orderlies, aides-de-camp, and adjutants, ate in a commissariat, and reportedly even socialized in an officers' mess. Female combatants were confined to a rôle scarcely less conventional than in regular armies. The rebels' self-conscious desire to act in a way that conformed to their idealized view of conventional military behaviour was particularly evident during the general surrender, when many spurned the opportunity to escape. Some, like Thomas Doyle, took pride in their swashbuckling comportment: 'Éamonn Ceant and General Lowe marched at the head of the men. Éamonn looked great: he had his shirt thrown open, his tunic thrown open and was swinging along at the head of his men. He looked a real soldier.'[60] This admiration for military values, which contributed to the popularity of volunteering before the outbreak of the Great War, was widely shared within contemporary society. Significantly, the rebels' belief that they had fought, as one put it, 'in a fair and clean manner', came to be shared by nationalist opinion, as did admiration for their stoical acceptance of a punishment that was widely regarded as unjust and vindictive.[61]

Yet, as Joe Good's account of the surrender highlights, the rebels' perception of their behaviour was not universally shared:

> The bearing and behaviour of the rebels was that of men who had done something laudable and, as their behaviour had been chival-

rous, they expected that military etiquette would be observed by the enemy. The British soldiers – officers and men – were obviously irritated and puzzled by the Volunteers. They were shocked at the small numbers that surrendered and at the variety and crudity of their arms. They regarded the Volunteers as shameless, impertinent traitors, and said so.[62]

One reason for the disparity in behaviour of the contending forces may have been the gulf between the rebels' idealized view of combat and the British army's use of the more brutal methods of modern war.[63] The wartime context explains much that seems otherwise inexplicable about the state's response: the frontal assault on Mount Street bridge, the devastation of the city centre by artillery, the imposition of martial law, the peremptory nature of the executions, and the counter-productive coercion that followed.

The relative restraint displayed by the rebels was encouraged by lack of personal animosity for their antagonists. The rebels did not know those that they killed. They generally described the Tommy in positive terms: 'a decent type of lad', 'a decent fellow', 'not a bad fellow'. Few statements convey much animosity between rebels and soldiers (many of whom were Irish nationalists), and many testify to a surprising degree of mutual respect or even admiration. But the tone changes in accounts of the end of Easter week, with descriptions of the humiliating overnight confinement of male and female prisoners without sanitary facilities outside the Rotunda, the taunting of leaders by G-men at Richmond barracks, and the executions and repression that followed.

The violence of 1916 must be understood within the context of the idealization of military values during the Great War, as well as the specific circumstances in which it occurred during Easter week. It should not be framed through the perspective of the violence that followed, even if it played a vital rôle in legitimizing that violence. Sectarian hatred, communal violence, tit-for-tat assassinations, reprisals, the war of terror against spies and enemies – the climate of fear so brilliantly evoked by Peter Hart's research on the Irish revolution – were largely absent in 1916. Considering what would soon follow, the Rising's reputation as a chivalrous fight may well be deserved.

NOTES

1. F. X. Martin, 'The 1916 Rising – a *coup d'état* or a "bloody protest"?', *Studia Hibernica*, 8 (1968), 106–37.

2. Sean Farrell Moran, *Patrick Pearse and the Politics of Redemption* (Washington 1994).

3. Fearghal McGarry, *The Rising: Ireland, Easter 1916* (Oxford 2010), pp. 95–102.

4. James Stephens, *The Insurrection in Dublin* (Gloucester 2008; 1st edn 1916), pp. 19–20.

5. Keith Jeffery, *The GPO and the Easter Rising* (Dublin 2006), p. 97.

6. *Ibid.* p. 94.

7. PD (HC), 5th series, lxxxii, cols 935–51.

8. *IT*, 28 Apr.–1 May 1916.

9. Clair Wills, *Dublin 1916: The Siege of the GPO* (London 2009), p. 89.

10. W. Alison Phillips, *The Revolution in Ireland, 1906–1923* (London 1923), pp. viii, vii.

11. *Ibid.* pp. 99–101.

12. Charles Townshend, *Easter 1916: The Irish Rebellion* (London 2005), p. 346.

13. F. X. Martin, 'Select documents: Eoin MacNeill on the 1916 Rising', *Irish Historical Studies*, 12 (1961), 226–71.

14. Townshend, *Easter 1916*, p. 354.

15. David Fitzpatrick, *The Two Irelands, 1919–1939* (Oxford 1998), pp. 59–60.

16. *Irish Independent*, 18 Apr. 2006.

17. Gabriel Doherty, 'The commemoration of the ninetieth anniversary of the Easter Rising' in Gabriel Doherty and Dermot Keogh (eds), *1916: The Long Revolution* (Cork 2007), p. 407.

18. George O'Flanagan, MAD, BMH Papers, WS 131.

19. Kevin McCabe, WS 926.

20. Joost Augusteijn (ed.), *The Memoirs of John M. Regan: A Catholic Officer in the RIC and RUC, 1909–48* (Dublin 2007), p. 95.

21. James Kavanagh, WS 889.

22. Peter Hart, *The I.R.A. at War* (Oxford 2003), p. 64; Anne Dolan, 'Ending war in a "sportsmanlike manner" ': the milestone of revolution, 1919–23' in Thomas E. Hachey (ed.), *Turning Points in Twentieth-Century Irish History* (Dublin 2011), pp. 21–38.

23. Seumas Grace, WS 310.

24. Michael Foy and Brian Barton, *The Easter Rising* (Stroud 2000) p. 167.

25. Joanna Bourke, *An Intimate History of Killing: Face-to-Face Killing in Twentieth-Century Warfare* (London 1999).

26. Con O'Donovan, ws 1750.

27. James and Thomas Walsh, ws 198.

28. *Ibid.*

29. Padraig O'Connor, ws 813; James and Thomas Walsh, ws 198.

30. William Christian, ws 646.

31. James and Thomas Walsh, ws 198.

32. John Austin, ws 904.

33. Bernard McAllister, ws 47.

34. Joseph Lawless, ws 1043.

35. Patrick McHugh, ws 677; Frank Martin, ws 236; Arthur Greene, ws 238; Hugh Kearney, ws 260.

36. Desmond Ryan, ws 724.

37. Revd Michael Curran, ws 687.

38. Jeffery, *The GPO*, p. 158.

39. Charles Donnelly, ws 824.

40. Lord Dunsany, *Patches of Sunlight* (New York 1938), pp 280–1.

41. *Weekly Irish Times* (comp.), *Sinn Fein Rebellion Handbook: Easter 1916* (Dublin 1998; from 2nd edn 1917), pp. 10–11; Diarmuid Lynch, ws 4.

42. Joe Good, ws 388.

43. Fitzpatrick, *Two Irelands*, p. 62.

44. Foy and Barton, *Easter Rising*, p. 167.

45. Frank Robbins, ws 585.

46. James O'Shea, ws 733. See also Foy and Barton, *Easter Rising*, p. 186.

47. Frank Robbins, ws 585.

48. Patrick Kelly, ws 781.

49. James O'Shea, ws 733.

50. Augusteijn, *John Regan*, p. 96.

51. Patrick Bermingham, ws 697.

52. Robert Barton, ws 979.

53. Townshend, *Easter 1916*, p. 189.

54. Foy and Barton, *Easter Rising*, p. 188.

55. E. Gerrard, ws 348.

56. Augusteijn, *John Regan*, p. 95. See also Foy and Barton, *Easter Rising*, pp. 186–7.

57. *Rebellion Handbook*, p. 23.

58. George Chester Duggan (son of the bank manager), ws 1071.

59. *Rebellion Handbook*, p. 45.

60. Thomas Doyle, ws 186.

61. John Shouldice, ws 162.

62. Joe Good, ws 388.

63. On militarism and the Great War, see Wills, *Dublin 1916*, pp. 91–2, 98–103.

5. The Sack of Balbriggan and Tit-for-Tat Terror

Ross O'Mahony

The town of Balbriggan they've burnt to the ground,
While bullets like hailstones were whizzing around:
And women left homeless by this evil clan
They've waged war on the children, the bold Black and Tan.[1]

In every part of Ireland that we visited we were impressed by the atmosphere of terrorism which prevailed. This is due to some extent to uncertainty: people are afraid that their houses might be burned: they fear that they might be arrested or even dragged from their beds and shot.[2]

The 'Sack of Balbriggan', on the night of 20–1 September 1920, has entered nationalist folklore as an infamous example of the so-called system of 'reprisals'. This chapter will assess its credentials as an act of state terror, documenting the historical context, the course of events on the night, and the people affected by it. Accounts of the Sack are contradictory, some depicting the targets as prominent republicans and their families, others as innocent victims of rampaging Black and Tans. The truth is more nuanced. The Sack prompted republican retaliation leading to a tit-for-tat campaign of terror in North Co. Dublin (Fingal). Ultimately, most of the victims were ordinary citizens whose lives were disrupted by the escalating violence.

In March 1920, the first Black and Tans arrived in Gormanstown camp, three miles north of Balbriggan. Eventually 9000 of these new recruits came through this heavily fortified camp, which provided a base for training and for local raiding. Fingal had a republican tradition dating back to the rebellion of 1798, and stories of that time had lived on.[3] The Fingal Brigade of the Irish Volunteers had distinguished itself in Easter 1916, when a force led by Thomas Ashe and Richard Mulcahy captured a police barracks and defeated a detachment of the RIC at Ashbourne.[4] The tactics adopted by Ashe and Mulcahy anticipated the guerrilla campaign of the IRA during the War of Independence. In accordance with orders sent through the Brigade, the Fingal Volunteers surrendered to a detachment of police from Balbriggan, being escorted by a company of the 5th Lancers to Swords, and thence to Richmond Barracks. The principal leaders of the Fingal Brigade, Thomas Ashe and Richard Coleman, both died in prison. Ashe died after being forcibly fed while on hunger strike in Mountjoy, on 25 September 1917. Coleman succumbed to influenza in December 1918, while incarcerated at Usk in Wales. Coleman's death prompted de Valera to remark: 'Fingal has contributed more than its fair share.'[5]

The events of the Rising and its aftermath might therefore suggest that Fingal was strongly republican and a hotbed of Volunteer activity. This did not, however, apply to Balbriggan, which had no involvement in the Rising and no Irish Volunteer company, despite attempts to form one.[6] Many townspeople were actively involved in supporting the war effort, businesses supplied the British army, and the Town Commissioners provided the town hall for war benefit events, resolving in January 1916 to form a local committee to encourage enlistment even as it was falling elsewhere. The largest local employers were two hosiery manufacturers, Deedes, Templer & Co., an English firm, and Smyth & Co., whose managing director (Lewis Whyte, JP) was a well-known loyalist.[7] For such a small town (with only 507 houses and 2273 inhabitants in 1911), a large number of men heeded the call to arms (292, of whom 41 were killed).[8] Balbriggan's reputation as a traditionally republican town is largely mythical. However, as the Great War dragged on and the threat of conscription loomed, nationalists in Balbriggan began to voice dissent and became involved with the rapidly expanding Sinn Féin and Volunteer movements. A Volunteer company was set up in the town by Thomas Peppard, a recently released veteran of the Rising, and ex-servicemen participated in its training. In the General

Election of December 1918 Frank Lawless, another veteran of the
Rising, was elected MP (or TD) for Sinn Féin in North Co. Dublin.
His vote more than doubled that of the veteran Home Ruler John
Joseph Clancy, who had represented the constituency since 1885.
The counting of votes and declaration of the poll took place in Bal-
briggan, giving rise to no disturbance apart from some expressions
of hostility from the RIC.[9]

Despite the local advance of republicanism, the presence of so
many ex-servicemen and their relations curtailed support for the
IRA. In the Fingal region, Swords, Rush and Lusk were far more
prominent in the military movement. The beginning of 1920 was
a period of rising prosperity for Balbriggan. Smyth & Co. had
just opened a new hosiery factory and had a large order book. Its
manager, Thomas M. Cashell, told the Board of Guardians that if
more housing were available then more staff could be taken on, and
that his workers could pay up to 10s. per week in rent. The Town
Commissioners had already embarked on a scheme to erect new
housing to facilitate this expansion.[10] On 15 January 1920, the first
municipal elections since 1914 provided a test of political conti-
nuity. Of the eight sitting councillors, only three (all unionists) were
returned, and the new chairman was (Michael) James Derham of
Sinn Féin.[11] Five months later, the elections for Balrothery RDC provided a clearer test of Sinn Féin's success in supplanting 'constitutional' nationalists. In Balbriggan, which contributed five members
to the Council, only 1077 valid votes were cast out of 1888 names
on the electoral register. Though Sinn Féin secured a majority,
Labour also polled strongly. On the first count, Christopher Brown
(264 votes) and James Derham (247) were elected for Sinn Féin,
along with Labour's Michael Brady (223). Peter Carr (Labour) and
Patrick Donegan (Sinn Féin) were elected on the second count.[12]

Republican activity in Balbriggan intensified, as courts sanctioned by Dáil Éireann were convened and republican police
imposed a curfew on the opening of public houses. The presence of
these courts and police, and other 'seditious' activities by local 'Sinn
Féiners', resulted in more frequent searches and arrests by the Black
and Tans. James Derham, the new chairman of the Town Commissioners, was arrested in February outside Swords, and afterwards

imprisoned in Mountjoy. Black and Tans moved into Balrothery Workhouse and began using it as an additional base for raiding the houses of republican suspects.[13] Local defiance of state authority was expressed in a resolution passed on 18 August 1920: 'That we, the Balbriggan Town Commissioners, hereby pledge our allegiance to Dail Eireann, as the legitimately constituted and elected Government of the Irish people: and bind ourselves to carry out any decrees issued by the Republican Local Government Department.'[14] Despite this affirmation, the ordinary system of Petty Sessions was still operating and well attended, suggesting that many in the town had not transferred their allegiance to the republic.[15] Meanwhile, the local IRA battalion and the Fingal Brigade as a whole began to plan a new series of attacks, though with little success. The commander of the Fingal Brigade, Michael Lynch, was admonished by Richard Mulcahy, CS, who told him that 'this sporadic shooting of the enemy, before the men were properly trained was just a waste of time, and that there were to be no more attacks until I was satisfied that the men were fit to go through with them and would not make a mess of them, through blundering'.[16]

The first reference to the Balbriggan district in the weekly returns of 'outrages', reported by the RIC, occurred in April 1920. On 13 and 14 April, the shops of Balbriggan closed in accordance with the nation-wide strike in support of the IRA hunger strikers in Mountjoy.[17] On the second night, when news of the prisoners' release reached the town, there were celebrations. The Town Commissioners met that evening and unanimously resolved:

> That this Council takes this opportunity of congratulating the Irish Republican Prisoners on their magnificent victory the greatest in the history of this country, and that we adjourn this meeting as tribute to this splendid courage and self sacrifice in the fight for Irish Freedom, and as a protest against callous brutality which has placed them at death's door.[18]

On a hill outside the town, a more impromptu gathering took place. A police patrol had seen a bonfire on Clonard Hill and Sergeant Patrick Finnerty and four other local policemen went to investigate. They found a crowd assembled with a Sinn Féin flag, singing the 'Soldier's Song', 'The Red Flag' and the 'The Felons of our Land'.

Sergeant Finnerty cautioned the leader, Thomas Lawless, who then
called for three cheers for the Irish Republic, de Valera and others.
When the crowd moved back to Balbriggan, the police followed. As
they entered Clonard Street, a shot was fired and Sergeant Finnerty
hit, but the crowd appeared not to notice. The wounded sergeant
was carried to a nearby house and then taken to the Mater Hospital, where he died from his wounds on 16 April, after twenty-five
years' service.[19] Some houses were raided after the shooting, but no
arrests made.

Shock and horror at Finnerty's killing were widely expressed.
In a sermon on 18 April, the parish priest remarked that it was the
first murder in the town for generations. He hoped that, as a result
of this shedding of innocent blood, the scourge of God would not
fall upon the parish.[20] An inquest was held on 1 May. The jury
vigorously condemned an attack that had discredited the town and
returned a verdict of murder by persons unknown: 'They all knew
very well what was happening throughout the country, but the
little town of Balbriggan had always been quiet and it should have
remained so.'[21]

On 29 April, however, another long-serving sergeant, John
Brady, had died from his wounds following an attack on Rush RIC
barracks. Again the attack was condemned by a local jury.[22] Republican animosity towards the police was evident in threatening letters
sent to Constables McDermott and Thorpe on 21 July and Head
Constable Hunter on 18 August. These letters do not appear to
have unduly worried the RIC and Hunter expressed the opinion that
they were sent just to annoy.[23] These three threatening letters were
the only incidents in Balbriggan over the summer to feature in the
weekly outrage summaries. Otherwise, republican activity does not
appear to have been increased to any great extent, a fact attributed
to the heavy presence of the RIC and Black and Tans.[24]

September 1920 saw a country-wide increase in outrages against
the police: 243 outrages were attributed to Sinn Féin in the week
ending 19 September 1920.[25] On 20 September Head Constable
Peter Burke was travelling in plain clothes from Dublin to Gormanstown camp, with his brother (Sergeant William Patrick Burke) and
a few colleagues. In Balbriggan they stopped at Mrs Smyth's public

house on Drogheda Street. A party of 'Black and Tans' was already in the bar, and reports conflict as to whether an argument broke out or merely singing. Mrs Smyth told the visitors that no more drink would be had and called for the local RIC to intervene, but on arrival they declined. While the Burke brothers and the Black and Tans were in Smyth's, two members of the local IRA were drinking in another public house, Connolly's on the corner of Bridge and Mill Streets. They were Michael Rock, intelligence officer, 1st Battalion, Fingal Brigade, and reportedly also James Derham, chairman of the Town Commissioners.[26] William Corcoran, another local IRA man, informed them of the presence of Black and Tans in Smyth's. Rock told Corcoran to get him a gun and he and Corcoran went to the other bar, where they found the Black and Tans holding local civilians who had been drinking in the pub. According to Rock's statement for the Bureau of Military History:

> I ordered them to clear out, instead of doing so, they made a rush at me and I had no option but to fire. I shot one of the Head Constables dead and wounded the other, who later recovered, and then my pal and I cleared out the back door and got safely away. The Derhams, Lawless, Gibbons and others were warned not to stay at home that night.[27]

In fact, Head Constable Burke died shortly afterwards from his injuries. He had been assigned to the RIC depot in the Phoenix Park to help train the Black and Tans, and was regarded as a popular officer.[28]

Word reached Gormanstown around 11 p.m. and immediately a party of Black and Tans (possibly accompanied by Auxiliaries) set out for Balbriggan. A detachment of Auxiliaries had recently joined the Black and Tans already based in the camp. Four motor lorries stopped outside the RIC barracks on Drogheda Street.[29] By this time Rock had returned the gun and, fearing he had been identified by local RIC, he fled the town.[30] Ten or twelve men proceeded down the street, breaking glass as they went and firing shots into the air. They then stopped outside John Derham's public house and started to break the shutters and windows of the pub before raiding the living-quarters upstairs. After forcing the Derham family from their home, they wrecked and then torched it. John Derham later told the American Commission on Conditions in Ireland that 'it was burned to the ground, and not a vestige left. Everything burned down. My neighbour's house, Connolly's, on the opposite corner, was the same way. Nothing but bricks and stones. Clonard Street, seventeen houses burned in that street, nine in one row.'[31] By the morning of 21 September, so it was reported, twenty-five houses had been burned, fifty had had windows broken, and four public houses, two groceries, a newsagency and the Deedes hosiery factory had been destroyed.

The police arrested two men during the night, James Lawless[32] and John Gibbons, who were taken to the barracks for questioning. Gibbons was secretary to the local Volunteers and was asked to name Head Constable Burke's killer.[33] Lawless was a barber, who had been cautioned in April 1920 for leading the republican demonstration at which Sergeant Finnerty had been fatally shot.[34] He too was asked for information on the shooting. Both men apparently refused and next morning their bodies were found with bayonet wounds on Quay Street, ten yards from the barracks.[35]

The police had reputedly received local information enabling them to target the homes and businesses of those responsible for the murders or closely linked to them, as Sir Henry Wilson observed in his diary for 23 September: 'At Balbriggan, Thurles and Galway yesterday the local police marked down certain SFS as in their opinion the actual murderers or instigators and then coolly went and shot them without question or trial. Winston [Churchill] saw very little harm in this but it horrifies me.'[36] This claim was confirmed in 1923 by the unionist historian W. Alison Phillips: 'The very night of the Balbriggan reprisal, for the first time, men came to the police to denounce the murderers, moved by fear that their own houses might be burned.'[37] The belief that the reprisals were accurately directed is also implied in local recollections of the attacks: 'Clonard Street, locally known as "Sinn Féin Row", was the most severely hit.'[38]

Some of the victims were indeed prominent republicans or implicated in outrages. The Derhams of Drogheda Street were perhaps the leading republican family in Balbriggan. John Derham was a Sinn Féin Town Commissioner.[39] His son James was not only chairman of that body but involved in IRA fund-raising, as well as being

present when the shooting was planned.[40] Mike Derham passed
on a message to his father to lock up the pub after the shooting.[41]
Connolly's public house, where the shooting had been planned, was
also destroyed.[42] The burning of Anne Corcoran's dairy in Clonard
Street avenged the fact that one of the two gunmen was her son
William, though this reprisal also put the widowed Mrs Corcoran
and her other six children out of their home.[43] Lawless and Gibbons
were arrested and killed because of their known involvement in the
Fingal Brigade, which had been conspicuous in the 1918 election
campaign as well as supporting the town's republican courts and
police.[44] It is worth noting that none of those targeted appeared in
the files of republican suspects compiled by the RIC's Crime Special
Branch at Dublin Castle.[45]

In many cases, however, the selection of targets for reprisal
does not suggest a directed attack based on accurate local information. The house of Burke's killer, Michael Rock, was raided but not
destroyed.[46] Yet the Auxiliaries set fire to the large purpose-built
hosiery factory of Deedes, Templer & Co., which employed 120
people on the premises and up to 300 out-workers. This seems to
have been deliberately targeted, as it lay 500 yards from the main
scene of reprisals in Clonard Street and was on the sea side of the
railway embankment dividing the town (see map, p. 84).[47] That the
firm was based in London did not insulate the factory from attack.[48]
The other hosiery factory in Balbriggan, Smyth's, was saved only
by the intervention of a local policeman.[49] Along with Derham's,
the Auxiliaries burned three shops in Drogheda Street: McGowan's
and McGlew's groceries and Reynolds's newsagency (with modest
annual rateable valuations of £12 or £13 each).[50] Most of the
targets had no confirmed association with the IRA or the republican
movement. The apparently indiscriminate character of these reprisals, and their grim consequences for homeless families and jobless
workers, have caused the event to be remembered ever since as 'the
Sack of Balbriggan'.

As already suggested, Balbriggan had hitherto seemed, despite
the general upsurge in revolutionary violence, a relatively quiet and
peaceful town. This fact intensified public shock and outrage after
the events of the 20–1 September. The *Drogheda Independent* said

the town looked like 'Hell on Earth'; the *Freeman's Journal* compared it to 'one of the Belgian towns that had been sacked by the
invaders'.[51] The *Westminster Gazette* headline was 'R.I.C. Reprisals –
Balbriggan Sacked.' The London *Daily News* commented on 'barbarous "reprisals" now being ... systematically and openly carried out
by the Black and Tans'. The *Manchester Guardian* talked of an 'An
Irish Louvain', declaring that 'to realise the full horrors of the night
one has to think of bands of men inflamed with drink raging about
the streets, firing rifles wildly, burning houses here and there, and
loudly threatening to come again tonight and complete their work'.
The *Birmingham Post* offered the most prescient comment. Although
supporting the restoration of order in Ireland, it observed that 'it is
not by means of a policy of reprisals that order can be restored'.[52]

Balbriggan was 'a veritable godsend to the Sinn Féin propaganda bureau', as the army commander in Ireland, General Macready, later pointed out. He greatly underestimated the extent of
the damage in his memoirs, claiming that it was barely noticeable.[53]
In fact, though the worst damage was concentrated in Clonard
Street, the destruction was considerable if not quite amounting to
a 'Sack'.[54] Along with the burning of central Cork on 11 December
1920, Balbriggan became the most notorious of British 'reprisals'
in Ireland. The British Labour Party's Commission to Ireland and
the American Commission on Conditions in Ireland (composed
of Quakers in order to suggest impartiality) each took evidence
from townspeople. The Labour Commission's report discussed the
episode at length:

> The burning of Balbriggan is regarded by the Chief Secretary for
> Ireland as a 'reprisal' for the shooting of a police officer. Men were
> shot, houses and other buildings were burnt, women and children
> terrified and driven to the fields. The police may or may not, in
> this terrible havoc, have punished those guilty of the death of the
> police officer. But even if they did it is a frightful procedure to
> inflict so much injury upon the many who are innocent in order
> that the very few who are guilty may suffer.[55]

The *New York Times*, in its report on the American Commission's
findings, had as its headlines 'Tales of Terrorism in Irish Districts'
and 'A Night of Yelling, Burning, and Shooting'.[56]

No policy for reprisals was officially sanctioned by the British government. However, according to Macready:

> Although these unauthorized reprisals at that time had a marked effect in curbing the activities of the I.R.A. in the immediate localities, and on these grounds were justified, or at all events winked at, by those in control of the police, I saw that they could only result in the police taking the law into their own hands ... and lost no time in protesting strongly to the Chief Secretary on the subject, urging him either to carry out reprisals as authorized and controlled operations, or to stop them at all costs. Unfortunately at that time certain persons in high places in London were convinced that terrorism of any description was the best method with which to oppose the gunmen, not realizing that apart from all other reasons the gunmen could always 'go one better'.[57]

One of those 'persons in high places' was the Chancellor of the Exchequer. As Austen Chamberlain wrote to his sister: 'It is a fact that the reprisals have secured the safety of police in places where previously they were shot down like vermin, has [sic] caused the people to warn them again & again of ambushes and the like, & together with the steps taken by Govt. is getting the murder gang on the run by degrees.'[58] Balbriggan was the first Irish town to experience a major reprisal, but this was swiftly followed by comparable events in Clare (Ennistymon) and Cork (Mallow and Fermoy).[59]

The Sack of Balbriggan resulted in a marked increase in 'outrages' against Crown forces and their supposed allies in the area, giving rise to a cycle of tit-for-tat terror. Leading figures in the IRA were convinced, like Sir Henry Wilson, that the police had acted on advice from local informers. Thomas Peppard and Michael Rock, intelligence officers for the Fingal Brigade and the local battalion respectively, believed that an ex-soldier named Jack Straw was responsible for guiding the perpetrators.[60] Police reports denied this, stating that he had been wrongly accused.[61] The IRA, however, court-martialled and executed Straw.[62] His body was found in a ditch outside Swords on 21 October. Six days later, Crown forces hit back by taking Volunteer John Sherlock out of his home in Skerries and shooting him dead. The houses of two other Skerries Volunteers, William McDonald and Matthew Derham, were burned down on the nights of 27 and 28

October.[63] In November, no republican outrages were reported from the Balbriggan district, but at least two were directed against republicans. On 21 November, a stonecutter and Labour representative named Matthews was shot twice at his home by Crown forces.[64] In the early hours of 22 November, Jack McCann, a well-known Volunteer (with two brothers serving in the British army) was taken from a house in Rush and shot dead by Crown forces.[65] Further incidents of terror were reported from the district in December. On 8 December, Farrell's public house in Balbriggan was raided and robbed by men dressed in police uniforms. Farrell was an RIC pensioner, but his assailants ignored this and robbed him of £5 6s., also searching other customers.[66] Later in the month Thomas Hand, a Skerries Volunteer, was taken from his brother's house and shot dead.[67]

Violence continued unabated in the New Year. Constable Samuel Green, a Black and Tan from London, was shot on 2 February in Mrs Smyth's public house, the scene of Head Constable Burke's murder. Green died of his wounds next day, having served in the RIC for only two months.[68] On 13 February, a police patrol from Swords was ambushed at Ballough outside Balbriggan, Constable John P. Lynch being fatally wounded after seventeen years' service.[69] In an ambush on 19 April, Sergeant Stephen Kirwan of the RIC in Balbriggan (with twenty-one years' service) and Volunteer Peter White were both shot, dying of wounds the next day.[70] Five days later, in the heart of the town, a police patrol was fired on and one civilian injured.[71] A wagon laden with stores for Gormanstown camp was torched on 9 May at the railway depot in Balbriggan.[72] Sergeant Joseph Anderson, a bandmaster at Gormanstown in his thirty-ninth year of service, was shot dead by four men at Hampton, Balbriggan, on 21 May.[73] Also shortly before the Truce, the Lusk IRA burned down a military establishment at the Remount Farm.[74] This facility for training cavalry horses was a significant local employer, and relations between townspeople and soldiers had remained good. Its destruction, like the earlier burning of factories in Balbriggan, put local people out of work.[75]

This record of tit-for-tat violence in the Balbriggan district made little impression on the Chief of Staff, Richard Mulcahy. In April 1921, he belittled the achievements of the Fingal IRA: 'The total loss inflicted on the enemy in three months in this Black-and-Tan infested area, is apparently 5 killed and 13 wounded. No damage to enemy war material has occurred, except bullet marks on a few lorries. ... From the standpoint of the war as a whole this can be described as negligible.'[76] In fact, as shown above, there had been a marked increase in armed conflict since the Sack of Balbriggan the previous September. Mulcahy was often dismissive when assessing reports from provincial units, even in a notoriously active county such as Clare: 'To me they indicate the absence of practically any military intelligence or technique. On the Volunteer side it shows constant watching for the Enemy in a district in which there is almost daily activity on the part of the latter, yet contact with the Enemy is only established on three days in the month.' David Fitzpatrick's analysis of IRA engagements in Mid Clare records attacks on three days in April 1921, four in May, and two in June.[77] Considering the unfavourable conditions under which the Fingal Brigade operated, their performance does not appear to merit Mulcahy's contemptuous assessment. In addition to precipitating a cycle of retributive terror, the Sack of Balbriggan probably consolidated local support for militant republicanism. Reprisals may have cowed many townspeople but also encouraged acquiescence, at least, in the IRA's campaign, as suggested by its increasing ability to mount attacks.[78] Indeed, all over the country reprisals seemed to have reinforced support for Sinn Féin and the IRA.[79]

Was the Sack of Balbriggan deliberately provoked by republicans in order to arouse outrage at home and abroad? Michael Hopkinson believes that 'a central, if unstated, aim of the IRA was to provoke a harsh response and hence to court publicity and international sympathy'.[80] This does not appear to have been the case in Balbriggan. According to Michael Lynch: 'No preparations were made against possible reprisals, and the tragedy was made worse by the fact that the Quartermaster, who had control of our rather scanty supply of weapons, was away in Drogheda and did not arrive back until the town had been destroyed.'[81] Further, it seems that the local IRA recognized this as a mistake and in subsequent operations, such as the attack on the Remount Farm, they occupied positions around the village in case of reprisals.[82]

A sheaf of compensation claims was presented to the Malicious Injuries Board of the Town Commissioners, who passed it
on to Dublin County Council. This file was evidently among books
stolen in a police raid on 11 Parnell Square on 23 November 1920,
though these claims were heard by the Recorder of Dublin early in
the New Year.[83] The tortuous process by which claimants eventually secured compensation for malicious injuries in discussed in the
next chapter. This was not the only means by which Balbriggan's
victims sought redress. In May 1922, a deputation representing the
Town Commissioners, those who had lost property, and town notables waited upon Michael Collins to seek his support for a special
scheme for reconstruction in the town, as in Cork, and Collins gave
them his support.[84] Yet, eleven months later, George Gavan Duffy
drew attention in the Dáil 'to the question of relieving the distress in
Balbriggan where a number of men, some of them married and with
families, have now been unemployed since 20th September 1920'.[85]

The Sack of Balbriggan was a tragedy. This essay has sought
to present a clearer picture of the events of the night, to uncover
who actually did the shooting and how it happened, to identify the
victims of the night, and to determine whether they were chosen
at random or targeted because of their involvement in the murder
or their prominence in the republican movement. The outcome is
mixed: while notable republicans were targeted, two being killed, the
majority of those attacked were victims innocent of any documented
complicity. These victims, often left homeless or unemployed, were
also the last to benefit from the promised reconstruction works.
Thus John Derham, whose son James had become a Treatyite TD,
received an advance reconstruction loan in September 1922, well
before other claimants had been looked after.[86]

David Fitzpatrick has stressed that 'the rapid intensification
of violence after 1919 was largely caused by the disorganization
and savagery of the "occupying" forces'.[87] Such intensification in
the Fingal region did not become marked until after 20 September
1920. Discussing the events at Balbriggan and the perceived failure
of the local IRA to hit back, Michael Hopkinson notes that 'the last
thing the local population needed as they rebuilt their lives was a
repetition of that violence'.[88] Unfortunately, the violence did not

cease, exacerbating popular uncertainty and fear. Sections of the police and the IRA both became more or less willing participants in tit-for-tat terror; those without the power to choose between peace and war were the ordinary inhabitants.

NOTES

1. The first couplet of this contemporary ballad is quoted in Sir Nevil Macready, *Annals of an Active Life* (2 vols, London 1924), vol. 2, p. 498.

2. *Report of the Labour Commission in Ireland*, (London 1921), p. 9.

3. Peadar Bates, *Rebellion in Fingal* (Loughshinny 1998), p. 25.

4. Col. J. V. Lawless, 'The battle of Ashbourne' in *Dublin's Fighting Story* (Cork 2009), pp. 60–6.

5. Quoted in Bairbre Curtis, 'Fingal and the Easter Rising 1916' in *Fingal Studies*, 1 (2010), p. 47.

6. *Ibid.* p. 42.

7. *Ibid.* pp. 43–4.

8. Bernard Howard, 'The British army and Fingal during the Great War' in *Fingal Studies*, 1 (2010); *Thom's* (1918), p. 1181b.

9. Thomas Peppard, MAD, BMH Papers, WS 1398, pp. 8–9.

10. Brendan Matthews, *The Sack of Balbriggan* (Dublin 2006), p. 16.

11. Balbriggan Town Commissioners, Minute Book, 1918–22 (30 Jan. 1920), pp. 123–4, Fingal Archives, Swords.

12. John Derham, in Albert Coyle (ed.), *Evidence on Conditions in Ireland: Comprising the Complete Testimony, Affidavits and Exhibits Presented before the American Commission on Conditions in Ireland* (Washington, DC 1921), p. 93; Matthews, *Sack*, p. 26.

13. Matthews, Sack, p. 32.

14. Balbriggan TC, Minute Book (Aug. 1920), p. 200.

15. Peppard, WS 1398, p. 25.

16. Michael Lynch, WS 511, p. 145.

17. *Drogheda Independent*, 17 Apr. 1920.

18. Balbriggan TC, Minute Book (14 Apr. 1920).

19. RIC, Weekly Summaries of Outrages against the Police, July, Apr. 1920, NAL, CO 904/108 (microfilm, TCD); Richard Abbott, *Police Casualties in Ireland, 1919–1922* (Cork 2000), pp. 69–70.

20. Matthews, *Sack*, p. 17.

21. *Drogheda Independent*, 1 May 1920.

22. *Ibid.*; Abbott, *Police Casualties*, p. 74.

23. Weekly Summaries, July, Aug. 1920.

24. Michael Rock, WS 1399, p. 13; Peppard, WS 1398, p. 25.

25. Weekly Summaries, Sept. 1920.

26. Other reports indicate that Derham had been arrested in July, for riding a bicycle at night, and was not released until 15 Oct. 1920 or even later: Derham, in Coyle, *Evidence*, pp. 93, 116–17.

27. Rock, WS 1399, p. 12.

28. W. Alison Phillips, *The Revolution in Ireland, 1906–1923* (London 1923), p. 188; Abbott, *Police Casualties*, pp. 122–3.

29. Derham, in Coyle, *Evidence*, p. 101.

30. Rock, WS 1399, p. 12.

31. Derham, in Coyle, *Evidence*, pp. 102, 108.

32. Though Thomas Lawless is named in the police report, the only Lawless matching the police description of age and profession in 1911 was James Lawless, the one Thomas Lawless being a fisherman aged 60: NAD, family schedules, Census of Ireland, 1911 (accessible online).

33. Derham, in Coyle, *Evidence*, p. 107.

34. Weekly Summaries, Apr. 1920.

35. Derham, in Coyle, *Evidence*, p. 107.

36. Extract in Charles Townshend, *The British Campaign in Ireland, 1919–1921: The Development of Political and Military Policies* (Oxford 1975), p. 116.

37. Phillips, *Revolution*, p. 191.

38. Matthews, *Sack*, p. 46.

39. Derham, in Coyle, *Evidence*, p. 94.

40. Rock, WS 1399, pp. 11–12.

41. Derham, in Coyle, *Evidence*, p. 97.

42. *Thom's* (1918), p. 1753. Its annual valuation was £32, a substantial sum.

43. Census of Ireland, 1911.

44. Peppard, WS 1398, p. 12.

45. 'Personalities' Files, CO 904/193–216.

46. Rock, WS 1399, p. 12.

47. Derham, in Coyle, *Evidence*, p. 112.

48. Curtis, 'Fingal', p. 43.

49. *Report of the Labour Commission*, p. 39.

50. *Thom's* (1918), p. 1753.

51. *Drogheda Independent*, 25 Sept. 1920; *Freeman's Journal*, 24 Sept. 1920.

52. D. G. Boyce, *Englishmen and Irish Troubles: British Public Opinion and the Making of Irish Policy, 1918–22* (London 1972), pp. 52–3.

53. Macready, *Annals*, vol. 2, p. 498.

54. Jim Walsh, 'The Sack of Balbriggan' in Balbriggan and District

Historical Society, *Balbriggan: A History for the New Millennium* (Dublin 1999), p. 201.

55. *Report of the Labour Commission*, p. 53.

56. *New York Times*, 19 Nov. 1920; Coyle, *Evidence*, p. 105.

57. Macready, *Annals*, vol. 2, p. 498.

58. Boyce, *Englishmen and Irish Troubles*, p. 55.

59. James S. Donnelly, Jun., '"Unofficial" British reprisals and IRA provocations, 1919-1920: the cases of three Cork towns', *Éire–Ireland*, 45, nos. 1–2 (2010), 152–97 (180).

60. Peppard, WS 1398, p. 22; Rock, WS 1399, p. 13.

61. Weekly Summaries, Oct. 1920.

62. Peppard, WS 1398, p. 13.

63. IG, MCR, Oct. 1920, CO 904/113.

64. *Freeman's Journal*, 23 Nov. 1920.

65. Peter F. Whearity, 'John Jack "Rover" McCann (1886–1920), Irish Volunteer' in *Fingal Studies*, 1 (2010), 68.

66. Weekly Summaries, Dec. 1920.

67. IG, MCR, Dec. 1920.

68. Weekly Summaries, Jan. 1921; Abbott, *Police Casualties*, p. 192.

69. Weekly Summaries, Feb. 1921; Abbott, *Police Casualties*, p. 199.

70. Weekly Summaries, Apr. 1921.

71. Weekly Summaries, Apr. 1921.

72. Weekly Summaries, May 1921; Abbott, *Police Casualties*, p. 223.

73. Abbott, *Police Casualties*, p. 245.

74. Rock, WS 1399, p. 4.

75. *Fingal Independent*, 19 Dec. 2003.

76. Quoted in Michael Hopkinson, *The Irish War of Independence* (Dublin 2002), p. 146.

77. David Fitzpatrick, *Politics and Irish Life, 1913–1921: Provincial Experience of War and Revolution* (Cork 1998; 1st edn 1977), p. 187.

78. Michael Laffan, 'Republicanism in the revolutionary decade: the triumph and containment of militarism, 1913–23' in Maurice J. Bric and John Coakley (eds), *From Political Violence to Negotiated Settlement* (Dublin 2004), pp. 49–50.

79. Paul Bew, 'Moderate nationalism 1918–23' in *ibid.* p. 73; Joost Augusteijn, *From Public Defiance to Guerrilla Warfare: The Experience of Ordinary Volunteers in the Irish War of Independence, 1916–1921* (Dublin 1996), p. 227.

80. Hopkinson, *War of Independence*, p. 79.

81. Lynch, WS 511, p. 144.

82. Peppard, WS 1398, p. 21.

83. Dublin Co. Council, Minute Book (Dec. 1920), p. 38, Fingal Archives.

84. Ministry of Economic Affairs, Minute Sheet, 26 May 1922, NAD, FIN 1/453; Balbriggan TC, Minute Book (May 1922), p. 333.

85. *DD*, iii, col. 128 (17 Apr. 1923).

86. Office of Public Works, Minute, M. Doolen, 21 Sept. 1922, FIN 1/453.

87. David Fitzpatrick, 'Ireland Since 1870' in R. F. Foster (ed.), *The Oxford Illustrated History of Ireland* (Oxford 1989), pp. 213–74 (250).

88. Hopkinson, *War of Independence*, p. 146.

6. The Price of Balbriggan

David Fitzpatrick

Most contributors to this book have touched on the human costs of the Irish revolution, whether in the form of deaths, personal injuries, destruction of property, or wreckage of lives. For survivors, the assessment of such costs was not merely a matter of historical curiosity but a vital step in the search for emotional and material redress. Part of that process, largely overlooked by historians of the revolution, was the provision of official compensation for criminal and malicious injuries suffered by non-combatants as well as protagonists of all affiliations. Using official returns in conjunction with personal data and press reports, it is possible to reconstruct a collective profile of those receiving compensation. This permits a more comprehensive analysis of the 'victims' of the revolution than could be obtained from any rendition of partisan or anecdotal sources.

Yet the principles by which recipients were selected, and a price assigned to their losses, ensured that those whose lives were most blighted by revolutionary and counter-revolutionary violence often received little or no compensation. The poor, having little property, secured negligible awards; injuries to the person carried a lower price than many injuries to property; forced loss of employment counted for nothing. Needless to say, no attempt was made to identify or compensate those experiencing trauma or psychological damage attributable to the conflict. Analysis of the compensation records confirms these inequities, but historians must search elsewhere for the uncounted victims who neither sought not received compensation. This chapter is restricted to investigating about seventy recipients of compensation for losses caused by 'the Sack

of Balbriggan' on the night of 20–1 September 1920, the horrific
episode contextualized in the preceding essay.

II

As in the current 'peace process', selecting an appropriate measure
of redress for victims was a major preoccupation for both new and
old régimes. In Northern Ireland, Sir James Craig's government
declined to reopen cases in which the courts had made decrees as
yet unpaid, instead instructing local authorities to pay out a proportion of each award, using grants amounting to £1,500,000 from
the British government, which accounted for two-thirds of the total
sum already decreed. This ensured that the Exchequer rather than
local ratepayers bore the cost of compensation. Furthermore, as
Craig explained in late June 1922, it averted 'a rehash of all those
sordid happenings, and having the harrowing details again served
up for relatives and friends, and where the passions of the people
were sufficiently high already'.[1]

The British and Provisional governments had already embarked
on a comprehensive 'rehash' of tens of thousands of cases involving
injury to property in Southern Ireland between 21 January 1919
and 11 July 1921. Instead of accepting the often exorbitant amounts
decreed by County Court Judges and urban Recorders during the
revolutionary period, the Provisional government agreed to the
creation of a quasi-judicial Compensation (Ireland) Commission,
charged with investigating each claim and assessing awards and
legal costs. These awards were invariably rubber-stamped by the
Ministry of Finance and promulgated in *Iris Oifigiúil*. After about
ten days' grace during which third parties could assert charges on
the injured property, they became due for payment, though vexa-
tious further delays were commonplace. As in Northern Ireland,
ratepayers were relieved of responsibility, payments being sanctioned initially through a vote of £5,000,000 by the virtually
penniless Dáil. The two governments agreed that each would be
responsible for injuries perpetrated by its own supporters. Since
the main origin of property claims was unofficial 'reprisals', most
of the bill was eventually paid by transfers from the British Trea-
sury. The Provisional government also undertook to honour unpaid

decrees for pre-Truce injuries against the person, without in this case submitting the claims to further scrutiny. In defiance of logic, the burden of responsibility was reversed. Since more supporters of the Crown than republicans had suffered injury or death, the Exchequer again funded most of the compensation. Separate provision was made for compensation relating to various categories of injuries sustained after the Truce.[2]

The three-man Commission convened on 19 May 1922 in the Green Street courthouse, by courtesy of the Recorder of Dublin who had determined the original Dublin decrees a year or so earlier. The British government was represented by a senior civil servant, the Provisional government by a businessman.[3] The Commission's first chairman was Lord Shaw of Dunfermline, a prominent Scottish Liberal lawyer and former MP with a reputation for opportunism (in 1909, he had abruptly abandoned his client in a major divorce case in order to persuade Asquith to make him a Lord Justice of Appeal when sudden death created a vacancy). Shaw's Irish and liberal credentials were impeccable, for in 1917 he alone among the Law Lords had condemned as illegal a Defence of the Realm Regulation allowing wartime internment.[4] Shaw promised to 'make a square deal' in settling each claim, avoiding any consideration of 'motive' on the part of either victims or perpetrators.

Despite some controversy, the decision to investigate and reassess awards was justified by the fact that scarcely any criminal injury claims had been contested by County Councils (on behalf of ratepayers) when originally brought before the courts in 1920–1, as there had been no practical prospect of payment. The councils, being under republican control, had made no attempt to raise the required rate; the British government, though responding to this challenge by withholding grants and loans from the recalcitrant authorities, had restricted compensation to injured agents of the Crown. Consequently, most malicious injury claims were presented with the aim of publicizing atrocities rather than actually securing compensation. The Commission was an ingenious device for providing redress without being bound by excessive awards in undefended cases. Hugh Kennedy, the Provisional government's Law Officer, welcomed the decision 'to consider the question of compensation in respect of damage sustained during the later Irish war for liberty, that, by such compensation, the score might be to some extent wiped out'.[5] If not quite a 'Truth and Reconciliation Commission', this initiative manifested the shared determination of the two governments to compensate victims of all political persuasions and, when necessary, to tear open half-healed wounds in order to verify the extent of the injuries inflicted.

After an initial flurry of highly publicized test cases, many relating to reprisals in Cork, the Commission tackled the massive revolutionary legacy of unpaid property claims, of which 37,000 had been lodged by February 1923. Most of its awards were already the subject of judicial decrees, but some had never passed through the judicial process including those arising from 'authorized reprisals' in the Martial Law zone. Disheartened by the obvious incapacity of the original Commission to investigate each case in a public hearing, Shaw resigned in November 1922. This prompted the two governments to devolve most of its work to a team of up to fifty officials who roved the country, inspected damaged premises, and in most cases persuaded claimants and local authorities to agree upon a reduced award.[6] After an interregnum of three months, the reformed Commission secured a new chairman, Sir Alexander Wood Renton (a former Chief Justice of Ceylon whose chief credential was his vice-presidency of the Egyptian Riots Indemnity Commission of 1919).

Undaunted by the magnitude of the task and oblivious of the Civil War, the investigators spent over three years demolishing the paper mountain. About 1500 awards were made in 1922 and 8407 in 1923. Since a large proportion of claims were outside the Commission's initial terms of reference, these terms were extended in January 1925 to embrace all injuries committed by agents of the Crown, whether or not authorized by superior officers, and claims resulting from occupation of buildings by Crown forces.[7] All told, the Commission determined 19,000 cases.[8] The final compensation bill exceeded £7,000,000, most of which was eventually refunded in various forms by the British government.[9] In addition, full payment was eventually authorized for over 500 outstanding personal injury decrees, most cases being determined after the Civil War, in the winter of 1923-4.[10]

Balbriggan's victims were compensated quite promptly, almost every property award being issued during the five weeks preceding the creation of the Irish Free State on 6 December 1922. With few exceptions, the published entries for Balbriggan give the name and street of the recipient, an indication of the types of property affected and the extent of damage, the street in which the injury occurred, the date and amount of the original decree (along with associated legal costs), and the amount of the award and costs finally authorized for payment. Though the date of the injury itself is not provided, press reports of the relevant judicial hearings suggest that all (or virtually all) of these cases relate to the reprisals of 20–1 September 1920. This information embraces seventy-one named claimants injured at Balbriggan, who submitted seventy-four distinct claims.[11] The total bill for compensation amounted to £83,727, equivalent to several millions today. More than half of the total Balbriggan payment (£45,000) went to Deedes, Templer & Co., the London-based hosiery manufacturer whose Balbriggan factory and cutting-edge machinery had been completely destroyed.[12] The smallest award was for £7, one-quarter of all awards fell short of £20, and the median figure was below £60 (see Appendix).[13] By April 1923, President Cosgrave could affirm, when questioned about distress in Balbriggan, that 'practically every claim which it is possible to pay has been discharged', £65,051 having been distributed.[14] Comparison with press reports in September 1920 indicates that almost all alleged victims of reprisals eventually received awards, with two notable exceptions. Both were siblings of Sinéad de Valera, who as Jane Flanagan had spent her infancy in Balbriggan.[15]

The schedules permit a rough analysis of sixty-five awards by type of injury, distinguishing injuries to premises (ranging from house-destruction to window-breaking) and also cases where part or all of the injured property was destroyed. Premises were affected in 45% of these cases, equally divided between cases of damage and destruction. Nearly half of the awards concerned destruction of moveable property (such as furniture, clothing, or 'personal effects'), while damage to property inspired the few remaining claims.[16] Press reports of the subsequent court hearings offer a less abstract catalogue of personal losses: two watches belonging to the dairy-keeper

Anne Corcoran; Owen Costello's 'totally exaggerated' claim for
pictures (£35) and delph (£48); John Derham's 'valuable' piano
(£80) and whiskey stock (£290); John McGowan's Collard piano,
books and novels; John Landy's jewellery. The shattered world of a
respectable spinster is evoked by the case of Margaret Gilsenan of
Dublin Street, a dressmaker aged thirty-seven, whose claim incorporated a window smashed by rifle-shot (£20), dress materials (£57),
antiques, a Crane piano (£35) and music.[17] Her substantial home
(with six rooms and three front windows) had been fire-bombed by
assailants who 'indulged in singing and piano-playing'.[18]

In ten cases, the award included a stipulation that part or all
of the award be devoted to 'reinstatement of structure' necessitated
by the destruction of buildings (in most cases a public house or
shop). These reconstruction grants, designed to promote the economic welfare of the locality and payable retrospectively, typically
exceeded the market value of the property before destruction and
resulted in a sharp increase in rateable valuation. The sums involved
ranged between £5000 and £1050, exceeding £3000 in four cases.[19]
In addition, at least fourteen smaller houses or cottages were
destroyed, most compensation being awarded to landlords rather
than occupiers (who could claim only for injured possessions). These
cases usually involved either labourers' cottages built and owned by
the Balrothery Rural District Council, or properties owned by the
O'Neill brothers who had invested their drapery profits in rental
property. The Council and the O'Neills were awarded £2000 and
£945 respectively, arising largely from the destruction of five Council
cottages and six O'Neill properties in Clonard Street. Though the
rateable occupiers were not named in the schedules, it has proved
possible to tentatively match all but one of these cottages with
tenants who received compensation for injuries to furniture or the
like.[20] This record of destruction is undeniably bleak, involving at
least 22 buildings in a town with about 500 occupied houses.

Lawyers representing the claimants secured over £1800 in awards
for costs, equivalent to 2.2% of the sum awarded to victims. Though
perhaps modest by today's standards, this further burden on British
taxpayers entailed a substantial windfall for William L. B. Cochrane
and Co., the solicitors (only recently established in Balbriggan) who

had handled almost all of the criminal injury claims in 1920–1.[21] The Deedes case entailed by far the largest award of costs (£472 10s.), but with a single exception costs were awarded for every claim, however small. Indeed, the smaller the amount of compensation, the greater the proportion of each award that was collected by lawyers. In the Deedes case, the ratio of legal costs to compensation was only 1.05% (a guinea per hundred pounds), and the ratio for the top quartile of awards (exceeding £200) was 1.62%. By contrast, the ratio for the second quartile was 14.3%, rising to 26.5% for the third quartile. For the lowest quartile of awards (£20 or less), the ratio was no less than 53.5%. Thus lawyers received £8 4s. 9d. for securing an award of £12 for doors and windows damaged in Patrick Burke's bootmaker's shop, while £10 for broken plate-glass windows in Phillips Wright's medical hall justified legal costs of £9 8s. 9d. Doubtless, this reflected not systematic discrimination against poorer applicants, but higher overheads in the case of small claims from any quarter. Yet, as in most crises, lawyers clearly made a killing in the aftermath of the Irish revolution.

Comparison of the awards with the original decrees confirms the thoroughness with which the Commission's investigators pursued their task. The total compensation bill for Balbriggan was reduced by about £25,000, mostly because of a drastic reduction in the award for Deedes (reduced from £62,324 to £45,000). This was due mainly to the fact that by June 1922 the company had decided not to reopen its Balbriggan business (the company was dissolved later that year).[22] Over two-fifths of the decrees (28 cases out of 66) were reduced after investigation, and none was increased. Predictably, lawyers were exempted from the squeeze, only one judicial award of costs being reduced by the Commission. Most assessments of legal costs were untouched, but in almost one-third of cases (21 out of 65) the allowed costs were actually increased. The Commission was particularly generous when reappraising larger awards, the assessment of costs being increased in three-quarters of the top quartile of awards, three-eighths of the second quartile, 12% of the third quartile and only 6% of the sixteen smallest awards. However parlous the state of public finances, the new state was not reduced to penalizing its legal profession.

III

If the published schedules of compensation were our sole source, little more could be divined about the victims of Balbriggan. Fortunately, most of the recipients can be confidently matched with names appearing in family census returns and valuation records. The census schedules for 1911 and 1901, now accessible online, provide extensive personal information (such as age, marital status and occupation) along with data on occupied houses (such as the number of outhouses, rooms and front windows, and whether walls or roofs were 'perishable'). Regrettably, the 1911 census for Balbriggan does not indicate streets within the town, making it difficult to match some awards with census schedules. This problem has been overcome by collating the census schedules for 1911 with those for 1901, which are subdivided by street name.

The revision books of the valuation (the basis for collection of local rates) give the names of occupiers and their 'immediate lessors' or landlords, the annual valuation of buildings and land (with acreage), a description of the types of building on each holding, and the date at which officials recorded changes of occupiers, lessors or valuation. Though understating the current rental and market value of buildings, the returns of annual valuation provide a fairly reliable index of relative value. Each holding is assigned a number within each townland or street, which enables it to be precisely located on annotated maps held at the Valuation Office in Dublin.[23] By linking census and valuation records with the compensation schedules, much vital information about most claimants has been assembled. The collective profile has been filled out by abstracting the annual lists of prominent citizens and shopkeepers in *Thom's Directory*, and by analysing press reports of the relevant court hearings in early 1921 and the reprisals themselves in September 1920.[24] Though extremely wearisome, similar prosopographical probes could in principle be applied to every other outbreak of reprisals.

The exercise of matching these nominal records testifies to the efficiency and accuracy (with some notable exceptions) of official record-keeping in that distant era. Of the 50 distinct properties in which injuries were sustained, no less than 46 (92%) have been matched with valuation records, 33 (66%) with houses occupied by claimants or their families in the census of 1911, and 25 (50%) with houses returned in 1901. Though considerable migration occurred within Balbriggan in the decade after 1911, partly because of the building of twenty labourers' cottages by the Balrothery RDC, few newcomers seem to have settled in the town despite the recent expansion of hosiery manufacture. Consequently, almost every claimant has been matched with family census schedules, apart from a few non-resident landlords and others who may have sustained injuries while visiting the town. In matters of detail, admittedly, the census returns compiled by householders and collected by the RIC were sometimes inaccurate. Comparison of the schedules for 1901 and 1911 reveals bizarre but predictable anomalies in the enumeration of ages and the quality of housing.[25] Despite such problems, householders seem to have taken considerable care to provide reliable information on essentials such as names, occupations and family status, creating a solid foundation for any collective profile of the victims of Balbriggan. A list of the recipients of awards, tabulating some of this information, appears in the Appendix.

IV

It would be wrong to assume that those compensated for property damage were invariably claiming for injuries sustained in their own homes. Of the 71 claimants, only 57 seem to have been occupiers (or relatives of occupiers)[26] of the 50 properties affected by reprisals. The remaining claimants included two contractors receiving minor awards: the Balbriggan Gas Co., Ltd., which claimed for fire damage to gas connections and cookers, and Smyth & Co., the surviving stocking manufacturer, which claimed for 'hose' burnt in various parts of the town. Three claims related to property losses occurring outside the claimant's home, including Patrick McMullen's horse and Dr William Fulham's clothing, probably damaged during his nocturnal vigil as he worked with the old RIC to stem the reprisals and save Smyth's factory from the fate of its gutted rival.[27] The remaining nine claimants were not occupants but landlords of the properties affected. My statistical analysis of claimants and properties is restricted to cases in which the damage was inflicted on, or in, the claimant's home.

MAP OF PROPERTIES AFFECTED BY THE SACK OF BALBRIGGAN

Map of Properties Affected by the Sack
of Balbriggan, 20–1 September 1920

○ Dwelling affected
● Dwelling destroyed
△ Shop affected
▲ Shop destroyed
▢ Major building (unaffected)
• House (unaffected)
13: 35 No. 13 in appendix: award £35

Scale (metres)   0   100   200

Sketch map by David Fitzpatrick, based on annotated town
plans of Balbriggan (1: 2500, 1909 edn), matched with
revision book (1912–31): Valuation Office, Dublin.

Just over half (26) of the 50 affected properties were private houses. The remainder, including most cases involving major awards, were shops and similar businesses (13) or public houses (8), along with the Deedes factory, the medical hall and a hay-shed. Most of the businesses were prominent enough to be listed in directories, which give details of 15 properties where injuries were sustained.[28] The 50 injured properties were spread through most major streets in Balbriggan, with marked concentrations in Clonard Street (22), Drogheda Street (12), Bridge Street (7) and Dublin Street (5). The sketch map indicates the location of each property, graphically confirming the impact of reprisals on clusters of neigh-bouring houses such as the row of neat labourers' cottages with small gardens, which the Balrothery RDC had built shortly before the Great War, on the south side of Clonard Street. The award schedules broadly confirm contemporary press reports of damage to 'thirty small houses, most of them thatched cottages, and some slated dwellings' in Clonard Street.[29] Though some houses were damaged or destroyed through fire spreading from neighbouring properties, most seem to have been attacked individually. With the exception of the Deedes hosiery, none of the town's factories or public buildings was attacked.

Despite the lure of thatch for arsonists, only 8 of the 33 prop-erties linked with census returns had 'perishable roofs'. Over two-fifths (14) were classified as first-class dwellings, 16 as second-class, 3 as third-class, and none as fourth-class. More detailed indicators of house quality all suggest both a wide range and over-represen-tation of superior premises (see Appendix). The number of rooms and also of front windows ranged between 14 and 1, with median figures of 6 and 5 respectively, while the number of house points varied between 21 and 3 (median 9, signifying an upper-second-class dwelling). Similar patterns apply to the alternative measure of annual rateable valuation, ascertainable for a much larger propor-tion of properties (46 out of 50, compared with 33 census matches). The valuation of affected buildings ranged between £115 for the hosiery factory and £1 5s, for four cottages (mostly thatched) occu-pied by a linen weaver, farm servant, fruit dealer and boat owner's wife. The median valuation was quite high by urban Irish standards (over £6), but one-quarter of the properties were valued at £2 10s. or less. Though all sorts of buildings from wretched thatched hovels to prosperous public houses were affected by reprisals, the targets tended to be relatively valuable shops or houses, which a cynical attacker might have deemed worthy of the expenditure of a petrol bomb, a bullet, or a match.

Over three-fifths (35) of the 56 claimants whose own households were injured (excluding the impersonal case of Deedes) were male. Half of the claimants were already married in 1911, while 12% were widowed and 38% remained single.[30] As the Appendix indicates, the median claimant was middle-aged by 1920 (37 in 1911); the age of claimants in 1911 ranged between 15 and 72; and one-quarter of claimants were already 49 or more in 1911. The demographic profile of Balbriggan's victims therefore differs sharply from that of republican activists, who were overwhelmingly male, young and unmarried.

It is worth noting that almost all claimants were literate Roman Catholics, born locally and claiming no knowledge of the Irish language. The migratory exceptions included four publicans: Patrick Connolly and Bernard O'Reilly from Cavan, John Landy from Louth, and Anastasia Morrissey from Tipperary. Other immigrants from beyond Co. Dublin were William Murray from Dublin City, an engine-fitter at a hosiery factory, Bridget O'Brien from Westmeath, a shopkeeper and police pensioner's widow, and Rose O'Brien from Cavan, a student at Loreto College in 1911. The victims included two Protestants: Elizabeth Moore of Dublin Street, a member of the Church of Ireland dependent on annuities from property; and James Phillips Evans Wright, a pharmaceutical chemist from Dublin City, who belonged to the Society of Friends. Every claimant could reportedly read and write except Thomas Richardson, an elderly farmer living in Clonard Street. The sole Irish-speaker was Dr William Francis Fulham, the dispensary officer from Drogheda, who did not, however, sustain any injury to his home or household in Drogheda Street. If Balbriggan's victims were enthusiasts for Irish Ireland, they gave no hint of this sentiment in their census returns.

The wide social range of claimants is demonstrated by their occupations, which could be ascertained in 55 cases (including a few unoccupied relatives who have been assigned the occupations of husbands or other family members). Of these, 4 were unskilled labourers or carters, 4 were involved in agriculture, and 7 were fishermen, sailors, or marine dealers. Only a few claimants could boast even faintly superior status (the chemist, 2 clerks, 2 annuitants and the secondary-school student). The textiles industry (including hosiery) accounted for 7 claimants, skilled trades for 5, and building and construction for a single claimant. Predictably, the dominant occupational groups were publicans (9) and shopkeepers (11). Whereas the town's élite escaped almost unscathed and its proletariat was under-represented, its retailers and small businessmen were disproportionately afflicted. In addition to those whose homes or business premises were injured, several rich townsmen suffered losses as landlords. These included James O'Neill (draper turned annuitant), William J. Cumiskey (coal, brick and slate merchant), Hugh Robert Scanlan (provision merchant), and William Ennis (a farmer in Clonard who also owned a substantial public house in Balbriggan).

In some cases indiscriminate, many of the reprisals were calculated to damage the economic life of the town regardless, so far as is known, of the political affiliations of victims. Though obnoxious, the selection of shopkeepers and businessmen as primary targets conforms to the economic rationale of reprisals as an instrument for efficiently punishing entire communities. While this doctrine was never adopted or generally applied as a concerted government policy, many politicians, soldiers and policemen believed that communities sheltering terrorists (such as the killers of the Burke brothers in Balbriggan) could be weaned away from condoning violent republicanism if their material interests were sufficiently threatened. The destruction of the Deedes factory was the outstanding local example of this strategy, harming hundreds of workers through a single act of destruction. By comparison, burning a row of cottages brought little benefit, by any calculation, beyond the momentary spasm associated with causing a conflagration and inspiring terror among the poor and the powerless.

V

To what extent did the distribution of compensation reflect the hierarchy of suffering generated by the reprisals in Balbriggan? As already stated, those with little property to lose secured little compensation, however intense their suffering; while indirect victims, such as the 300 or 400 workers formerly employed by Deedes, had no redress whatsoever. This inequity was somewhat alleviated by the creation on 24 September of a committee of thirty-two prominent townsmen and local notables, including Protestant as well as Catholic clergy, which launched a subscription fund 'for the relief of the existing destitution'. Four of the eventual claimants for compensation were subscribing members of the committee, and ten other claimants were named among the early contributors. With the exception of Hugh Scanlan (£5), a provision merchant and landlord who was to recover £1050 for the destruction of two of his houses, none of these benefactors had themselves suffered serious losses.[31] The subscription list also included William Cochrane, whose contribution of £50 may be set against his ample takings as solicitor for the claimants. One of the most smartly trousered philanthropists was 'Mr Erskine Childers, Balbriggan' (£1), otherwise a leading republican propagandist resident in Bushy Park Road, Terenure.[32]

Whereas the poorest sufferers had little access to public compensation and were therefore dependent on private relief, some wealthy businessmen may have secured double compensation through insurance payments. Admittedly, according to a visitor from Newfoundland, few of the properties damaged in Balbriggan recouped their losses from insurers since no payment was granted unless 80% of the risk value of the property had been insured.[33] However, as the major insurance companies were themselves among the first recipients of compensation, it is clear that many Irish enterprises were sufficiently insured to qualify for reimbursement.[34] Like the legal profession, the insurance industry may actually have benefited from mayhem in Ireland, being largely insulated from punitive pay-outs and presumably boosted by heightened public awareness of the need for adequate cover.

In Balbriggan, there is strong evidence that those receiving the largest awards subsequently prospered, thanks to the generous grants reserved for 'reinstatement of structure'. In 1924, the Civil War having subsided, all private properties in Balbriggan benefiting from awards above £800 were revalued upwards. Those who rose from the ashes on a cloud of compensation were the publicans Patrick Connolly (whose valuation was raised from £32 to £43), Joseph McGowan (£11 15s. to £30 in 1925), John Derham (£18 to £40) and John Landy (£10 5s. to £30); along with the dairy-keeper Anne Corcoran (£9 to £21), the shopkeeper Bridget O'Brien (£5 to £15), and the marine dealer Mary Costello (£16 to £20).[35] By contrast, not a single property securing an award of £800 or less attained higher rateable valuation in 1924. Six cottages occupied by recipients of compensation (all but one rented from landlord claimants such as Terence O'Neill) were reassessed in 1924 as 'down' or in 'ruins' and valueless.[36] Otherwise, the devastation of September 1920 left virtually no official imprint on the valuation of Balbriggan.[37]

Those who suffered serious personal injury or the loss of a relative were meanly treated by comparison with wealthy publicans whose premises had been destroyed or damaged. The Burke brothers, whose murder and attempted murder outside Mrs Smyth's public house in Dublin Street had provoked the reprisals, were priced at £1500 and £1000 respectively, whereas seven claimants for injury to property received £1700 or more. In strict accordance with legal principles of compensation, the Recorder of Dublin had halved the sum claimed by Head Constable Peter Burke's dependents, and reduced the compensation sought by his severely wounded brother and fellow policeman, Sergeant William Patrick Burke, from £3500 to £1000. These reductions cannot be ascribed to nationalist tendencies on the part of the Recorder, Thomas Lopdell O'Shaughnessy, who had achieved notoriety for his severity in dealing with republican prisoners after 1916. Though an alumnus of Belvedere College and presumably the product of a mixed marriage, O'Shaughnessy was a strong unionist who had once declined an invitation to stand for a Glasgow constituency.[38] He would have been horrified by the killing of the 34-year-old Galwegian head constable, notable for his active service against the IRA in Co. Clare; and by the fearful attack on his brother, recently appointed as Weights and Measures Inspector in Balbriggan and a thrice-wounded veteran of the Irish Guards in the Great War.[39] The reduced decrees were doubtless based on the relative salaries of a head constable and a sergeant, and would have been paid out of the levy deducted from local authority funds in the case of decrees concerning injuries affecting agents of the Crown.

The Recorder's impartiality was evident in his award of £1750 to the widow and eight children of James Lawless, the 41-year-old barber of Bridge Street who had been fatally wounded during an attack on his shop by 'soldiers' (later identified as policemen, bent on revenge, whose acts could be lawfully construed as criminal injuries). This was determined on the precedent of awards to dependents in 'the Wicklow Hotel case',[40] regardless of the Recorder's qualms: 'It was hard on the ratepayers to have this burden imposed on them, but that was not for him to discuss.' Though the award for Lawless amounted to scarcely one-third of the original claim of £5000, it still exceeded that for Head Constable Burke. The smaller award for the dairyman James Gibbons, reduced from £3000 to only £500 and shared among his three unmarried sisters, probably reflects the fact that several members of the family were at work.[41] The modest price attached to human life doubtless reflected the principle that survivors were only partly dependent on earnings lost through death or injury, whereas restitution of property destroyed or damaged as a result of criminal or malicious acts was a legal entitlement.

The Recorder's drastic reduction of many claims for injuries to property, as well as the person, reminds us that the search for legal redress was not merely a quest for justice but part of a massive propaganda campaign. Each stage in the process launched by a reprisal gave republican strategists ample opportunities for demonstrating to Irish, British and international audiences the futility and brutality of the administration of Ireland during the year preceding the Truce. The events at Balbriggan received detailed and indignant news coverage in the unionist as well as nationalist press, quickly followed by the publication of photographs depicting ruined houses and dignified victims, the creation of a relief committee, and an invitation from the American Commission on Conditions in Ireland to send a delegate to the United States to confirm the shocking details of the 'Sack'.[42]

The court hearings that followed, between January and March 1921, offered further opportunity for republican theatre, in which often extravagant claims were presented without any contest apart from the Recorder's probing questions. Whereas certain County Court Judges (such as Matthias McDonnell Bodkin in Clare) willingly colluded in this exercise, O'Shaughnessy did not hesitate to reject implausible claims for furnishings, rebuilding costs, architects' fees (for Deedes), or stock lost by a reformed tax-evader (John Landy) with no surviving books or accounts. After the second hearing of Balbriggan cases, he protested 'that it was not fair to the ratepayers to put forward inflated and exaggerated claims, especially as the ratepayers on whom the burden fell were not represented'. He had already noted sarcastically 'that it was stated a Relief Committee had been appointed to bring up witnesses, and yet in nearly instance so far the persons examined were of substance'.[43]

Press reports indicate that his decrees disappointed many claimants, with reductions in 22 of the 25 reported cases. Those affected including Deedes (which claimed £100,000 but was decreed £62,324); publicans such as Patrick Connolly (cut from £14,000 to £9500), Joseph McGowan (£9800 to £7000), John Derham (£8600 to £7200) and John Landy (£8500 to £4300). The fact that further reductions were subsequently imposed by the Compensation Commission in such cases suggests that O'Shaughnessy's instinct was sound. Even so, as already reported, all of these publicans emerged from the revolution with properties of much higher value in 1924 than in 1920. Paradoxically, the propagandist impact of hearings relating to Balbriggan was enhanced by the Recorder's evident scepticism and unionist sympathies. His acceptance of the substance of the claims before him testified to the inhumanity and often arbitrary terrorism of the perpetrators more tellingly than the nationalist bombast of a Bodkin or de Valera.

Setting aside exaggerated claims and propagandist exploitation, the available records confirm the shocking social impact of the Balbriggan reprisals. The price of Balbriggan for its citizens was measured by the range of compensation awarded, inadequate and inequitable though it now seems. But Lloyd George's government paid an even higher price than the compensation bill for the folly of its forces and the failure of its Irish policy. Episodes such as Balbriggan undermined Britain's credentials as a liberal democracy, negated the gains from decades of reconciliation and reform, persuaded nationalist doubters and many former unionists that Irish terrorists were less arbitrary and malign than the forces of the Crown, and conferred moral legitimacy on the emerging republic. The price ultimately paid by Britain for Balbriggan, and many comparable atrocities, was the irrevocable loss of Ireland.

NOTES

1. *IT*, 23 June 1922.

2. See *Irish Free State. Compensation for Injury to Persons and Property. Memorandum* (9 Apr. 1923), HCP, 1923 [Cmd. 1844], xviii, 115.

3. C. J. Howell Thomas, Deputy Chief Valuer of the Board of Inland Revenue, and James C. Dowdall of the Incorporated Chamber of Commerce and Shipping.

4. See Lord Macmillan's rather bitchy entry on Shaw in the old *Dictionary of National Biography*.

5. *IT*, 20 May 1922.

6. *PD (HC)*, 5th series, clx, col. 1647–8 (26 Feb. 1923). Of the first 27 inspectors, 23 were qualified lawyers, engineers, architects or valuers, 17 had been resident in Ireland at the time of appointment, and 13 were on secondment from the civil service: *IT*, 6 Dec. 1922 (HC report).

7. *Compensation (Ireland) Commission. Warrant of Appointment* (8 May 1922), HCP, 1922 [Cmd. 1654], xviii, 523; *Compensation for Damage to Property in Ireland. Summary of the Terms of an Agreement* (7 Jan. 1925), HCP, 1924–5 [Cmd. 2445], xxiii, 293.

8. Statistics are derived from the schedules of awards periodically published in *Irish Oifigiúil* between October 1922 and April 1926 (of the 54 schedules compiled by the Ministry of Finance, schedules 1 and 2 were evidently not published, while the supplement containing schedule 27 has not been located). Since the Commission had determined 1250 awards by late Nov. 1922, it may be inferred that the missing first and second schedules incorporated about 1000 cases: *IT*, 29 Nov. 1922 (HL report). I am grateful to Jane Leonard for alerting me to this neglected source and supplying photocopies of most of the schedules containing references to Balbriggan.

9. *PD (HC)*, 5th series, clxxxvi, cols 5–6 (6 July 1925) and ccvii, cols 6–7 (30 May 1927); *DD*, xxiii, col. 796 (3 May 1928).

10. Statistics are again derived from *Iris Oifigiúil*, which published 25 schedules relating to personal injuries (all issued between Mar. 1923 and Oct. 1924). 186 of the 527 awards were promulgated in the final quarter of 1923 and 188 in the following quarter.

11. One claimant received 2 awards; 2 joint claimants received 3 separate awards; and 3 other awards were each made jointly to 2 named individuals. Multiple awards to the same recipients have been aggregated in the statistical analysis.

12. *IT*, 27 June 1922. This was the only known Balbriggan award reported in the press but not in *Iris Oifigiúil*. Detailed reports of the Deedes case appear in *IT* and *II*, 22, 23 Sept. 1920, 1 Feb., 8 Mar. 1921.

13. For explanation of terms, see Appendix.

14. *DD*, iii, col. 128 (17 Apr. 1922). Cosgrave's statement referred to 71 Balbriggan cases, closely matching figures derived from other sources. Later issues of *Iris Oifigiúil* listed 4 additional Balbriggan awards worth £922, while a couple of awards not relating to injuries on 20–1 Sept. may have been included in Cosgrave's figures. The monetary discrepancy is largely accountable to grants withheld pending 'reinstatement of structure' (see below, n. 19).

15. Damage was reported to the houses of Sinéad's brother Laurence Flanagan and Mrs Andrew White (evidently her sister Catherine): *IT*, 22 Sept. 1920. Inspection of census and valuation records indicates that in 1911 Catherine Flanagan was still living with her aunt Catherine Byrne, a shopkeeper in Drogheda St, and that occupancy of the shop passed to Andrew White in 1924 and Catherine White in 1958. Sinéad's father and brother, both named Laurence Flanagan, were living in Dublin in 1901 and 1911, the family having vacated a house in Hampton St, Balbriggan, by 1880. It may be this property, subsequently occupied by Philip Curwen, which was identified in the press as the house of de Valera's brother-in-law.

16. 14 claims involved destruction of premises, 15 damage to premises, 32 destruction of moveable property, and 4 damage to moveable property.

17. *IT* and *II*, 29 Jan., 1 Feb., 9 Mar. 1921; *Drogheda Independent*, 5 Feb. 1921 (cuttings kindly shown to me by Ross O'Mahony).

18. *II*, 22 Sept. 1920.

19. 2 awards for reinstatement of structure referred to several properties (£1885 for the 5 RDC cottages and £1050 for 2 houses belonging to Hugh Scanlan). The sum alocated to reinstatement grants was £24,705.

20. Press reports and valuation records for Clonard St, discussed below, revealed that 5 claimants occupied holdings for which the Balrothery RDC was immediate lessor, while 5 more were tenants of Terence O'Neill (the sixth unfortunate tenant remains unidentified). Since the Council claimed for damage to 15 cottages in addition to the 5 destroyed, it is possible that

some of those destroyed were in fact rented to tenants who made no separate claims.

21. Entries in *Thom's Directory* indicate that Cochrane's had moved from Bailieborough, Co. Cavan, to Balbriggan in 1918.

22. *IT*, 27 June 1922.

23. I am grateful to the Superintendent, Valuation Office, for permission to consult the revision books, copy the maps and reproduce the resultant information.

24. Information is derived from issues of *Thom's Directory* for 1911, 1915, 1918, 1922 and 1927 (and *Macdonald's Irish Directory* for 1910), and relevant issues of the *IT*, *II* and *FJ* (all accessible online).

25. Of 48 claimants whose ages were returned in both 1901 and 1911, only 19 aged by precisely 10 years over the decade, another 10 by 9 or 11 years, 9 by less than 9 years, and 10 by more than 11 years. Of 15 properties housing claimants in both 1901 and 1911, only 8 scored the same number of points in each year, whereas 4 scored one point more or less, and 3 at least two points more in 1911. House points were based on the number of rooms and front windows, with bonus points for houses with 'imperishable' walls or roofs.

26. This category includes Peter Cunningham, awarded £18 for personal effects destroyed in Bridge St, who was identified in press reports as a grocer's assistant with Patrick Connolly, recipient of the second-largest award (£7500) for the burning of his public house, shop, home and stock.

27. The third 'visitor', Julia Bates, was returned as a resident of Dublin St, where her property assessed at £20 was destroyed; but the only census match in 1911 was a carpenter's wife living in Donabate, Co. Dublin.

28. In 5 other cases, directories listed claimants (or their relatives) whose losses arose from their position as landlords, contractors or visitors.

29. *IT*, 22 Sept. 1920. On the same date, the *II* reported that about 20 houses had been 'set alight' in Clonard St, in addition to 'a row of eight small thatched houses', and that windows had been smashed in the houses that escaped burning.

30. Data on marital status are available for 52 of these 56 claimants. In a few cases, information on marital status is based on either the census of 1901 or the compensation schedules.

31. *IT*, 30 Sept., 8 Oct. 1920. The other claimant-benefactors in the first and second subscription lists were Smyth and Co. (subscription £50, award £18); William J. Cumisky (£50, £20); Hugh Kennedy (£50, £30); Dr Fullam (£25, £8); Bernard O'Reilly (£25, £122); Margaret Corcoran (£20, £20); Catherine Darby (£10, £15); Anastasia Morrissey (£5, £30); Mrs Mary Jane Hall (£5, £20); Michael J. Sharkey (£5, £52); Philip Wright (£5, £10); and Charles and Mary Graham (£10 and £5, joint award £40).

32. *IT*, 30 Sept. 1920.

33. I am grateful to Jane Leonard for discovering and supplying transcripts of Billy Browne's letter to his mother, 10 Nov. 1920, when a student at Merton College, Oxford (made available online at www.brownepapers.com by a grand-daughter of this alert Newfoundlander, later a prominent Canadian politician).

34. By early 1923, the Free State government had paid £330,498 to insurance companies with respect to advances of £552,002 already made by those companies to policy-holders: *PD (HC)*, 5th series, clx, col. 838 (20 Feb. 1923).

35. The respective amounts awarded for reinstatement of structure in these 7 cases were £4000, £3500, £3000, £1800, £1400, £1700 and £1400.

36. 17 other hitherto inhabited properties in Balbriggan were reportedly in ruins in 1924, including 14 with immediate lessors who were also claimants yet failed to claim for these properties. The octogenarian annuitant Elizabeth Moore was lessor of 6 ruined houses in Dublin St and 5 in Moore's Lane, but received only £13 for property destroyed in Dublin St (probably in her own house). It is possible that a couple of the ruined houses had been damaged in unreported acts of reprisal.

37. All labourers' cottages rented out by the RDC remained at the same valuation (£2) as before, as did every other affected property except James McGlew's public house (reduced from £16 to £12 10*s*. in 1924), for which £80 had been awarded for damage to premises.

38. See obituaries in *IT* and *Irish Press*, 8 Mar. 1933. He was buried by the headmaster of Mountjoy School, a Church of Ireland clergyman.

39. *II*, 22 Sept. 1920; *IT*, 23 Sept. 1920.

40. The precedent arose from the killing by armed men of William Doran, night porter at Dublin's Wicklow hotel, on 29 Jan. 1921. Doran, aged 45 and father of 3 young children, was officially stated to have 'been on friendly terms with the police'. The Recorder reduced his widow's claim from £6000 to £1750, of which £300 was awarded to each child: *IT*, 31 Jan., 9 Mar. 1921.

41. *IT*, 11 Mar. 1921. The awards for Lawless and Gibbons were promulgated in *Iris Oifigiúil*, 6 Mar. 1923, but were not paid until 13 July: *DD*, iv, col. 893 (17 July 1923). Neither family appears to have received a separate property award, though the barber's shop was reportedly destroyed.

42. John Derham, TC (publican and claimant), accepted the invitation in place of his imprisoned brother on 24 Sept. 1920, and was granted a passport and visa 6 weeks later: *IT*, 25 Sept., 9 Nov. 1920.

43. *IT*, 1 Feb., 29 Jan. 1921. In addition to distributing weekly relief to 332 recipients, the relief fund provided temporary loans to 20 claimants for compensation, 'pending the settlement of their claims': *IT*, 5 Nov. 1920.

In President Cosgrave's typically enigmatic words: 'The exhaustion of the funds of the Relief Committee cannot be ascribed wholly to the extent of unemployment prevailing in the town': *DD*, iii, col. 128 (17 Apr. 1923).

Appendix: RECIPIENTS OF BALBRIGGAN PROPERTY AWARDS

NOTES TO STATISTICAL SUMMARY

Since most statistical distributions in these tables are highly skewed, the best indicator of an 'average' is not the mean (ubiqitous in historical studies yet wildly misleading) but the median (the midway figure when a series is arranged in rank order). For non-statisticians, skewness is most clearly conveyed by citing a few other figures at set points in that rank order (here, the maximum, upper quartile, lower quartile, and minimum). The upper or lower quartile figures respectively apply to observations midway between the median and the maximum or minimum.

STATISTICAL SUMMARY

Category	Cases	Max.	Upper Q.	Median	Lower Q.	Min.
Awards for Criminal Injuries to Property in Balbriggan (£):						
Compensation	68	45,000	225	58	20	7
Costs	68	472	16	12	9	0
Decrees for Criminal Injuries to Property in Balbriggan (£):						
Compensation	66	62,324	275	69	27	8
Costs	65	98	16	11	8	5
Houses where Criminal Injuries were Sustained, 1911 Census (no.):						
Rooms	33	14	10	6	4	1
Front Windows	33	14	9	5	3	1
House Points	33	21	15	9	7	3
Buildings where Criminal Injuries were Sustained, 1920 (£):						
Valuation (£)	46	115	13.5	6.25	2.5	1.25
Claimants in Whose Homes Criminal Injuries were Sustained, 1911 Census:						
Age in 1911 (yrs.)	47	72	49	37	27	15

SOURCES

Awards and decrees for Balbriggan appear in *IT*, 27 June 1922 and *Iris Oifigiúil*, 6 Nov., 6 Dec. 1922, 27 June 1923, 27 Jan., 9 June 1925 (NLI). Census data were derived from family schedules and house and building returns for Balbriggan, 2 Apr. 1911 and, where necessary, 31 Mar. 1901 (accessible online). Valuation data for Balbriggan DED (Urban) were abstracted from the revision book, 1912–31 (Valuation Office, Dublin), linked with earlier and later books to establish succession to holdings and changes in valuation.

NOTES TO TABLE OF RECIPIENTS

The following table presents a few salient facts about each award and recipient, drawn from a spread-sheet of several hundred columns for each case. Numbers refer to properties affected by awards, as marked on the sketch-map. *Secondary Claims* involve smaller awards relating to properties already listed and numbered under *Occupiers and Relatives*. Joint claims and awards are signified by *J*. *Names* are taken from the published lists of awards, incorporating italicized additions from census or valuation returns. *Streets* include one townland within the urban area (Tankardstown) and one rural townland in Balbriggan DED (Salmon), given in parentheses. *Premises* are categorized according to the house and building returns of the census for 1911 supplemented by valuation records. *Valuation* figures indicate the annual rateable valuation of buildings (excluding land). *Census* data relate to 1911, except in three cases (italicized) where information is available only for 1901. *HP* refers to house points, recorded in the house and building returns and defined in note 25. *Age* is that returned in 1911. *MS* refers to marital status in 1911, distinguishing m(arried), s(ingle) and w(idowed). *Occupations* in parentheses refer to those of householders, husbands, etc., of claimants without specified occupations in the census. Merch(ants) include those trading in T(ea), W(ine) and S(pirits). A few entries for occupation or marital status from extraneous sources are italicized. All information on premises, valuation and housing refers only to properties affected by compensation awards, excluding properties occupied by claimants compensated for losses incurred away from home.

TABLE OF RECIPIENTS OF BALBRIGGAN PROPERTY AWARDS

Claimant Surname	Name	Street	Claim (£)	Decree	Award	Premises	Valn (£) 1920	1924	HP	Age	MS	Census, 1911 Occupation
Occupiers & Relatives												
1 Deedes, Templer & Co		(Tankardstn.)	100,000	62,324	45,000	Factory	115	R				*Manufacturer*
2 Connolly	Patrick	Bridge	14,000	9500	7500	Pub. ho.	32	43	16	30	s	Lic. vintner
3 McGowan	Joseph	Drogheda	9800	7000	6700	Pub. ho.	11.8	30	15	34	m	Lic. vintner
4 Derham	John	Clonard	8600	7200	6000	Pub. ho.	18	40	16	49	m	Publican
5 Landy	John	Drogheda	8500	4300	3800	Pub. ho.	10.3	30	10	37	m	Publican
6 Corcoran	Anne	Clonard	3300	2850	2225	Private	9	21	11	42	w	Dairykeeper
7 O'Brien	Bridget	Clonard	2600	2250	1900	Shop	5	15			m	*Shopkeeper*
8 Costello	Mary	Clonard		1650	1400	Dealer	16	20	5	57	w	Marine dealer
9 Gilsenan	Margaret	Dublin	1000	600	425	Private	6.5	6.5	8	27	s	Dressmaker
10 Dowling	Michael	Drogheda	600	400	350	Private	7	7	8	26	s	Carpenter
11 Richardson	Thomas	Clonard		255	255	Private	3.75	3.75	6	60	m	Farmer
12 Canty	Lawrence	Dublin	345	275	250	Private	6.5	6.5	8	30	m	Hosier
13 Hughes	Mary Anne	Clonard		300	225	Private	1.25	R	7	37	s	Linen weaver
14 White	Catherine	Drogheda	400	220	200	Private	5.5	5.5	8	25	s	Hosier
15 O'Reilly	Bernard	Bridge		122	122	Pub. ho.	36	36	20	48	m	S&W merch.
16 Kiernan	Thomas	Clonard		100	100	Private			8	26	m	Comm. clerk

17	Costello	Owen	Clonard	260	100	100	Dealer	1.5	R	3	25	m	Gen. dealer
18	Dunne	Nicholas	Clonard		105	100	Private	2	2		50	m	Gen. lab.
19	Hammond	John	Clonard		84	84	Private	1.25	R	5	52	w	Farm servant
20	McGlew	James	Drogheda	80	80	80	Pub. ho.	16	12.5	15	49	s	Vintner
21	McMahon	John	Clonard		76	76	*Private*	2	2		44	m	*Trade calling*
22	Reynolds	Ellen	Drogheda	200	95	75	Stationer	13	13	14	32	s	Shopkeeper
23	Smith	Elizabeth	Dublin	150	73	73	Private	2.75	2.75		32	w	Dressmaker
24	Connolly	Margaret	Drogheda	84	72	72	Shop	9.5	9.5			m	*Shopkeeper*
25	McCullen	James	(Salmon)		65	65	Private			16			*Farmer*
26	Fanning	Mark	Clonard	150	75	60	*Fruit de.*	1.25	R		46	m	*Fruit dealer*
27	Seaver	John	Drogheda		60	60	Private	1.5	R		60	m	Sailor
28	Kildea	Catherine	Clonard		48	48	Private	2	2		39	m	(Fisherman)
29	Carton	Mark	Clonard		40	40	Private	2	2		42	s	Railway carter
30	Graham	Charles	*Bridge*			40J	Hotel	35.3	35.3	20	57	m	Hotelkeeper
30	Graham	Mary	*Bridge*			40J	Hotel	35.3	35.3	20	55	m	(Hotelkeeper)
31	O'Brien	Patrick	Drogheda	25	36	36	Private						RN
32	Delaney	Edward	Bridge+		30	30	Shop	11	11				
33	Costello	Richard	Clonard		35	30	Dealer	3	3	9	26	s	Marine dealer
34	Kennedy	Hugh	*Mill*		45	30	Private	3	3	7	15	s	Linen clerk
35	McMahon	Owen	Clonard		30	30	Private				40	s	Ag. labourer

	Claimant Surname	Name	Street	(£) Claim	Decree	Award	Premises	Valn (£) 1920	1924	HP	Age	MS	Census, 1911 Occupation
36	Morrissey	Anastatia	Bridge		36	30	Pub. ho.	19	19	21	25	s	T&W merch.
37	Donnelly	James	Clonard		25	25	Private	2	2		45	m	Railway lab.
38	Costello	Michael	Clonard		27	20	Private	3	3	10	35	m	Undertaker
39	Corcoran	Margaret	Clonard		40	20	Private	1.25	1.25		50	m	(Boatowner)
40	Hall	Mary Jane	Drogheda	20	20	20	Greengr.	11	11	9	38	w	Shopkeeper
41	Comerford	Anne	Clonard		19	19	Private	2.5	2.5	6	45	m	(Ship carpr)
42	Murray	William	Clonard		17	17	Private	3	3	6	30	m	Engine fitter
43	McGarry	Richard	Bridge		15	15	Smithy	7.25	7.25	14	25	s	Gen. smith
44	Darby	Catherine	Bridge		15	15	Shop	30	30			m	Shopkeeper
45	Herbert	Bridget	Drogheda		15	15	Private	3.25	3.25	8	72	w	Lodging hkr.
46	Moore	Elizabeth	Dublin		12.5	12.5	Private	23.3	23.3	12	72	s	Annuity (house)
47	Burke	Patrick	Clonard		12	12	Bootshop	6	6	17	65	s	Bootmaker
48	Connellan	Martin	Quay		20	12	Hayshed	5	5				
49	Wright	Jas. Phillips	Drogheda		10	10	Med. hall	13.5	13.5	18	32	m	Pharm. chemist
50	Heeney	Margaret	Dublin			7	Hardware	20	20	17		m	(Building Contr.)
Secondary Claims													
7	Reynolds	Jn. Corvin	Clonard	1200	850	800	Shop	5	15	5	31	s	Cycle agent
8	Costello	Joseph	Clonard	700	600	600	Dealer	16	20	5	20	s	Marine dealer

#	Surname	First name	Address				Type				Age		Occupation
18	Dunne	Mary Ellen	Clonard		75	75	Private	2	2		24	s	Seamstress
31	O'Brien	Rose	Drogheda		30	30	Private				15	s	Student
18	Dunne	Patrick	Clonard		25	20	Private	2	2		26	s	Gen. lab.
2	Cunningham	Peter	Bridge	20	18	18	Pub. ho.	32	32				*Grocer's ass.*
Landlords & Relatives													
	Balrothery	RDC (Lusk)	*Clonard*	3100	2088	2000	Private						
51	Scanlon	Hugh Robt	Dublin	2000	1050	1050	Grocery	14	14	11	45	m	Prov. merch.
	O'Neill	James A.	Clonard+		2600J	945J	*Private*				39	s	Annuity (house)
	O'Neill	Terence	Clonard+		2600J	945J	*Private*				31	s	*Draper*
52	Ennis	Wm. Joseph	Drogheda		55	55	Pub. ho.	20	20		26	s	Farmer's son
53	Sharkey	*Michael J.*	Drogheda		73	52	Drapery	11.5	11.5	13	44	s	Draper
	Fegan	Rose	Clonard		30J	30J	Private				21	s	Dressmaker
	Fegan	Anne	Clonard		30J	30J	Private				54	m	(Mason)
	Cumisky	*William J.*	Hampton	8	8	8	Coalyard						*Coal merch.*
Contractors													
	Balbriggan	Gas Co.	Dublin	127	110	110	Private						
	Smyth	& Co.	Dublin		18	18	Private						
Visitors?													
	McCullen	Patrick	Drogheda		45	45							*Farmer*
	Bates	Julia	Dublin		20	20					35	m	(Carpenter)
	Fullam	William Fr.	Dublin		34	20					48	m	Med. prac.

7. 'English Dogs' or 'Poor Devils'? The Dead of Bloody Sunday Morning

Jane Leonard

I

'Are there any more of your English dogs that you want to be slain?' asked the Quaker writer Rosamond Jacob in her diary for Thursday, 25 November 1920. That morning she had watched a British military cortège pass along the Dublin quays with the coffins of men killed by the IRA the previous Sunday morning. Another republican diarist, the progapandist Erskine Childers, was more humane: 'poor devils'.[1]

'All slain at fixed hour' was how the *New York Times* of 22 November described the breakfast-time assassinations. IRA units had entered about a dozen boarding-houses and hotels seeking guests they suspected of being British intelligence officers. Some on their list were out or managed to escape unhurt. At eight addresses, they found their quarry. Nineteen men were shot in bedrooms, hallways and gardens. Fourteen were killed on the spot and a fifteenth died of wounds weeks later.

The breathless tone in contemporary reports of 'the Blackest Sunday in Irish history' or 'Dublin's ghastly Sabbath of Terror'[2] still infuses present-day depictions. In his diary for 20 June 1995, Neil Jordan was struck by 'the amount of violence in Bloody Sunday. Find a way to make it gripping, not nauseating.' In his film, *Michael Collins*, the dead men were 'the elite of the British secret service. Churchill hand-picked them.'[3] A 'factsheet' for children visiting the GAA Museum at Croke Park describes the IRA as 'an elite assassination unit' under orders 'to take out the backbone of the British Intelligence network in Ireland'. A recent guide to the period, by a serving

British army officer, is no less emphatic: in killing 'a crack undercover team', the IRA had 'blinded the British Secret Service' in Dublin.[4]

This essay suggests that those killed were more disparate and less experienced than most have assumed. Only a minority were natives of England, and less than half appear to have been undercover intelligence officers.[5] The majority were in fact a medley of courts-martial officers, recent police recruits, uniformed staff officers, and Irish civilians.[6]

Despite the vast amount written on Bloody Sunday and the release over the last decade of relevant British military records, the names and essential biographical details of Bloody Sunday fatalities are seldom cited accurately by historians. While the murky circumstances of the day and the clandestine nature of intelligence work naturally contributed to a blurred collective portrait at the time, it is odd that the victims' identities remain opaque ninety years later. Correct identification of victims is an essential element in affirming the humanity of the dead in any conflict. When *Lost Lives*, the monumental necrology of the Northern Ireland conflict, first appeared in 1999, some bereaved families expressed their hurt in cases where next of kin were omitted, names misspelt, or nicknames used in place of given names. This essay aims to assemble what is reliably known about each victim, through brief biographical profiles of all those fatally wounded on Bloody Sunday morning. These 15 fatalities account for over one-third of the 41 deaths resulting from political violence that occurred on Bloody Sunday (including 36 in Dublin).[7] All of these victims are identified in the Appendix, which records place of death, affiliation, and those responsible for each fatality.[8] Although not the first Sunday to acquire the adjective, in Irish terms it was certainly the bloodiest.[9]

That afternoon, the murder tally increased by ten at Croke Park, when Crown forces opened fire during a Gaelic football match. Four more among the sixty wounded at Croke Park died subsequently. Before midnight, Crown forces killed one civilian out after curfew, fatally wounding another.[10] Never before had Dublin's street lamps remained alight until dawn. At Dublin Castle, four deaths took place before daylight. Of three killed while in custody, two were the IRA's most senior officers in Dublin while the other was a Clare civilian. Another death resulted from the suicide of an Auxiliary Cadet. Elsewhere in the city, an 18-year-old army private died in obscure circumstances.[11]

Outside Dublin, three others died before midnight. The IRA killed a policeman in West Cork, while troops killed civilians in Mayo and Meath. Further shootings that eventually proved fatal involved policemen attacked while discussing with friends the news from Dublin. Head Constable John Kearney, shot after completing evening devotions in Newry's Dominican church, died of wounds the next day. Constable Isaac Rea, attacked while chatting to a greengrocer's daughter in Cappoquin, Co. Waterford, survived until just after Christmas. His death completes the necrology of Bloody Sunday. With the exception of three boys and a woman, all of the dead were men.

Most published studies of Bloody Sunday have either focused on its impact on intelligence and propaganda, or treated the morning's events as a brisk prelude to the subsequent drama at Croke Park and Dublin Castle. More recently, historians have mined the testimony of IRA veterans to investigate the mixture of remorse and sang-froid displayed by those who pulled the triggers that morning. With the exception of Charles Townshend's pioneering exposition of a bereaved mother's quest for justice, scholars have yet to consider Bloody Sunday as an occasion of grief, mourning, trauma and aphasia.[12]

The naming of the Hogan stand at Croke Park, McKee barracks and Clancy barracks reflects the pre-eminence of IRA members in the hierarchy of Bloody Sunday's victims.[13] The civilians, like the dead officers, are scarcely remembered. This neglect is epitomized by adjoining unmarked graves in Glasnevin cemetery, where two victims (an ex-officer from the morning, a child from the afternoon) lie buried. Yet some vestiges of such victims remained. On the sixth anniversary of Bloody Sunday, the *Sunday Independent* carried an *in memoriam* notice for Brigadier Dick McKee, placed by Charlie Dalton and his comrades. Dalton had taken part in the IRA's assassination of three officers in Upper Pembroke Street. The same column carried two notices for Jack Fitzgerald, a convalescent police officer killed that morning.

II

1. John Joseph Fitzgerald

No 'English dog', Fitzgerald, like Michael Hogan, was from a well known Tipperary GAA family. He was staying at 28 Earlsfort Terrace, a boarding house near UCD. His father was Dr Joseph Fitzgerald, a dispensary doctor at Cappawhite for decades and a patron of its GAA club.[14] Jack, the fifth of eleven children, lost his mother while still a boy. The children were raised by their father and an aunt, until old enough to board in Dublin at Sion Hill and Blackrock College.

A schoolboy when the War began, Fitzgerald joined up in 1915 before his seventeenth birthday. Two siblings, William and Noreen, also served.[15] Commissioned into a battalion of his local regiment, the Royal Irish, he served with the 16th (Irish) Division. During the battle of the Somme, he was wounded at Guinchy in September 1916. On recuperating, he was transferred to the Royal Flying Corps early in 1917. He joined the 60th Squadron that autumn, but was soon taken prisoner when his plane crashed. Not yet twenty, Fitzgerald escaped from his POW camp early in 1918 but was recaptured crossing the German border. He was repatriated just before Christmas 1918 and mentioned in despatches for his exertions in captivity. During 1919, by now a flight commander, he served against the Bolsheviks with the North Russian Expeditionary Force at Archangelsk. That autumn, he was demobilized.[16]

Earlier that year, on leaving the Durham Light Infantry, his elder brother William had completed a law degree at Trinity. In 1920, he joined the colonial service and was posted to Nigeria.[17] Following William's example, Jack Fitzgerald applied for a cadetship in the colonial police. It was a natural choice for a 'rock boy', for the school's civil service section crammed candidates for the colonial police as well as the RIC. Pending a posting, he sought a few months' practical experience and enrolled in the RIC in June 1920. Its depot in the Phoenix Park, where his service commenced, was also a training centre for colonial police cadets.

Like other ex-officers who joined the RIC pending acceptance for the colonial police, he attested as an ordinary constable but was assigned to be a defence-of-barracks sergeant. When the Auxiliary

Division was formed later that summer, the main rôle of these sergeants was to instruct new recruits in the defence of small rural barracks. While in Clare, Fitzgerald was taken prisoner when the IRA attacked his barracks. He was taken into a field to be shot, but escaped. As he struggled free, his arm was wrenched from its socket. After surgery in a Dublin hospital, he convalesced at Earlsfort Terrace. A Tipperary newspaper reported that he was intending to transfer to the Auxiliaries; but his family later testified that his passage from Ireland to take up a colonial cadetship was booked for 5 December.[18]

The gunmen who called to Earlsfort Terrace that morning enquired for a Mr Fitzpatrick. A maid responded that they only had a Captain Fitzgerald in residence, but helpfully pointed out his room. Staff and guests heard a scream and a series of shots. When the killers had departed, two fellow lodgers, both medical students, found him dead in bed, with a perforated wrist and gunshot wounds to the head, neck and chest. His landlady told the military court of inquiry that letters he had received included several anonymous death threats.[19]

2. Geoffrey Thomas Baggallay

Captain Baggallay had lodged at 119 Lower Baggot Street since the summer. Promoted to Judge Advocate General in the recollections of one of his killers,[20] he was in reality a junior courts-martial officer (CMO). Born in 1891, he was the son of a London architect. After attending the Merchant Taylors' school, he became a solicitor's clerk in Lincoln's Inn Fields, passing the intermediate Bar examination in 1914.

As a Territorial in the Artists' Rifles, he joined the colours in August 1914 and was in France by October. Commissioned into the Welsh Regiment in 1915, he later joined the South Wales Borderers. At Cambrai in November 1917, his leg was amputated. Months later, as the bone end had not healed, three additional inches were removed from the stump. While convalescing, he passed his final legal examination and was called to the Bar in May 1919. His stump was now sound enough to bear an artificial limb, though he still limped heavily.

After a year as a CMO at Catterick, Baggallay was posted to Ireland in July 1920. A month later, he became engaged to the daughter of his local vicar in Wimbledon.[21] He was one of about forty junior barristers and solicitors hastily recruited from outside Ireland in consequence of the Restoration of Order in Ireland Act.[22] With the Irish legal profession reluctant to conduct prosecutions against IRA suspects, generous salaries and allowances encouraged struggling barristers from England and further afield to risk a military posting in Ireland.[23] As a further incentive and also to make assassination in retirement less likely, those becoming CMOs in Ireland were promised a leg up into the Colonial Legal Service. This proved harder to arrange after 1922.[24]

Baggallay's selection for assassination was attributed to his reported involvement in the killing two months earlier of John Lynch, a Kilmallock businessman. According to an IRA intelligence report, Baggallay was the duty officer at Ship Street barracks who answered a telephone request from a British intelligence officer to despatch reinforcements to the Royal Exchange hotel, Parliament Street, where Lynch was shortly afterwards shot dead.[25]

On the eve of his death, Baggallay acted as assistant prosecutor in the court martial of Michael O'Rourke, accused of the murder in Co. Limerick of a private in the Machine Gun Corps. Next morning, at his lodgings, callers told the maid that they had a letter from Dublin Castle for 'Capt Bagelly a one-legged man', and she directed them to his room. He died from gunshot wounds to the head and chest. His killers (allegedly including Seán Lemass, a future taoiseach) stole his papers.[26] Baggallay's family later appealed unsuccessfully for the return of personal correspondence.[27]

3. William Frederick Newberry

Captain Newberry, another CMO, also died in Lower Baggot Street, at no. 92. He was born in Exeter in 1875 and educated at Cheltenham College. He then spent a year in the Royal Marine Light Infantry but resigned his commission in 1895. On marrying in 1898, he entered Gray's Inn. His legal career was no more stellar than Baggallay's. Newberry's wife, who ran a Brighton boardinghouse, supported him until he was called to the Bar in 1909. While a student, he had spent several years as a Territorial officer. He practised for two years in London before heavy losses on investments led to his emigration to Canada in 1913. By that stage, the only child of the marriage, a daughter, had died. His wife remained in England while he practised at the Manitoba Bar. He returned to London when war broke out. Unlike the other victims, Newberry had no overseas war service but remained in England with various reserve battalions. After the Armistice, he taught elementary law to troops awaiting demobilization. Posted in this capacity to Dublin with the Wiltshire Regiment in 1920, he was promoted to brigade education officer in June. That autumn, he finally secured a decent salary on appointment as a CMO.[28]

His wife was visiting from London when the IRA broke into his ground-floor lodgings. The couple initially tried to secure their bedroom door with chairs. Mrs Newberry then sought to shield her husband as he attempted to climb out the window. He was shot in the head, stomach and leg, dying on the window-sill. His killing evoked particular revulsion in press and parliamentary reports of the morning, prompted by his wife's presence and the fact that his dangling corpse remained visible to passers-by for some hours until its removal to St Vincent's hospital.

According to two contemporary accounts of Bloody Sunday (by Mrs Woodcock at Pembroke Street, and two Australian free-lance journalists, husband and wife, wintering in Dublin), the morning resulted in a further fatality. A grief-stricken pregnant wife miscarried and died shortly after seeing her husband 'butchered'. In 1962, she was identified as Mrs Newberry in James Gleeson's attempted refutation of 'the fable and fiction' surrounding Bloody Sunday.[29] For fifty years, historians have accepted and occasionally embellished this attribution. If such an event occurred, it must have involved a lover rather than a wife, as none of the widows died in the immediate aftermath of Bloody Sunday. Madeleine Helen Henrietta (Hettie) Newberry, aged 45 in 1920, was alive in June 1921, when her compensation claim was heard and her husband's will proved, and was still resident in Golders Green in the following year.

4. Thomas Herbert Smith

Herbert Smith was the resident landlord at 117 Morehampton Road. He was born in 1873 in Longwood Avenue, Portobello. Within a decade, the area had become Dublin's Little Jerusalem as refugees from the Lithuanian pogroms settled there. By 1891, his birthplace was occupied by a rabbi. His father, William Smith from Limerick, was an accounting clerk in a carrier's firm on the Dublin quays. A decade later, William had prospered sufficiently to move his wife and eight children from the inner city to a new villa near Sutton. The family were prominent members of the Church of Ireland in Howth. Two cousins served as Anglican and Quaker missionaries.

Like his father, Herbert Smith became a clerk. He later managed a painting business owned by another Howth family. In 1908, Smith married his employer's daughter, Anna Marie Antoinette Jones. Twin sons were born in 1910, but one died in infancy. On census night in 1911, the couple and the surviving twin, Percival, were living in Drumcondra. Later that year, they moved back to Sutton.[30] The family then spent a couple of years in Queensland, where Smith worked in the building trade.

On returning from Brisbane in May 1914, he invested his Australian savings in renovating rental properties. He was the only victim not to serve in the Great War. By 1918, he had moved to Morehampton Road, where his parents joined him a year later, moving into a house two doors down. Another son and a daughter had arrived by November 1920. Percival's playmates included the children of a neighbouring property developer and republican named Batt O'Connor, with whom Michael Collins often stayed while 'on the run'.[31]

5. Donald Lewis MacLean

The Smiths' lodgers were Scots. Donald MacLean, his wife Kate and 6-year-old son James Bertram had moved from Prestwick to Dublin some months earlier.[32] MacLean was born in Ayrshire in 1889. He joined the Ayrshire Constabulary in 1907 and was stationed in Alloway (birthplace of Burns) before enlisting, like many Scottish policemen, in the Scots Guards. In 1917, he was commissioned into the Rifle Brigade. He suffered facial injuries during the

War. Demobilized early in 1920, he was recalled for army service
in June and posted to the Dublin District. MacLean was the only
victim directly identified as an intelligence officer in the official
British casualty lists issued after Bloody Sunday. His widow's compensation claim revealed that a married intelligence officer with
one child earned £1 16s. 3d. per day.[33]

A few weeks earlier, Kate MacLean's younger brother, John
Caldow, had come from Prestwick to stay with them while looking
for work. Caldow was an unemployed blacksmith whose father was
a pithead labourer. The only non-officer among the victims, he had
served with the Royal Scots in Gallipoli and France. He planned to
join the RIC. Like Fitzgerald, he was a 22-year-old bachelor.[34]

The adults were still in bed when the IRA burst past 10-year-old
Percival, who answered the front door. Smith and MacLean both
asked not to be shot in front of their wives and were taken with
Caldow into a bedroom away from their families. Mrs Smith was
allowed into another room to hush her toddler. When the killers
had departed, she rushed for help to a neighbouring doctor's house,
while Kate MacLean stayed with the children and the bodies. Dr
William McElhinney found the three victims lying on the bedroom
floor. MacLean had died instantly from several shots to the chest
and heart. A bullet through Smith's mouth had penetrated his skull
and paralysed him on one side. He was unconscious, but died before
an ambulance arrived. Caldow was taken to Baggot Street hospital
with thigh and stomach wounds, but survived.[35]

6. Henry James Angliss

Among the lodgers at 22 Lower Mount Street were office clerks,
UCD students and three undercover intelligence officers. The guest
registered as 'Mr Mahon' was in reality Lieutenant Henry James
('Paddy') Angliss. Also known as 'MacMahon' while in Dublin, he
was the only victim known to have used an alias. Angliss was apparently born in 1891 in Dublin, while his father, a Fermanagh soldier,
was stationed there. Raised in England, he enlisted in a Scottish
regiment in 1909. In 1916, he became a non-commissioned officer
and was awarded the DCM for leading a trench raid by the Highland
Light Infantry and rescuing wounded companions. In 1917, he was

commissioned into the 11th Inniskilling Fusiliers, so becoming one of the few Catholic officers to serve in the 36th (Ulster) Division. He later served with the Machine Gun Corps, involving an intelligence posting during 1919 in North Russia. A widower, he remarried in the same year. Though demobilized in March 1920, Angliss was soon recalled to the army as an intelligence officer, serving in Dublin from the summer onwards.[36]

According to IRA reports, Angliss was responsible for John Lynch's murder and had revealed this when drunk to a female lodger. Like many agents targeted that morning, the Lower Mount Street Three were easy to keep under surveillance, as they generally stayed at home during the day. Their nocturnal sallies usually ended in local shebeens.

The agents he lodged with escaped unhurt. Both were identified only by the first letter of their surnames in evidence heard, months later, at the court martial of those accused of killing Angliss. 'Mr P', in fact Charles Peel, was a naturalized German merchant sailor from Bournemouth who occupied the adjoining bedroom. He managed to barricade his door and escaped injury, despite a fusillade through the door.[37] 'Mr C' was in bed with Angliss when the killers entered their bedroom. He was a reluctant witness for the prosecution, having deserted in England on the day he was due to travel to the court martial. Arrested and brought to court by military police, he became its star turn. Though censorship curtailed Dublin newspaper coverage, the Scottish press reported that 'Mr C' claimed to be an ex-officer with neurasthenia, who had dropped out of studying medicine at Glasgow University and rejoined the army as an intelligence officer some months earlier. Cross-examination revealed that the legal team was surprisingly well informed about his family background and his reputation for drunkenness and brawling. Having given his evidence, he was soon quietly dismissed from the army.[38]

Though mentioned by surname in Mark Sturgis's diary and fully identified in court-martial records, 'Mr C' has retained his 'elusive' and 'notorious' reputation in many historical accounts. In fact, Lieutenant John Joseph Connolly was a Wexford graduate of UCD. A decorated (yet cashiered) veteran of the 16th (Irish) Division, he received an honorary BA (War) degree in 1917. He returned to UCD on a scholarship after the War, but dropped out in 1920 and became a temporary civil servant. His record in civvies was as chequered as in khaki. Despite failing to repay his grant, running up further debts and being arrested for drunkenly assaulting a publican, he was engaged as an intelligence agent. Under these circumstances, it seems reckless and futile to have placed him in lodgings with UCD students.[39]

In his testimony, Connolly recalled that when five gunmen entered the bedroom and demanded the agents' weapons, Angliss showed them where they were, and pleaded irrelevantly that he and Connolly were Catholics. Meanwhile, firing broke out outside the house as passing Auxiliaries intervened. Inside the bedroom, a gunman fired several shots at the bed as Connolly and his companion tried to escape. Connolly avoided injury by rolling under the bed, while Angliss died from chest and buttock wounds.[40]

7. Frank Garniss

A draft of newly arrived Auxiliaries, marching from the depot at Beggars Bush barracks to Westland Row station, had heard the commotion in Lower Mount Street. The house was surrounded and two Cadets were despatched back to barracks for reinforcements. The killers escaped except for Frank Teeling, who was wounded and captured. Frank Garniss and Cecil Morris only got as far as Mount Street bridge before meeting IRA lookouts. They were killed in the back garden of 16 Northumberland Road, becoming the first confirmed fatalities in the Auxiliary Division.[41]

Garniss, a council warden's son, was born in Hull in 1885. He became an apprentice bricklayer before enlisting as a teenager in the West Yorkshire Regiment. By 1914, he had soldiered for over a decade, including a posting in the Punjab. During the War, he was promoted to sergeant and later commissioned into the Leicestershire Regiment. He married while on leave in 1915. A son, also Frank, was born before the Armistice and a daughter, Grace, followed in summer, 1920, when he had returned to Hull after demobilization. Following enlistment in the Auxiliaries on 18 October 1920, his service in Ireland was restricted to a few days at Beggars

Bush barracks. Yet 200 members of the Yorkshire Constabulary walked behind his coffin when he was buried in Hull.[42]

8. *Cecil Augustus Morris*

Morris, killed with Garniss, was aged twenty-four. A Londoner, he grew up in Croydon, where his father had a barber's shop, and attended the local Church of England primary school. Until conscripted in 1915, he worked in the family business and taught Sunday school. Of the war veterans killed that morning, he was the only conscript. A private in the Middlesex Regiment, he married in late 1915 and was serving in France by July 1916. A year later, having recovered from wounds, he secured a commission in the same regiment, before transferring to the Machine Gun Corps in 1918. A son, also Cecil, was born before the Armistice.

After demobilization in early 1919, Morris briefly resumed hairdressing before becoming a tram conductor. Laid off in autumn, 1920, he joined the RIC on the same day as Garniss. On the day of their death, both men were preparing to join G Company of the Auxiliary Division, stationed at Killaloe, Co. Clare.[43]

9. *George Francis Bennett*

A day earlier, George Bennett and Ashmun Ames had moved into lodgings at 38 Upper Mount Street, near the Peppercanister church. The house was formerly the home of John Kells Ingram, author of 'Who Fears to Speak of '98'. It was one of several boarding houses in the street used by military personnel and their families.[44]

Bennett was born in Java in 1892, the son of an English engineer and a Dutch mother. The family settled in Bournemouth when he was a small child. From 1906 until 1911, he was at Sherborne in Dorset, becoming head of school. He then took a law degree at Magdalen College, Oxford and worked briefly as an engineer before enlisting in November 1914.

Though commissioned into the Army Service Corps in 1916, his subsequent service was with the Intelligence Corps. This included periods at GHQ in France and as an agent in Holland, where having a mother from Rotterdam must have proved useful. Mentioned in despatches in 1918, he was demobilized in the following year. He lived in Pimlico for a period before being recalled for special service in Ireland in early summer, 1920. He had recently converted to Catholicism, a move perhaps influenced by his long friendship with Aylmer Maude, a prominent lay Catholic.[45]

10. *Peter Ashmun Ames*

Born in Pennsylvania in 1888, Ashmun Ames was named after a New York ancestor who had fought in the American Revolution. His father, who died when Ames was three, was an accountant who worked in Canada before returning to the United States. Ames grew up in his mother's home town of Morristown, New Jersey. After high school, he studied at the Stevens Institute of Technology in Hoboken. An elder brother, Joseph Bushnell, was a prolific writer of science fiction and children's novels. He founded the Boy Scout movement in New Jersey and wrote screenplays for early cowboy movies. Another brother, Ernest, worked in London, and Ashmun joined him there in 1912. He worked as a secretary before joining the army.[46]

Ames was commissioned into the Grenadier Guards in late August 1917, having trained with an officer cadet unit. It is unclear when his military service had begun. By his mother's later account, he had joined up early in the War after becoming a British citizen. Prior to being commissioned, he had twice been invalided from the front.[47] Her account cannot be substantiated from his surviving military record, and seems at odds with evidence that he was still an American civilian in February 1917 when applying to renew his passport. This application stated that he was a secretary who required the passport for 'war relief work' in France. However, if Ames was already working in British intelligence, the renewed passport may have been required to allow him to pose as a neutral working for a war charity. American entry into the War, two months later, presumably terminated such a rôle, and instead he joined the Grenadiers. By August 1918, when he acted as best man at the remarriage of his widowed brother at the Franciscan Church in Ascot, he had been promoted to lieutenant.[48]

Though demobilized in April 1920, within weeks he was recalled for special service in Dublin and arrived there in June. Before coming to Ireland, he had a flat beside the Albert Hall in Kensington and a girlfriend, Millicent, the daughter of Lady Orr Ewing of Berkeley Square. Ames's previous Dublin billet, shared with Bennett, was at 28 Upper Pembroke Street. Having moved into their new lodgings at 38 Upper Mount Street on Saturday, 20 November, they returned to Pembroke Street for dinner and bridge with various residents and guests, among them the American Consul, Frederick Dumont. Though pressed to stay until the curfew ended, the two officers and the consul went home in the early hours of Sunday.[49]

In the opinion of the IRA men who drank with them, 'Colonel Aimes' and his flatmate 'Major' Bennett were the most senior agents operating in Dublin. In fact, both were temporary lieutenants and junior in rank to two of the agents with whom they had previously lodged in Pembroke Street (Price and Dowling). That the IRA could track them to their new home was reportedly due to the porter at Pembroke Street. Later court-martialled for allegedly assisting the Pembroke Street assassins, James Green had asked colleagues whither Ames and Bennett had moved, ostensibly to return their laundry.[50]

On Sunday morning, Ames was taken out of his bed and brought into Bennett's room, where the two were lined up and shot. Both received several bullet wounds in the chest, back and arm. Ames was also shot in the leg and Bennett in the head. Before he fired the pistol, Vinny Byrne experienced a pious twinge: 'The Lord have Mercy on your souls.' Having lived and died together, the two officers, both Catholics, were buried in the same row in a London cemetery.[51]

On the day after Bloody Sunday, the engagement of Ashmun Ames to Millicent Ewing was announced in the New York Times. A day later, the same paper printed his death notice, 'killed by Sinn Feiners'. In New Jersey, his family received an equally grim sequence of telegrams.[52] On the Friday, Millicent sprinkled holy water over his grave.

11. Leonard Price

The Dublin Service Flats Ltd operated several properties (including nursing homes where wounded officers recuperated) in the streets around Merrion and Fitzwilliam squares. At 28 Upper Pembroke Street, it provided ten flats and a basement dining room.[53] Apart from an elderly widow, the tenants were all military officers, including four bachelors and three whose wives had joined them in Dublin. Two others (Ames and Bennett) had moved out on the eve of Bloody Sunday. Whereas the married men were either regimental or staff officers, the bachelors were undercover agents. It is puzzling that agents posing as commercial travellers chose to lodge alongside uniformed personnel.

One agent escaped because he was out on a raid. Robert Jeune, who had trained with Bennett and come to Ireland at the same time, was busy searching the Inchicore rail depot.[54] Six of the officers he lodged with were in bed or dressing, as the raiders entered through the front door and over the rear garden wall. Like many of the houses targeted that morning, no. 28 offered excellent side and rear access. Lanes beyond the garden led to Fitzwilliam Square and Leeson Street (Plates 11, 12).

The two men shot in their third-floor flat were both Londoners. The son of a stockbroker, Leonard Price was born in Islington in 1885, raised on the south coast, and sent to Brighton College. After his parents died, he lived with a cousin on the Isle of Wight. After school, he moved to Hampstead, became a clerk, and served as a Territorial in the Honourable Artillery Company.

By September 1914, Price was serving in France. Commissioned into the West Yorkshire Regiment in 1915, he subsequently won a Military Cross with the Middlesex Regiment. He was wounded and taken prisoner during the German advance in April 1918, when Portugese troops serving alongside his unit broke and fled. Repatriated just before Christmas 1918, he served as a staff officer in Scotland until demobilized as a temporary major in autumn, 1919. A bachelor, he returned to the Isle of Wight before being recalled for service in Ireland in June 1920.

After training at Hounslow, Price and a future housemate at Upper Pembroke Street, Randolph Murray, were gazetted together as junior intelligence officers. In early official lists of Bloody Sunday fatalities, he was initially described as a sapper officer at headquarters (a common cover for agents).[55] A schedule of his possessions conveys the pre-war Edwardian clerk turned battle veteran: tennis flannels, pince-nez, pipe-lighter, Military Cross and 1914–15 Star.[56]

12. *Charles Milne Cholmeley Dowling*

Price and his flatmate, 'Chummy' Dowling, were taken from their beds and shot in the chest. Both died instantly. Decades later, their fellow lodger Robert Jeune recalled Dowling as 'a grand ex-Guardee'. Although Dowling was born in smart Belgravia, his parents had met in the rougher world of Gold-Rush Australia. His mother was a Tasmanian; his father, also Charles, was a second-generation Ulsterman who had emigrated to Victoria in the 1850s. His paternal great-grandfather was a Church of Ireland clergyman. Charles senior prospered in Australia and become a ranger on the Ballarat goldfields and a colonial magistrate. A widower, he remarried in 1885, retired to London, and died in 1893 when his son was two.[57]

Dowling had a privileged upbringing in Eaton Square, as shown by a sketch of him, aged seven, as a pageboy in white satin when his cousin married a Russian prince. Twenty-one years later, now a Grenadier Guards officer, he was one of the mourners at her funeral.[58] After attending Rugby from 1905 to 1908, he crammed for the army and was commissioned in 1910, becoming a lieutenant a year later. During the War, he was thrice wounded in France. A staff officer by 1917, he was stationed for some months after the Armistice in Germany, before returning to England.[59]

While on leave in France during spring, 1920, Dowling resigned his commission, citing a job offer. As a reservist, he was recalled for an intelligence post with the Dublin District, Irish Command, in June 1920. A remobilization memorandum instructed him to report for training to Hounslow, bringing uniform and civilian clothes including a 'varied assortment of overcoats, caps etc.'[60] Once in Dublin, Captain Dowling posed as a representative of various Ulster linen companies, doubtless making good use of his family ties to Lough Swilly.[61]

13. *Hugh Ferguson Montgomery*

In the hallway and on the stairwell below, four more shootings took place. Hugh Montgomery was shot as he and his wife Ethel emerged from their ground-floor flat. She was grazed on the knee, but he sustained more serious injuries to the chest and shoulder.

Montgomery was aged forty. Like both parents, he was born

in India. His mother's family were Bengal civil servants and Indian army officers, but his father's lineage was dominated by Irish clergy, several generations having ministered at Moville, Co. Donegal and Ballinascreen, Co. Londonderry. His father returned from Bengal in 1899 and became a rector in Somerset. An uncle, Henry, became bishop of Tasmania before returning to London in 1901. Montgomery spent many holidays with his cousins (who included a future field marshal, Bernard Law Montgomery) in Somerset and Donegal (at New Park, the ancestral home near Moville).[62] At Marlborough College from 1893 to 1898, his talent as a right-handed cricketer blossomed. He played on the first XI in his final year and for Somerset from 1901 to 1908. His last representative game was for the Navy against the Army in 1912.[63]

Montgomery joined the Royal Marine Light Infantry in 1900 after a year at the Royal Naval College. A dull decade followed in ports on the south coast of England, alleviated in 1906 by marriage, which however yielded no children. In 1910, he had a year at Staff College. Its commandant (another future field marshal) was unimpressed by his tendency 'to lapse into detail and lose sight of the main issue', but sagely predicted that he would improve with experience.[64]

In 1911, Montgomery was posted to the Admiralty's Intelligence Department. Joining its War Staff a year later, he helped to devise a special service unit within the Royal Marines. Seconded to the army in 1913, he returned to the Admiralty when war broke out. The army soon requested him again, and from 1915 to 1918 he served chiefly as a staff officer on the Western Front. Throughout the War, he kept in contact with his younger cousin, Bernard. Though Montgomery survived the Somme, the Ancre and the Lys unscathed, his only brother, Neville, was killed serving with the Canadians at Lens in 1917. The most decorated of Bloody Sunday's victims, he was frequently mentioned in despatches, particularly for his conduct at Cambrai in December 1917 and again in the final phases of the War.[65]

After the Armistice, Montgomery, now a brevet lieutenant-colonel, spent a further year as a staff officer. He returned from Germany to the Royal Marines at Chatham for a few months before yet another army secondment in February 1920. He was now considered to be among the most promising Royal Marine officers of his generation. By contrast, cousin Bernard, at Staff College that year and soon to go to Cork, was then regarded by superior officers as 'a bloody menace'.[66]

Hugh Montgomery's new posting to Dublin, as a senior staff officer with the Irish Command, appeared in the *Quarterly Army Lists* throughout 1920. That this uniformed officer was accompanied by his wife further indicates that he was not an undercover agent. As a GSO1, collation of intelligence was naturally part of his job, but his widow's compensation claim was emphatic that his rôle was not clandestine: he 'had nothing to do with special operations in Ireland but was doing educational training'. When he inspected the 1st Cadet Battalion, Royal Dublin Fusiliers, at Portobello Barracks, the event was reported in the press.[67]

After being shot on Bloody Sunday, he was taken first to a neighbouring nursing home and then to the George V military hospital. His wife's knee was patched up and, like all wives living in flats, she was hastily moved into barracks that evening. Montgomery recovered enough to return to the nursing home to convalesce, but relapsed a fortnight later and died in hospital on 10 December.[68] Though all officers killed as a result of Bloody Sunday received military funerals, Montgomery was apparently the only victim whose death on active service in Ireland was explicitly recorded on a war memorial.[69] This reflects his status as the third most senior British military fatality in Ireland between 1920 and 1922.[70]

The other three wounded officers included two regular officers of the Lancashire Fusiliers, Lieutenant-Colonel Wilfrid Woodcock and Captain Brian Keenlyside. Woodcock was shot on the stairs as he prepared to leave for the Sunday church parade at his barracks. Keenlyside was lined up in the hall and shot with Lieutenant Randolph Murray. At Dublin Castle in the following days, Mrs Woodcock and Mrs Keenlyside stoically appeared for press interviews and photo-calls (Plate 15). The pregnant Biddy Keenlyside's pluck, in struggling with her husband's attackers, added much to the drama of the day, as did Caroline Woodcock's press interviews and subsequent published narrative of what happened after she witnessed a gunman climb over the garden wall.[71] Woodcock and Keenlyside both recovered and soldiered on until 1928. Alongside

honours won in Gallipoli and France, Woodcock later included
'Ireland. Wounded 1920' in his entry for *Who's Who*.[72]

Lieutenant Randolph Murray shared a top-floor flat with the
absent Jeune. Mrs Woodcock recalled that he was in bright blue
pyjamas when shot along with Keenlyside. Murray appears to be
the sole Cairo Gangster among the dead and injured of Bloody
Sunday, if that retrospective term denotes an intelligence officer
with prior service in Egypt. He was the son of an Edinburgh lawyer
and local politician. After attending George Heriot's school, he
joined the Royal Scots and served in Gallipoli, France and India.
While on attachment to the Indian army, he was appointed special
intelligence officer and served in the Middle East, first at Ismailia in
Egypt and then in Palestine.

Murray was shot in both lungs and was not expected to live.
His parents were summoned and left for Dublin that evening. After
several months in hospital, Murray was invalided out of the army
with a permanently collapsed lung, but remained a Territorial for
some years. Though unfit for heavy work, he put his Irish experience
to good use as a commercial traveller for an Edinburgh brewery,
until killed in a car crash in 1938.[73]

14. Leonard Aidan Wilde

Guests staying that weekend at the Gresham hotel, on Sackville
(O'Connell) Street, included Leonard Wilde, a grocer's son born
in Reading in 1891. He was educated locally and then at 'University
College' – exactly which college, like many aspects of his life,
remains obscure.[74] He became a language tutor, fluent in French
and Spanish, and spent some years abroad before the War; he was
in Cuba in 1913. His presumed conversion to Catholicism may date
from this period.

By the outbreak of war, he had entered an enclosed French
(and Francophone) Benedictine community at St Michael's abbey,
Farnborough, taking the 'simple vows' of a novice. This may have
prompted the substitution of Aidan (after the Lindisfarne saint)
for William as his middle name. At Farnborough, the community
nursed convalescent French and Belgian troops. Clerical students
like Wilde helped out as medical orderlies. When monks of military

1. 'The tank preserving the peace in disordered Dublin'

2. 'A motorist being searched by one of the military pickets'

Hosiery Mills, Balbriggan

3. 'Hosiery mills, Balbriggan'

4. 'The Square, Balbriggan'

THE SQUARE. BALBRIGGAN.

5. 'The campaign of lawlessness in Ireland'

6. 'Part of a row of cottages which were destroyed by fire'

PART OF A ROW OF COTTAGES WHICH WERE DESTROYED BY FIRE
About two hundred people were rendered homeless by the havoc.

7. 119 Lower Baggot St, sidelong view

8. 92 Lower Baggot St

9. 38 Upper Mount St

10. 'A house of death', 22 Lower Mount St

A HOUSE OF DEATH: THE HOUSE, 22, LOWER MOUNT STREET,
where Mr. Mahon, a civilian, was assassinated.

11. 28 Upper Pembroke St, portico

12. 28 Upper Pembroke St, rear

MURDER MOST FOUL IN DUBLIN
THE BLACKEST SUNDAY IN IRISH HISTORY

THE MURDERED OFFICERS: 1, CPT. L. PRICE, M.C.; 2, LT. G. BENNETT, late R.A.; 3, MAJ. DOWLING, Gren. Gds.; 4, CADET F. GARNISS; 5, CPT. BAGGALAY

13. 'Murder most foul in Dublin: the blackest Sunday in Irish history'

14. 'A field of death: where Hogan fell in Croke Park football ground struggle'

15. Mrs Woodcock and Mrs Keenlyside

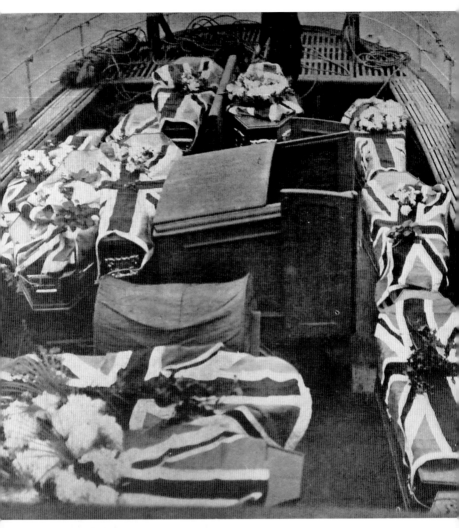

16. 'The Martyrs of the Macroom Massacres'

age were recalled to France for army service, Wilde himself joined the Royal Army Medical Corps in January 1915, but was medically discharged after only a week.[75]

Six months later (as Leonard William Wilde), he managed to secure a commission in the Sherwood Foresters. By that stage, he had joined the English Benedictines at Downside abbey near Bath.[76] He was wounded in France in autumn, 1915. After convalescing at Downside he resumed service for another six months, before being invalided out with shell-shock. Exactly four years before Bloody Sunday, a medical board noted his stammer and 'feeling of utter inability to face the firing line'.[77] Realizing that he was more suited to warmer climates, the board approved the Foreign Office's offer to use Lieutenant Wilde's skills as a temporary vice-consul in neutral Spain.

A month later, he moved to Barcelona. His work included monitoring enemy shipping and investigating whether trade continued with Germany. Wilde's linguistic skills and clerical contacts proved valuable. In spring, 1917, he was asked to translate and pass on to his 'clerical friends' an article on the British Catholic war effort by Monsignor Francis Bickerstaffe-Drew, a senior army chaplain. An anonymous propaganda pamphlet, published later that year and widely circulated in the Hispanic world, appears to have been based on this article.[78] Though the text made no mention of the French Benedictines, Wilde's involvement is suggested by a photograph of a Farnborough monk or novice tending wounded French soldiers.[79]

Scandal soon sullied his piety. Having run up debts of £544 (including 1000 pesetas owed to the abbot of Montserrat near Barcelona), and allowed a few cheques to bounce, Wilde was sacked by the Foreign Office in September 1917, and fled to Paris. A later attempt to rejoin the British forces failed, but the War Office (apart from refusing permission to use his military rank) did not obstruct his recruitment there, in May 1918, by the United States Air Service. The nature and duration of his American service is unclear.

Neither laicization nor scandal damaged his standing with the Catholic Church during his time in Paris.[80] Cardinal Amette, the archbishop of Paris, gave the blessing when Wilde married an American army nurse at Notre Dame in February 1919, in the

presence of the *curés* of the Spanish Church and many Allied officers.[81] His bride, Frances Rabbitts, a former language teacher and
a Sorbonne graduate, returned to the United States within months
of the wedding to visit her dying father.

Marriage had reformed him, so Wilde declared months later,
when he returned to Spain and offered to reimburse the consulate,
which had been forced to settle his debts. His former consular
colleagues, unimpressed by his offer, were uneasy that Wilde had
been let back into Spain and that he appeared to still be in contact
with a former Admiralty agent in Barcelona. The Foreign Office,
though, ruled that Wilde be refused a visa to leave Spain until he
had reimbursed the consulate. It is unclear how long this took, how
he was employed, or by whom. His demobilization papers, issued in
London in August 1920, merely stated that the final theatre of war
in which he had served was Spain, 'on consular duties'.

In the three weeks he stayed at the Gresham hotel, Wilde, who
registered as a commercial traveller, made little impression on staff
and guests. Yet three days before his death, he claimed to be *au fait*
with Irish political and ecclesiastical affairs. This claim was made
in a letter supporting the British Labour Party's position on Ireland,
which he sent to its leader, Arthur Henderson. In volunteering his
services as propagandist, Wilde cited his long-standing knowledge
of Ireland and his contacts within the Irish Catholic Church. Henderson released the letter to the press after Wilde's death.[82]

On opening the door of his hotel room that morning, Wilde was
shot in the head at close range and died instantly, parts of his brain
having been blown out. Mark Sturgis, writing in his diary at Dublin
Castle that night, recorded 'two Secret Service men assassinated
in the Gresham Hotel'. Two days later, though, Sturgis learned
that one (MacCormack) was in fact a vet who had been 'killed by
mistake'. He gave no further information on Wilde.[83]

Early press and parliamentary accounts said that he was a serving
lieutenant. Few biographical details emerged other than a report in
Monday's *Daily Mail* that he had attended Stonyhurst and later been
in Spain. Newspapers in Ireland and Britain fell silent, once Wilde's
unsettling letter to Henderson had appeared. Though Spanish newspapers that week ran many columns on the '*sangrientas jornados*' in

Dublin, including coverage of events at '*el hotel de Gresham*', Wilde seems not to have been mentioned.[84]

When funeral arrangements for the serving army and police officers were announced days later, his name was not listed. Whereas coffins for the eight army officers were ordered by the Irish Command from a firm in High Street, Wilde was buried by another undertaker. No death notice appeared with details of his funeral Mass in Dublin's pro-cathedral, followed by burial in Glasnevin cemetery. This took place on the day after the London state funerals for serving personnel killed on Bloody Sunday. Wilde's grave remains unmarked.[85]

Nor was his name included in the official fatality lists for Bloody Sunday that continued to appear until the following spring,[86] or in the Irish Command's list of fatalities between 1920 and 1922. Eleven other victims of Bloody Sunday were recorded in that roll of 180 names, produced for a memorial service on the second anniversary of Bloody Sunday in the chapel of the Royal Hospital, Kilmainham, shortly before the army's departure from Southern Ireland.[87]

What was Wilde's rôle and who employed him? According to later testimony for the Bureau of Military History by one of his killers, Wilde was delightfully guileless. On seeing a man 'of foreign appearance' emerge from his hotel room, James Cahill challenged him to give his name: 'Alan Wilde, British Intelligence Officer, just back from Spain.' The implausibility of this exchange is compounded by Cahill's far-fetched explanation: 'The fact that Wilde was a new arrival and probably mistook us for a British raiding party would explain his readiness to give us information regarding himself.'[88]

Perhaps Wilde was the nameless victim cited in another Bureau statement by Captain Edward Gerrard, a Dubliner then serving in the Royal Field Artillery. He recalled being told by Major-General John Joseph Gerrard, the senior army medical officer in Ireland in 1920, that 'there was an extra officer shot – they could not find out for a long time who he was. He was a Scotland Yard man sent over independently of the military. He was found out and shot with the others.'[89]

In England, even Wilde's solicitor was unsure of his status, as a letter sent months later to the War Office makes clear. The solicitor enquired whether his late client was owed any salary, either by the army or by any other government department, up to the date of his death, and whether his widow was entitled to any pension.[90]

Wilde's widow remained in Paris but remarried in 1924, in the American Legation in Tehran. Like Wilde, her new husband had been a language teacher before the War, in which he served as an army officer and interpreter in Paris, before becoming a diplomat and State Department expert on Afghanistan and Russia. Unlike Wilde, he survived all his postings.[91]

French (and English) Benedictine, army officer turned consul, presumed intelligence agent murkily implicated with the Admiralty, the Americans, and Scotland Yard, Leonard Aidan (or William) Wilde still eludes our grasp.

15. *Patrick Joseph MacCormack*

Unlike Wilde in the room below, Paddy MacCormack was well known to the Gresham's staff as an intermittent resident over several months. The hotel was a natural base for anyone as involved as he with the Irish horse industry.

MacCormack, born in Castlebar, Co. Mayo in 1877, was the only child of Patrick and Kate (née Feeney), drapers in the main street. The family were strong Catholics and Home Rulers. His mother was related to Michael Davitt and equally proud of her own part in the Land War. An uncle, Francis Joseph, whose first name he took at confirmation, became bishop of Galway.[92] Another uncle, Dr Charles Joseph MacCormack, ended his official career as inspector of reformatory and industrial schools at Dublin Castle.

The family were keen on horses and sent their son to be educated by the Vincentians at Castleknock College in Dublin, where pupils were allowed to ride and to hunt at Luttrellstown with the Royal Meath. Many former pupils became veterinary surgeons, others successful jockeys. MacCormack, however, worked initially in the family firm, run by his mother since his father's death in 1892.

In the early 1900s, he became an apprentice jockey with the famous Edwards brothers, who ran stud farms in Wiltshire and Limerick. A professional by the time he entered Dublin's Royal Veterinary College in 1906, he found a way to keep racing. He reputedly became the first Irishman to revoke his professional status for that of gentleman jockey. An annual fee of three guineas allowed him to enter amateur races.[93]

After qualifying in 1909, he practised in Castlebar but continued to race. Though he owned a few horses, he also rode occasionally for the celebrated trainer, James J. Parkinson.[94] From 1910 to 1917, MacCormack regularly entered races in the west and the midlands. He had a few wins with Waterside; but his biggest success, with the unfancied Nellie Mac, was at Limerick in 1915.

Unlike cousins in Castlebar and Athlone who joined up when war was declared, MacCormack remained a veterinary inspector with Mayo County Council for several years. In 1915, the bishop of Tuam presided at his wedding in the University church on St Stephen's Green. His bride was Mollie O'Connor, daughter of a prominent Roscommon draper and hotelier. Their daughter, Grace Mary, was born a year later.

In 1917, he joined the Royal Army Veterinary Corps. His first year's service in Kildare, where racing continued despite the War, passed pleasantly. In August 1918, while travelling by rail through France *en route* for Egypt, he made a will. It bore the crossed-out letterhead of Curragh camp. Underneath, Lieutenant MacCormack ruefully scrawled: 'I only wish it was.' In case anything 'unforeseen happen me, which I trust to God will not, while in the East', he left everything to his widow apart from an insurance policy for £300. This he cannily bequeathed to his mother, 'provided she has handed over her own £1000 policy' to his widow and child. He asked his mother and in-laws to help Mollie guide their daughter in the choice of a husband, and apologized for not leaving her better provided.[95]

The life of an army vet in Cairo was neither dangerous nor arduous, with plenty of time for racing. A barrister cousin, Frank MacCormack, who had moved from the Connaught Circuit to the healthier climate of Cairo, doubtless provided companionship and useful introductions. While awaiting demobilization in summer, 1919, MacCormack tried out as starter for the Gezira Sporting Club in Cairo and the Alexandria Jockey Club. At Abassia, where he had horses in training, he was among the season's winners. His progress in Cairo was mentioned in the Irish racing journals, newspapers in

Dublin and Mayo, and his school magazine. Many contemporary and also posthumous reports confused his prospective employers with the more sedentary Cairo Turf Club and the more famous Alexandria Sporting Club. By late 1919, the two clubs that he had tried out for merged, hiring ex-Captain MacCormack as the permanent starter at an annual salary of £1250.[96]

The Parkinson connection opened up excellent prospects in the protectorate, as many Egyptians began to develop stables and employ European trainers.[97] He was soon receiving an additional salary of £120 as secretary of the Egyptian Owners' and Breeders' Assocation, along with commission payments as the Irish Bloodstock Agency's agent in Egypt. His reputation and earnings were enhanced by wins for Star of Amen, one of the first horses he imported from Ireland.[98]

In August 1920, MacCormack came home on leave *ar muin na muice*, flush with a cheque for £1200 from an Egyptian buyer. His wife and daughter were to accompany him back to Cairo. Earlier that year, his wife, having lodged with her parents in Roscommon while he was in the army, had felt sufficiently secure to advertise for a 'mother's help, RC'.[99]

During that autumn's season, though he purchased some horses, most of the cheque was splurged on entertainment and display. A huge bill was run up at the Gresham, and his family was fitted out expensively for their new life in Egypt.[100] Hotel staff later recalled that he rarely rose before late afternoon, unless there was a race meeting on.[101] Lie-ins were facilitated by the fact that the Irish Bloodstock Agency and the Irish Horse Breeders', Owners' and Trainers' Association, with which he had regular dealings, met in the Gresham.

The MacCormacks' planned departure in mid October was postponed, when two of his new horses became ill and unfit for immediate shipment. Moreover, his wife wanted to remain in Ireland for her sister's wedding to the champion jockey, Tommy Burns.[102] The MacCormacks rebooked their departure from Dublin for 2 December, and his wife returned to Roscommon to help her sister get ready for the wedding in late November.

The racing season was nearly over. A few days before Bloody Sunday, MacCormack enjoyed the last day of the Curragh races, where his prospective brother-in-law almost won the Hibernian Plate.[103] MacCormack was affectionately remembered by racegoers in the West of Ireland for his singing and his ability to record a good night in rhyme. At the Gresham, fellow guests recalled his cheeriness and fraternization with serving officers staying in the hotel. On his last evening, he went to confession in the pro-cathedral before dining at Jammet's restaurant on St Andrew's Street.[104]

When the IRA arrived on Sunday morning, they inspected the hotel register and tore out several pages, before ordering staff to show them upstairs to two bedrooms. In no. 24, MacCormack, awake much earlier than usual, was breakfasting in bed and reading Saturday's *Irish Field* when gunmen burst into the room and shot him four times in the head and body.

In Castlebar, next morning, family members were attending a memorial mass for his bishop uncle when news of his death arrived. Amidst widespread shock at the killing of an ex-officer of 'an old and honoured Mayo stock', rumours circulated that this was the result of his having given his former rank when signing the hotel register.[105] In Mullingar, where he had often raced, the local paper indignantly declared that he 'had nothing to do with the Government of Ireland'.[106] In Dublin Castle, Mark Sturgis heard that MacCormack 'was occupying another man's room at the Gresham and was obviously killed by mistake'.[107] Though Sturgis was an *habitué* of Irish race meetings, later becoming friendly with J. J. Parkinson, his diaries offer no hint that MacCormack was employed in intelligence.

In Roscommon, the wedding plans were ruptured. A brief notice informed guests that, due to a family bereavement, the wedding would now take place quietly in Dublin on 1 December.[108] Mollie MacCormack and 4-year-old Grace, known as Gay, set off instead for his funeral in the pro-cathedral, on Wednesday 24 November. It was the second Mass offered that day for an Irish sportsman killed on Bloody Sunday. Mass had been said at 8 a.m. for Michael Hogan, before his remains were taken to Kingsbridge station *en route* for Tipperary.[109]

At Castleknock, where he became the third former pupil killed by the IRA since September, things were 'moving in a steadily more Gaelic direction'. The priests were learning Irish, hurling had been introduced, and invitations to play cricket against army teams were being declined, though rugby still prevailed. When the *Castleknock College Chronicle* later recalled incidents while 'the Terror was at its height', its focus was on the feats of former pupils on the run, rather than the fate of one shot while breakfasting in bed.[110] Two Vincentian priests attended his funeral, but MacCormack's name never again featured in school folklore.[111]

For the next three years, Mollie's family had to support her and MacCormack's mother while she faced litigation from his creditors. Perhaps these problems encouraged her to choose a Roscommon bank manager as her second husband. Having had another daughter and once again been widowed, she retired to Newbridge, where she and Paddy had been newly-weds before he left for Egypt. Gay MacCormack married a doctor and had a daughter, but died in her twenties. A bon vivant like her father, she used to hunt in Mayo and dance at the Gresham.

For a couple of years, MacCormack's mother kept his public memory alive through *in memoriam* notices (from which her daughter-in-law was pointedly excluded after remarriage).[112] Privately, though, this septuagenarian Land War veteran launched a courageous campaign, first unearthed by Charles Townshend in the 1970s, for acknowledgement of his civilian status.[113] Her letter was addressed to the Minister for Defence, Richard Mulcahy, who asked Michael Collins to provide details for a draft reply. Collins revealed that 'several of the 21st November cases were just regular officers. Some of the names were put on by the Dublin Brigade.' He thought that MacCormack was among the names added to the list, but recommended that Mulcahy's reply simply state 'that there was no particular charge against her son, but just that he was an enemy soldier'. In challenging this reply, she pointed out that her son had long been demobilized. The correspondence ended with Mulcahy lamely declining to advance 'any more definite reasons'.[114]

In every war and every campaign of terror, innocents have been slaughtered because they were in the wrong house or street, or were mixed up with or mixed with the wrong people. Yet the case of MacCormack is exceptional for the pathos of his mother's attempt to defend his name, and the callousness of the replies she received.

Her son was no anonymous British officer, posing as a commercial traveller, but a familiar and popular figure in Dublin, whose return to civilian life had been widely reported in Ireland for over a year before his killing. Paddy MacCormack was not a spy or would-be assassin. The fabled intelligence network of the IRA had murdered a charming chancer.

III

Five days later, nine victims (seven officers and two Auxiliary Cadets) received state funerals in London. The choreography of this event enabled the British public to grieve for individuals rather than a symbolic figure, such as the Unknown Warrior whose remains had been taken on the same gun carriage to Westminster Abbey a fortnight earlier. Cardinal Francis Bourne ruled that the funerals of Catholic victims in Westminster Cathedral should be an occasion for mourning all Catholic members of the forces killed in Ireland,[115] so counterbalancing Bishop Peter Emmanuel Amigo's recent homage to Terence MacSwiney at Southwark cathedral.[116]

While MacLean and Fitzgerald were buried with full military and police honours, the other Dublin funerals were private. The graves of nine serving officers (including MacLean's plot at Grangegorman cemetery in Dublin) subsequently came under the care of the CWGC.

In Ireland, though *in memoriam* notices appeared for a couple of years, family commemorations were muted. Aphasia, a useful designation for the suppression of public Irish remembrance of the Great War, may likewise be applied to the Irish legacy of Bloody Sunday morning. Though a nephew recalled that 'Uncle Jack' Fitzgerald was included in bedtime prayers when he was a child, he knew only that his uncle had died young in Ireland. Yet, at Blackrock, his memory endured. A Holy Ghost priest had officiated at his funeral, and until the 1990s a private Mass was offered for Jack on each anniversary of Bloody Sunday.[117]

In addition to the four victims born in Ireland, several had close family ties there. Seven of the fifteen were born in England, and two left next-of-kin in the United States. Most were in their late 20s or early 30s, their ages at death ranging between 22 and 47. No fewer than six were Catholic, the remainder being Anglican. Most were educated at English or Irish public schools and two were university graduates, but three had only primary schooling. Nine were married, six were fathers, and two were engaged.

Of the fourteen who served in the Great War, mostly on the Western Front, all but two were pre-war regulars, Territorials, or early volunteers. By the Armistice, all were officers, of junior rank with the exception of Montgomery. Only two served with Irish regiments. Three were decorated for gallantry and a couple of others were mentioned in despatches.

Twelve members of the Crown forces died: eight serving army officers, a GHQ staff officer on secondment from the Admiralty, and three policemen. Two others were civilians, while Wilde defies confident classification. The army officers comprised six deployed on intelligence duties and two CMOs. Apart from Montgomery, the officers had served in Ireland only since the summer, while the two Auxiliaries had only just reached Dublin.

The six intelligence officers had previously served in Europe and Russia, but not Egypt. If there was a 'Cairo Gang', as republicans retrospectively claimed, and if this term denotes where intelligence skills were honed rather than where agents enjoyed a coffee (allegedly the Café Cairo in Grafton Street),[118] then these men were not in it. The moniker might more accurately be applied to prominent agents who survived to be posted from Ireland to Egypt. Walter Carandini Wilson, the officer in charge of military intelligence on Bloody Sunday, moved on to Cairo in 1922, as did others in his 'gang'.[119]

Most sites associated with Bloody Sunday have survived, though the interiors have been changed utterly. By the 1950s, Irish dancing classes were held in what had been the ballroom of the Café Cairo, while Bord na Móna (the Turf Board) occupied 28 Upper Pembroke Street. Nowadays a boutique guesthouse, 92 Lower Baggot Street still advertises vacancies (see Plate 8). At 117 Morehampton Road, unimproved from the outside, Herbert Smith would no doubt have applauded the addition of a jacuzzi with gold taps by a later property developer. Yet even today, cycling past these 'houses of death' on a winter Sunday morning when the streets are empty, it is hard to avoid shivering.

NOTE ON SOURCES

It is impracticable to give specific citations for every snippet of biographical information drawn from standard sources, including morning, evening and weekly Dublin newspapers and many provincials (especially death and *in memoriam* notices); *The London Gazette* and *The Times* (online); *The Illustrated London News* and *The Graphic*; *Thom's Official Directory*; *Who's Who* and other biographical compendia; published school, university, professional and denominational rolls of honour; monthly, quarterly and supplementary *Army Lists*; published cemetery registers and online records of the CWGC, and the author's transcriptions and photographs from Glasnevin and Grangegorman cemeteries; burial records of the Glasnevin Trust; family and institutional schedules of the Census of Ireland, 1901 and 1911 (NAD, online); military and RIC service records and pension files (NAL); accounts of the circumstances of death in CILI reports (NAL, WO 35); original wills (NAD); Dublin City Coroner, Register of Inquests, 1916–33 and Register of Inquiries, 1916–27 (NAD); court-martial evidence (Michael Noyk Papers, NLI); Church of Ireland and other registers accessible through churchrecords/irishgenealogy.ie.

Many passenger lists, indexes to wills, census schedules for England, Scotland, Canada and the United States, registers of births, deaths and marriages, British medal index cards and service records for the Great War, and other standard genealogical sources for various countries have been consulted online through 'Ancestry Library Edition' (Libraries NI, cited as 'ALE'). Certain personal service files for officers in NAL (for Connolly, Dowling, Newberry and Wilde) have been read solely in versions reproduced on cairogang.com (cited as 'CG'), an extraordinarily wide-ranging and ever expanding resource for military and police careers. Use has also been made of digests of officer files for Ames, MacLean and Garniss in William Sheehan, *Fighting For Dublin: The British Battle for Dublin, 1919–1921* (Cork 2007). All other cited files for army, naval and airforce officers were consulted directly by the author.

My thanks to the following for assistance and information: the family of Jack Fitzgerald, and the late Dr Michael O'Carroll, CSSP (Fitzgerald); Michael O'Shea of St Mary's cemetery, Kensal Green (Ames and Bennett); Kate Cunningham, BL, and Theresa Thom, archivist of Gray's Inn (Newberry); Dr Gabriel Sanchez (Spanish newspapers); Dr Paul Harris (Staff College war memorial); Edmund Ross (access to the former Café Cairo); the abbot of St Michael's abbey, Farnborough (French Benedictines); Dr Jean Marc Oppenheim (Egyptian equestrianism); and David Fitzpatrick (bicycle).

NOTES

1. Rosamond Jacob, Diary, NLI, MS 32,582/38; extract from Childers, Diary, in Leonard Piper, *Dangerous Waters: The Life and Death of Erskine Childers* (London 2003), p. 203. A traumatized Bloody Sunday assassin features in Jacob's novel, *The Troubled House: A Novel of Dublin in the 'Twenties* (Dublin 1938), written some months after the event.

2. *The Graphic*, 27 Nov. 1920; *Irish News*, 22 Nov. 1920.

3. Neil Jordan, *Michael Collins: Screenplay and Film Diary* (New York 1996), pp. 47, 148.

4. Selina O'Regan and John Campbell, *The GAA Through History & Documents, 1870–1920* (Dublin 2008), factsheet no. 8; Peter Cottrell, *The Anglo–Irish War: The Troubles of 1913–1922* (Oxford 2006), p. 53.

5. The term 'intelligence officer' incorporates military personnel recruited for 'special service' in Ireland, as well those officially returned as such.

6. My thanks to the late Peter Hart, a Workshop comrade since 1990, for many discussions about sorting out agents from bystanders.

7. This figure excludes those dying on 21 Nov. from wounds received prior to this date (such as Arthur Bundry or Boundary, an army private, in Belfast), or late on the Saturday night (such as John McSwiggan, shot around midnight by troops in Magherafelt: CILI, NAL, WO 35/154).

8. Certain details in the Appendix differ slightly from those given in the succeeding essay on the basis of sources abstracted for *The Dead of the Irish Revolution*.

9. First used in the twentieth century of St Petersburg in 1905, early Dublin applications of the term 'Bloody Sunday' include the labour riots of 31 Aug. 1913 and the Bachelors Walk killings of 31 July 1914. Most headlines for 22 Nov. 1920 preferred 'Red' or 'Black', apart from *FJ* ('Dublin's Bloody Sunday') and the *Irish News* ('a veritable Bloody Sunday').

10. William Barnett, a Methodist chandler killed in Mountjoy Square, and William Cullinane, a Catholic seminarian, who died two days after being shot in Lincoln's Place.

11. Private E. W. Powell, Worcestershire Regiment. The cause and date of death of an unknown man drowned in the Liffey, erroneously reported to have been found in Auxiliary uniform, has not been determined: CILI reports; Coroner's Register of Inquiries; *Belfast Telegraph* and *Dublin Evening Herald*, 23 Nov. 1920; *The Times*, 24 Nov. 1920.

12. Published studies relating to Bloody Sunday morning include Christopher Andrew, *Secret Service: The Making of the British Intelligence Community* (London 1985), pp. 366–70; Tom Bowden, 'Bloody Sunday – a reappraisal', *European Studies Review*, 2 (1972), 25–72; Anne Dolan, 'Killing and Bloody Sunday, November 1920', *Historical Journal*,

49 (2006), 789–810; T. Ryle Dwyer, *The Squad and the Intelligence Operations of Michael Collins* (Cork 2005); Michael Foy, *Michael Collins's Intelligence War: The Struggle Between the British and the IRA, 1919–1921* (Stroud 2008; 1st edn 2006); David Leeson, 'Death in the afternoon: the Croke Park massacre, 21 November 1920', *Canadian Journal of History*, 38 (2003), 43–67; Paul McMahon, *British Spies and Irish Rebels: British Intelligence and Ireland, 1916–1945* (Woodbridge, Suffolk 2008), pp. 24–49; and Charles Townshend, 'Bloody Sunday – Michael Collins speaks', *European Studies Review*, 9 (1979), 377–85.

13. The eponymous victims were Michael Hogan, Dick McKee and Peadar Clancy.

14. John Kelly, *Ceapach na bhFaoiteach: The Cappawhite GAA Story, 1886–1989* (Cappawhite 1989), pp. 38, 48, 57.

15. *Veritas* (1916).

16. *Weekly IT*, 27 Oct. 1917; *Tipperary Star*, 12 Mar. 1921; Fitzgerald, officer file, NAL, AIR 76/162.

17. Sir William Fitzgerald became the last British Chief Justice of Palestine.

18. *FJ*, 9 Mar. 1921; *Clare Champion* and *Tipperary Star*, 12 Mar. 1921; *Nenagh Guardian*, 27 Nov. 1920. Fitzgerald's RIC record gives only his date of enlistment and rank, with no details of subsequent service or resignation.

19. CILI, WO 35/159B.

20. Interview with Matty MacDonald, OMN, P17B/105 (75–6), quoted in Dolan, 'Killing and Bloody Sunday', 799.

21. Baggallay, officer file, NAL, WO 339/30321; *The Times*, 3 May, 18 Aug. 1919, 20 Aug. 1920.

22. See Colin Campbell, *Emergency Law in Ireland, 1918–1925* (Oxford 1994), pp. 67–70, 118–23. The Act received royal assent on 9 Aug. 1920.

23. A CMO's annual pay was about £700, with a daily allowance of 8s. 6d.

24. These included lawyers from Australia, New Zealand and Canada. English CMOs who did not secure colonial legal posts after 1922 included 2 future MPs, one of whom committed suicide.

25. Piaras Béaslaí, *Michael Collins and the Making of a New Ireland* (Dublin 1926), vol. 2, pp. 56–8.

26. *Sunday Independent*, 21 Nov. 1920; statement by Matty MacDonald, quoted in Dolan, 'Killing', p. 799.

27. *II*, 22 Dec. 1920.

28. Newberry, officer file (CG); *IT*, 10 June 1921; information from Theresa Thom, archivist of Gray's Inn.

29. [Caroline Woodcock], 'Experiences of an officer's wife in Ireland',

Blackwood's Magazine, ccix (May 1921), 553–98 (585); Joice M. Nankivell and Sydney Loch, *Ireland in Travail* (London 1922), pp. 98–9; James Gleeson, *Bloody Sunday* (London 1962), p. 125.

30. Will of Thomas Herbert Smith, 18 Oct. 1911, NAD.

31. O'Connor's daughter, a nun, recalled playing with Percy Smith: Tim Pat Coogan, *Michael Collins: A Biography* (London 1990), p. 162.

32. *FJ*, 28 Jan. 1921.

33. *The Scotsman* and *Glasgow Herald*, 23 Nov. 1920; *FJ*, 28 Jan. 1921; Weekly *IT*, 4, 11 Dec. 1920.

34. *Glasgow Herald*, 23 Nov. 1920; medal roll. Though the *Herald* reported that he had joined the RIC and had a brother already serving as a Cadet, the RIC records contain no matching records.

35. *FJ* and *II*, 28 Jan. 1921.

36. There is conflicting evidence concerning his and his father's birthplaces: Angliss, officer file, WO 339/102450.

37. Entry for Peel (CG).

38. *Scotsman* and *Glasgow Herald*, 29 Jan. 1921; *Sunday Independent*, 30 Jan. 1921; Connolly, officer file (CG); Noyk Papers, NLI, MS 36222 (2).

39. David Foxton, *Revolutionary Lawyers and Crown Justice, 1916–23* (Dublin 2008), p. 238 (for Connolly's name and regiment); Connolly, officer file (CG); UCD *Calendar* (1917–18, 1919–20). Sturgis recorded on 28 Jan. 1921 that 'Conolly, I'm told, gave his evidence today well': Michael Hopkinson (ed.), *The Last Days of Dublin Castle: The Diaries of Mark Sturgis* (Dublin 1999), p. 117.

40. Noyk Papers, MS 36222 (3); *Anglo-Celt*, 27 Nov. 1920.

41. The first fatality was William James Anderson, accidentally shot at Beggars Bush barracks on 10 Oct. 1920; the first Cadets killed by the IRA were Bertram Agnew and Lionel Mitchell, kidnapped near Macroom in early Nov. 1920. Their bodies were never located: Richard Abbott, *Police Casualties in Ireland, 1919–1922* (Cork 2000), pp. 315, 322.

42. CG; Abbott, *Police Casualties*, p. 152; *Newsletter*, 30 Nov. 1920.

43. The sending of a wreath from G Co., Auxiliary Division, was noted in an obituary in his parish magazine, reproduced in irishconstabulary.com.

44. Though forbidden after Bloody Sunday to live out of barracks, within months British officers were again lodged in Upper Mount St. The agent living opposite no. 38, Frank Carew, did not return there, having been wounded when attempting to halt the killers.

45. *The Times*, 23 Nov. 1920. Maude, Bennett's former neighbour in Bournemouth and contemporary at New College, acted as executor of his will and applied for his medals. He became a papal chamberlain.

46. J. B. Ames's *The Emerald Buddha* (New York 1921) was dedicated to the memory of Ashmun, '*Patriae fidelis*'.

47. *London Gazette*, 19 Sept. 1917; *New York Times*, 23 Nov. 1920. A digest of Ames's officer file in Sheehan, *Fighting For Dublin*, pp. 159–60, dates his first commission as 30 Mar. 1917, 6 months prior to the date given in the *London Gazette*. Ames's medal index card, with date of first overseas service, has not survived.

48. Application for US passport renewal, 2 Feb. 1917 (ALE); *The Times*, 31 Aug. 1918.

49. Woodcock, 'Experiences', 585. Carl Ackermann reported that Dumont 'knew all the intimate facts upon which a government based its policy': *New York Times*, 7 Aug. 1921.

50. Coogan, *Collins*, p. 159; Noyk Papers, MS 36221.

51. Vinny Byrne, MAD, BMH, WS 423. Though Bennett's headstone at Kensal Green is damaged, Michael O'Shea informs me that the inscription 'killed in the service of his country' remains legible.

52. *New York Times*, 22, 23 Nov. 1920; see also *Baltimore American* and *New York Tribune*, 23 Nov. 1920.

53. The accommodation extended into the adjoining house. TDs were among later tenants of Dublin Service Flats, which survived until the 1940s.

54. Capt. Robert Dyne Jeune, Memoir (typescript, 1970s), IWM.

55. *Weekly IT*, 27 Nov. 1920. In the list of fatalities in the *Monthly Army List* for Mar. 1921, Price returned to the Middlesex Regiment.

56. Price, officer file with list of belongings, WO 339/42755.

57. Jeune, Memoir. From distant Tasmania and Belgravia, Dowling's father placed family notices in Irish newspapers: *FJ*, 20 Feb. 1861, 7 Oct. 1885.

58. She became Princess Alexis Dolgorouki: *The Standard*, 12 July 1898; *The Times*, 2 Sept. 1919.

59. Dowling, officer file (CG).

60. Memorandum, 30 June 1920 (CG). For the Hounslow spy school, see McMahon, *British Spies*, pp. 33–4.

61. *The Times*, 23 Nov. 1920.

62. Family tree in Henry Montgomery, *A Generation of Montgomerys* (Ballinascreen 2006; 1st edn 1895); Brian Montomgery, *A Field Marshal in the Family* (London 1973), pp. 134–5.

63. Philip Bailey *et al.*, *Who's Who of Cricketers* (London 1984), p. 712.

64. Confidential report by Brig. W. R. Robertson, 8 Dec. 1910, in Montgomery, officer file, NAL, ADM 196/63

65. Montgomery's DSO (1917), CMG (1919), and *Croix d'Officier de la Légion d'Honneur* (1919), are in the Royal Marines Museum.

66. Donald F. Bittner, *The Royal Marine Officer Corps of 1914* (Eastney 1984), p. 40; Brian Montgomery, *Field Marshal*, p. 179.

67. *II*, 8 Mar. 1921; *IT*, 23 Feb. 1920.

68. Weekly *IT*, 18 Dec. 1920; *The Times*, 14, 15 Dec. 1920. His remains were taken by destroyer to England and he was buried with full military honours in Brompton Cemetery, London.

69. Some are named on local war memorials, but without place of death. Montgomery is among 5 past students of Staff College honoured on its 'Ireland, 1920–22' memorial plaque at Camberley. This also records Field Marshal Sir Henry Wilson, despite his being killed in London. A family plaque in their father's church in Somerset also honours Montgomery and his younger brother.

70. Ranked above him among those on the Irish Command's list of fatalities, 1920–22 (in Order of Service, 21 Nov. 1922, Jeudwine Papers, IWM), were Col.-Comdt. Hanway Robert Cuming (killed Clonbanin, 5 Mar. 1921) and Col.-Comdt. Thomas Stanton Lambert (killed Athlone, 21 June 1921). Their names also appear on the Camberley plaque.

71. The Keenlysides' baby arrived the following spring and served in World War II. Caroline Woodcock's article (see note n. 29) appeared as a book in July 1921, reissued in a partly rewritten version, introduced by Tim Pat Coogan, as *An Officer's Wife in Ireland* (London 1994).

72. *Who's Who* (1948 edn). Keenlyside died in 1941, Woodcock in 1960.

73. *The Scotsman*, 23, 25 Nov. 1920, 29 Oct. 1938; *IT*, *II*, 8 Mar. 1921.

74. Wilde, officer file, and Foreign Office correspondence and consular despatches (CG; originals in NAL). Wilde's name has not been found in published war lists, calendars and alumni rolls of the various institutions he claimed to have attended.

75. Private Leonard Aidan Wilde, attestation record, in WO 364/4679.

76. Such a move was highly unusual as the two orders were unconnected.

77. Medical board recommendation, 21 Nov. 1916, in Wilde, officer file (CG).

78. *Los Catolicos del Imperio Britanico y la Guerra* (London *c.*1917). My own copy has the ink-stamp of the Pro Aliados Comision de Propaganda in Cordoba, Argentina.

79. Another photograph shows a feast-day procession at the Abbey.

80. Others among the hierarchy knew more: Archbishop Patrick Clune of Perth (uncle of another Bloody Sunday victim, Conor Clune), who had visited Allied troops in France during the war, later told the Gresham's manager that Wilde had been a British agent expelled from Spain: James Doyle, WS 771.

81. *The Times*, 18 Feb. 1919.

82. *Manchester Guardian* and *The Times*, 23 Nov. 1920.

83. Hopkinson, *Last Days*, pp. 76, 80.

84. *ABC* and *La Epoca* (Madrid), 23, 25 Nov. 1920.

85. Wilde, burial record (Glasnevin Trust, Cemetery Management Systems).

86. Bloody Sunday fatalities appeared in the *Monthly Army List* until Mar. 1921.

87. Order of Service, 21 Nov. 1922, Jeudwine Papers. The 11 names on the roll included Cadets Garniss and Morriss, the only policemen included in the service.

88. James Cahill, WS 503.

89. Edward Gerrard, WS 348.

90. Wilde, officer file (CG).

91. She was the last Bloody Sunday widow to die, in 1983, 18 years after the death of her second husband.

92. His initials are often given as P. F. in family and racing notices.

93. His form can be tracked through the *Irish Racing Calendar* (1912–20), the *Irish Field*, and turf notes in the Dublin press.

94. A vet from Waterford, later a senator. Parkinson's son William J., schooled at Castleknock, became a champion jockey.

95. Will of P. J. MacCormack, NAD.

96. *II*, 18 Aug. 1919; *Connaught Telegraph*, 2 Aug. 1919; *Castleknock College Chronicle* (June 1920).

97. The Turf Club, a social not a racing institution, was burnt down in Egypt's own Black Saturday in 1952.

98. *II*, *FJ*, *IT*, 10 June 1921; *Castleknock College Chronicle* (June 1920); *Irish Field*, 27 Nov. 1920.

99. *II*, 8 Jan.1920.

100. Kate MacCormack to R. J. Mulcahy, 23 Mar. 1922, Collins Papers, MAD, A/0535.

101. James Doyle, WS 771.

102. A Scot who moved to Ireland to avoid conscription, Burns also rode (far more successfully) for J. J. Parkinson. A lengthy career produced over 2000 wins, including the first Irish St Leger in 1916.

103. *Sunday Independent*, 21 Nov. 1920; *Irish Telegraph*, 22 Nov. 1920.

104. *Sport*, 27 Nov. 1920; *Tuam Herald*, 4 Dec. 1920; *Irish Field*, 27 Nov. 1920.

105. *Connaught Telegraph* and *Tuam Herald*, 4 Dec. 1920; *Ballina Herald*, 9 Dec. 1920.

106. *Westmeath Examiner*, 27 Nov. 1920.

107. Hopkinson, *Last Days*, p. 80 (23 Nov. 1920).

108. *II*, 26 Nov. 1920.

109. *Dublin Evening Herald*, 25 Nov. 1920.

110. James H. Murphy (ed.), *Nos Autem: Castleknock College and Its*

Contribution (Dublin 1996), p. 109; *Castleknock College Chronicle* (July 1923).

111. While Philip Kelleher, DI, RIC, was included in a list of deceased past pupils, MacCormack and DI Philip Brady were not: *Castleknock College Chronicle* (June 1921).

112. 'In sad and loving memory of my dear son Capt. Paddy F. Mac-Cormack – on whose soul, Sweet Jesus, Thy will be done – inserted by his sorrowing mother and only child Grace.' *IT*, 21 Nov. 1924.

113. Townshend, 'Bloody Sunday'.

114. Collins Papers, MAD, A/0535.

115. *Belfast Telegraph*, 25 Nov. 1920.

116. For a highly coloured defence of Bourne's decision to honour the 'Catholic Three', see Ernest Oldmeadow, *Francis Cardinal Bourne* (London 1944), vol. 2, pp. 180–1.

117. Information from the celebrant, now deceased.

118. The Café Cairo, at 59 Grafton St from the Boer War until the Civil War, extended to South King St, where its famous ballroom was located. Selling crystallized fruit and Egyptian cigarettes as well as coffee, it was popular with students and actors. Catering to a *paróiste forleathan*, its staff had a Mass offered for the repose of Kevin Barry's soul a week before Bloody Sunday.

119. Exactly a century before Ireland defeated England at Croke Park in 2007, Wilson had played centre three-quarter for England in the corresponding fixture. Ireland also won that match.

Appendix: DEATHS RESULTING FROM POLITICAL VIOLENCE ON 21 NOVEMBER 1920

Name	Location	Status	Killers	Died
	Dublin: Morning			
Ames, P. Ashmun	38 Ur Mount St	IO	IRA	
Angliss, Henry J.	22 Lr Mount St	IO	IRA	
Baggallay, Geoffrey T.	119 Lr Baggot St	CMO	IRA	
Bennett, George F.	38 Ur Mount St	IO	IRA	
Dowling, C. M. Cholmeley	28 Ur Pembroke St	IO	IRA	
Fitzgerald, John J.	28 Earlsfort Tce	RIC	IRA	
Garniss, Frank	16 Northumberland Rd	Auxiliary	IRA	
MacCormack, Patrick J.	Gresham hotel	Civilian	IRA	
MacLean, Donald L.	117 Morehampton Rd	IO	IRA	
Montgomery, Hugh F.	28 Ur Pembroke St	ADM/AR	IRA	10 Dec.
Morris, Cecil A.	16 Northumberland Rd	Auxiliary	IRA	
Newberry, William F.	92 Lr Baggot St	CMO	IRA	
Price, Leonard	28 Ur Pembroke St	IO	IRA	
Smith, T. Herbert	117 Morehampton Rd	Civilian	IRA	
Wilde, Leonard A.	Gresham hotel	Uncertain	IRA	
	Afternoon			
Boyle, Jane (Jennie)	Croke Pk	Civilian	CF	
Burke, James	Croke Pk	Civilian	CF	
Carroll, Daniel	Croke Pk	Civilian	CF	23 Nov.
Feery, Michael	Croke Pk	Civilian	CF	
Hogan, Michael	Croke Pk	Civilian*	CF	
Hogan, Thomas	Croke Pk	Civilian	CF	26 Nov.
Matthews, James	Croke Pk	Civilian	CF	
O'Dowd, Patrick	Croke Pk	Civilian	CF	
O'Leary, Jeremiah (Jerome)	Croke Pk	Child	CF	
Robinson, William	Croke Pk	Child	CF	22 Nov.

Ryan, Thomas	Croke Pk	Civilian*	CF	
Scott, John William (Billie)	Croke Pk	Child	CF	
Teehan, James	Croke Pk	Civilian	CF	22 Nov.
Traynor, Joseph	Croke Pk	Civilian*	CF	

Evening

Barnett, Wm. H. W.	Mountjoy Sq	Civilian	CF	
Clancy, Peter (Peadar)	Dublin Castle	IRA	CF	
Clune, Conor	Dublin Castle	Civilian	CF	
Cullinane, William	Lincoln Place	Civilian	CF	23 Nov.
McKee, Richard (Dick)	Dublin Castle	IRA	CF	
Powell, E. W.	Dublin	Army	?	
Spenle, Henry Emile	Dublin Castle	Auxiliary	Self	

Outside Dublin

Cowley, Austin Francis	Navan, Co. Meath	Civilian	CF	
Jays, Henry Clement	Leap, Co. Cork	RIC	IRA	
Kearney, John Joseph	Newry, Co. Down	RIC	IRA	22 Nov.
Lyons, Thomas	Knappagh, Co. Mayo	Civilian	CF	
Rea, Isaac James	Cappoquin, Co. Waterford	RIC	IRA	28 Dec.

NOTE TO APPENDIX

ADM/AR indicates secondment from the Admiralty to the army; CF represents members of unidentified branches of the Crown forces; CMO signifies military courts-martial officers; IO includes military personnel recruited for 'special service' in Ireland as well as those officially returned as 'intelligence officers'. Civilians listed on IRA rolls of honour are marked by an asterisk; dates of death for those subsequently dying of wounds (derived from CILI reports, coroners' registers, and death notices in the press) appear in the right-hand column; forenames in parentheses appeared in family death notices.

8. Counting Terror: Bloody Sunday and *The Dead of the Irish Revolution*

Eunan O'Halpin

I

This chapter concerns those killed on Bloody Sunday, in the context of a statistical survey of deaths attributable to political violence in revolutionary Ireland. The record of fatalities on 21 November 1920 was exceptional for three reasons: (1) the targeting and killing by the IRA of so many suspected intelligence operatives and two bystanders in a single ruthless and co-ordinated attack on Bloody Sunday morning; (2) the indiscriminate and sustained firing by Crown forces in Croke Park, which resulted in eleven civilian fatalities that day; (3) the subsequent death in custody in Dublin Castle of three men, including two senior officers in the Dublin IRA. By contrast, the death in various circumstances of six others (three members of Crown forces and three civilians) was unremarkable, just another day's dirty work associated with the Anglo–Irish conflict.[1]

The dramatic events of Bloody Sunday morning (analysed in the preceding chapter) had such an effect on British opinion that what happened that afternoon, evening and night became almost a footnote. A leading article in *The Times* denounced the murders 'of at least fourteen British officers and ex-officers', excoriating both 'the leaders of political Sinn Fein', who 'now see the harvest of their own wicked folly', and the government for tolerating 'an army already perilously indisciplined, and a police force avowedly beyond control'. The editorial offered no reflections on events at Croke Park, described elsewhere in the newspaper as 'a serious affair' in which Crown forces returned fire at IRA scouts, causing the crowd to stampede. There was no immediate coverage of other violent deaths that occurred on that day in Ireland. This was not a function simply of the scale of killings during the morning, but also of their horrific character and callousness. On Tuesday, when *The Times* finally provided a few details of the events in Croke Park, it took the official line.[2]

News of the overnight deaths of the IRA officers Dick McKee and Peadar Clancy, and of the hapless Conor Clune, only emerged after midday on the Monday. In its report next day, *The Times* reproduced Dublin Castle's highly problematic and implausibly intricate account of an intense struggle in a guard room, allegedly packed with weapons and a box of grenades as well as the prisoners and their guards, which had led to the deaths around midday of the 'Sinn Fein leaders'. Published in parallel with accounts of the funeral arrangements for the officers and ex-officers killed on Bloody Sunday morning, and of one Auxiliary Cadet who had killed himself in Dublin Castle during the afternoon, this report conveyed a grim message – 'an eye for an eye'.[3]

The British government's account of how and when McKee, Clancy and Clune had died was dismissed by republicans. It was generally believed that the three men, in custody since the Saturday night, had been tortured and then murdered during the late evening of Bloody Sunday. John Fitzpatrick, in whose home McKee and Clancy had been arrested and who had been arrested with them, gave a vivid account of his own experience. After being taken to the Castle with McKee and Clancy, he and other prisoners had been moved on to Beggar's Bush infantry barracks. As he said goodbye, 'McKee said to me "if you get through give my love to my mother, sisters, brothers & all the boys". He looked very pale & sad.' Clancy just 'smiled goodbye'.[4]

Republicans believed that Clancy, McKee and Clune were then interrogated and killed by a Captain [J. L.] Hardy. Fitzpatrick was later singled out in Beggar's Bush by 'a tall young fellow, good-looking, with a stiff leg', who said: 'I am after putting three bulletts [*sic*.] through your two f— Sinn Fein pals' hearts and I am coming back to do the same to you in a few minutes.' During subsequent interrogation, Fitzpatrick was shown the three bodies in an effort to make him identify them, though each corpse was already correctly labelled. McKee's 'face was battered up a lot. He had big marks all around his face. Some marks looked as if pieces of flesh was knocked out of them. He had bayonet wound in side & his fingers were all cut where he had grabbed Bayonette [*sic*.].' Clancy's 'face looked as if it had got a good beating. His forehead was marked over the eye. Also it stuck out well over his face & it looked as if it was burnt. His face was all yellow.' Medical examination of the three bodies revealed a number of broken bones and abrasions consistent with prolonged assaults, and bullet wounds to the head and body; yet this evidence did not deter the court of inquiry from quickly determining that the men had been lawfully killed.[5]

The eleven people who died on Bloody Sunday, after Crown forces opened fire on spectators at Croke Park, were unarmed and, so far as the RIC men who shot them were aware, all were civilians (they were not to know that the one footballer they killed, Michael Hogan of Tipperary, was an IRA officer). All eleven died of wounds rather than suffocation (as might have been expected with a stampede for cover). Three other civilians wounded at Croke Park were to die over the following days. An Auxiliary officer furnished a damning account, saying that 'I did not see any need for any firing at all and the indiscriminate firing absolutely spoilt any chance of getting hold of any people in possession of arms. The men of the Auxiliary Division did not fire.'[6] The fatalities included one woman, Jane Boyle, a butcher's assistant due to be married the next week, and at least two boys, 14-year-old Billy Scott and 10-year-old Jeremiah O'Leary. O'Leary's father, an ex-soldier employed as a military clerk, was in turn shot by unidentified gunmen in Mountjoy Square on 28 June 1921. He cried out: 'I'm shot. My God. I have done nothing to anybody.'[7] He survived. The eight adult men who died on Bloody Sunday as a result of the Croke Park shootings – five labourers, a barman, a launderer and a farmer – were unremarkable in themselves. One, Michael Feery, a 44-year-old unemployed labourer, was an ex-serviceman. None except Hogan had proven IRA connections, and the Crown did not attempt to portray them as republicans.

The conflicting testimony concerning Bloody Sunday exemplifies the problem that deaths can be categorized under a number of different headings, all problematic and dependent on the perspective of the classifier. What for the British authorities and military courts of inquiry were justifiable killings of prisoners attempting to escape lawful custody (McKee, Clancy and Clune in Dublin Castle), for republicans were obvious cases of murder committed by Crown forces in reprisal for the killings on Bloody Sunday morning. What for the authorities were unfortunate killings in self-defence at Croke Park, after Crown forces had allegedly come under fire from unidentified individuals in the crowd, were for republicans and others unprovoked, indiscrimate and unjustified killings of unarmed civilians carried out as acts of revenge.

Similar conflicts of interpretation apply to other fatalities that happened to occur on 21 November 1920. What for the IRA was the efficient killing of an oppressor, Constable Harry Jays, as he set out to intimidate the community in Leap, Co. Cork, was for the British government and its forces the cowardly assassination of a vulnerable policeman as he did his duty.[8] What for the army was the legitimate killing of the blacksmith Thomas Lyons in a field near Westport, Co. Mayo, when he failed to heed an order to halt (a military court of inquiry heard RIC evidence that he was on good terms with them, and had previously come to the aid of a wounded policeman), was for the local population the outcome of systematic brutality, which had so terrified the blacksmith that he ran rather than stopping to be searched. Such shootings of people for allegedly disobeying orders to halt became notorious in 1920–1, as were those of men supposedly trying to escape from lawful custody.[9] In Navan, Co. Meath, a sentry shot dead an elderly journalist, Austin Francis Cowley, who being deaf did not heed a challenge.[10] In Belfast, a soldier, Arthur Boundary, died from unspecified injuries received some time before.[11] In Dublin, not half a mile from Croke Park, a comfortably-off chandler, reputed Orangeman and Freemason named William Henry Barnett was shot around 11.40 p.m. on Mountjoy Square, as he went to check his premises. His silver watch was taken, and witnesses spoke of hearing a motor car and seeing a uniformed man with two others. This killing suggests the work of off-duty members of Crown forces rather than the IRA, although other cases show that it is dangerous to jump to conclusions.[12]

The various events of Bloody Sunday had left at least 35 people dead: 16 civilians, 16 associated with the Crown forces and 3 members of the IRA. How typical were Bloody Sunday's victims of the entire spectrum of violent fatalities during the revolutionary years?

II

This chapter draws extensively on data assembled for *The Dead of the Irish Revolution*, a project intended to identify all deaths arising from Irish political violence in the period from April 1916 to December 1921. The project gathered as much personal, occupational and other material as possible about each fatality, including personal background, how each person died, and by whose hand. No single set of official or private records, newspapers, recollections or other material provides a comprehensive, definitive list of fatalities. Notwithstanding the benefits of well-established administrative systems and unique service numbers for recruits, records of police and military casualties in Ireland are incomplete. So too are the lists compiled by related official bodies such as the Commonwealth (formerly Imperial) War Graves Commission.[13] On the separatist side, despite the impressive power of family and local memory and commemoration in Ireland, lists of fallen comrades are also inadequate. Some people were overlooked or perhaps deliberately omitted, others who met their death but never served in the IRA were claimed as members after the event. The identification and contextualization of civilian deaths present particular challenges, especially in the case of sectarian conflict in Belfast. A more prosaic but pervasive problem is confusion over the spelling of placenames and personal names, compounded by the frequent use of variant and sometimes questionable Irish versions.

Key primary sources included British military and administrative records in the National Archives, London (particularly those of the War Office, Home Office and Colonial Office). Records and other material held by various regimental museums were consulted, along with papers and oral history recordings in the Imperial War Museum. In Ireland, the project drew on collections in the UCD Archives (particularly those of Richard Mulcahy, Maurice Twomey, Ernie O'Malley, C. S. Andrews and Sighle Humphries);

in the National Library of Ireland (including those of Diarmuid
Lynch, Piaras Béaslaí, Liam Deasy, Florence O'Donoghue and Seán
O'Mahony); and in the Military Archives of Ireland (the so-called
Collins Papers and witness statements collected by the Bureau of
Military History). Use was also made of various collections held
by the Monaghan County Library, the Tomás Ó Fiaich Library in
Armagh, the Cork Archives Institute, the Leitrim County Library
and private owners. Unidentified deaths were pursued using the lists
of 'unknowns' in the indices to the General Registers of Deaths.
The census of 1911, which came online when the project was well
advanced, was used selectively to check details such as place of
birth and religion. The project has also made extensive use of the
national and local press in Ireland and in Britain, aided to some
extent by digitalization.

Completion of the project was helped by the recent release
of many British and Irish official records previously suppressed.
The most significant of these are the Bureau of Military History
witness statements, painstakingly collected in the 1940s and 1950s
but withheld from public gaze until 2003. In preparation for the
forthcoming decade of centennial commemorations marking events
between 1913 and 1923, the Bureau's records will shortly be com-
plemented by the phased release of an even vaster collection, the
records generated by various Military Service Pensions Acts and
held by the Department of Defence. These provide astonishingly
detailed information about individuals who took part, or claimed
to have participated, in the Irish revolution, and about the membership and activities of republican organizations down to company
level. There are also plans eventually to release the so-called 'medals
files', dealing with the award of '1916' and 'Black and Tan' medals.
These will provide future historians with enormous amounts of
fresh material on the activities of republicans and of their families
and descendants.[14]

The multiplication of records relating to republican activities
and fatalities presents problems of balance for researchers studying
terror in Ireland. There is no systematic repository of British or
of Ulster loyalist testimony comparable to the Bureau of Military
History statements or the Military Service Pension records, although

Crown forces and loyalists were together responsible for almost as
many deaths in Ireland as the IRA. While many personal accounts
by men whose service included Irish postings survive in scattered
locations such as military museums, these often give little insight
into their experiences in Ireland. In contrast to their IRA opponents,
former Black and Tans, Auxiliaries, military personnel and armed
loyalists seldom recorded their responses to events in revolutionary
Ireland except in official reports. Those involved in problematic killings only occasionally expressed remorse or reflected in public on
what they had done and why. Unlike the republican veterans who
lived and relived their brief experiences of violence for the rest of
their lives, most who had served the Crown were evidently content
to put Ireland behind them rather than dwelling upon a presumably
distasteful phase of their careers.

On the British side, most of the relevant documentation, apart
from police and military intelligence reports, is of administrative or
quasi-judicial origin. The records of military courts of inquiry constitute the most significant single source.[15] These courts of inquiry
were cursory and unsatisfactory, usually conducted within a day
or two of the death under investigation, often held in camera, and
without legal representation for relatives of the dead or any opportunity for independent cross-examination of witnesses. The military
officers who constituted the courts usually had no specialist training
or experience. When conflicts of evidence arose between members
of the Crown forces and other witnesses, or where the official evidence was problematic or implausible (as in many cases where civilians or republicans were killed while allegedly attempting to escape
from custody or avoid arrest), the courts of inquiry almost always
accepted the military or police version.

The rough and ready nature of these inquiries is reflected in the
recollections of Douglas Wimberley, adjutant of the 2nd Battalion,
Queen's Own Cameron Highlanders, stationed in Cork in 1920–1:

> we in the orderly room ... had to take on the local registration of
> births, deaths and marriages, and even hold all the inquests, of
> which, at such a time, there were certainly plenty. I well remember
> one occasion when I, and my Assistant Adjutant ... held an inquest
> in the orderly room, on the body of a new born infant, who had

been found suffocated with a rag in its throat, close to our camp. He and I had many other rather macabre inquests as well as this one, when we had the poor baby's body on the orderly room table.

After one cursory inquiry, he found that a man shot by unknown assailants had died as a result of a feud with 'some opposing Irish faction and I returned a verdict of death by an unknown hand. Many years later it was revealed to me that the man had in fact been shot, or even murdered, by a certain Cameron, who had been out on his own secretly at night.'[16]

The findings of military courts of inquiry were only occasionally rejected or challenged by higher authorities. In a few cases involving the killing of women by the security forces, senior officers expressed concern about findings that appeared to exonerate soldiers or police. An example is the notorious murder in December 1920 of Kate Maher, a middle-aged woman 'of dissolute habits' living in Dundrum, Co. Tipperary, who was found comatose and bleeding to death from internal wounds to her vagina. A few feet away lay Private Thomas Bennett, insensible from drink. He and other soldiers of the Lincolnshire Regiment had earlier been seen with her in a pub. The battalion OC blamed the incident on the absence through illness of a key NCO. Bennett was eventually court-martialled for murder but acquitted, partly on the ground that another suspect had been precipitately transferred to Russia before he could be charged.[17] Another court finding leading to expressions of unease by higher authorities involved the apparent suicide in February 1921 of the Scottish chorus girl Sarah Fitzpatrick ('Connie Curzon'). She had supposedly taken a gun from her ex-boyfriend, District Inspector Albert 'Tiny' Purchase, and shot herself in the breast as they walked to her lodgings from a pub after curfew in Dublin.[18] A rare case involving a male victim was that of Richard Leonard, taken from his home and shot on the night of 30 December 1920 by three drunken officers. Efforts to prosecute Captain W. Davis of the Northumberland Fusiliers for murder ran into legal difficulties and were dropped.[19] The courts of inquiry arising from violence on Bloody Sunday all found in accordance with the evidence presented by Crown witnesses.

III

In identifying those included in *The Dead of the Irish Revolution*, care has been taken to achieve consistency in procedure and accuracy in detail. In almost every case, at least two independent sources were used to confirm that a death occurred, and to determine that it was in some way connected with the political conflict. This rule of thumb may have occasioned the exclusion of some deaths that were in fact attributable to political circumstances. For example, the elderly Mary Jane Garland died of a heart attack on her Co. Monaghan farm in June 1921. Her family believed that what caused her death was the sight of an IRA party moving through the fields nearby – in Monaghan, Protestant farms were subject to sporadic raiding by the IRA, sometimes with fatal results. Her death certificate simply records that she had suffered from chronic heart disease. No reference to the circumstances of her death has been found elsewhere in official records such as police reports, or in newspapers. Consequently, Mary Jane Garland is missing from our list of revolutionary fatalities.[20]

Certain fatalities included in *The Dead of the Irish Revolution* were probably attributable to personal or local disputes more than to political considerations. Agrarian motives were clearly behind the shooting in Galway of a prominent landowner, Francis Shawe-Taylor, in March 1920. Another example is the shooting of Bridget Walpole, a farmer's widow, near Tralee in 1921. Although her body carried a card naming her as a spy, the local IRA disclaimed responsibility and attempted to investigate. It was generally believed she was killed because, being childless, it was feared she would give the farm to a relative from outside the area.[21]

The enumeration includes deaths arising from road accidents involving police and military vehicles; deaths accidentally inflicted on their fellows by members of the police, military, IRA, Special Constabulary and other organizations; self-inflicted deaths and suicides; and deaths arising from other kinds of misadventure (such as those of Neil and Kathleen McConvey and Minnie Kelly, who died in their sleep in Belfast on 21 November 1921 after a stray bullet pierced a gas pipe in their home).[22] British military fatalities arising in Ireland in 1917 and 1918 from causes such as training mishaps,

road and rail accidents, drownings, accidental shootings and suicides have been excluded, on the principle that they were linked primarily to the First World War rather than to Irish political violence.
The total does not include people who died after 31 December
1921, even if the cause was wounds, illness or injury contracted
on or before that date. The 482 fatalities in 1916 attributable to
the Rising and its aftermath require separate treatment because of
their concentrated character, the great majority having occurred in
a single week in Dublin City. They are not discussed in this chapter.

   The roll of fatalities includes a few who were unidentified at
the time and since. Among genuine 'unknowns' recorded in the
General Registers of Deaths was a man in his forties, believed to
be 'of the farming class', found shot dead on 3 July 1921 outside
Tyrrellspass, Co. Westmeath, a rosary clasped in his right hand and
two rifle casings lying nearby.[23] Other 'unknown' fatalities in those
registers turned out to be IRA men killed in action whose families
did not identify them for fear of reprisals, and who later recovered the bodies and reburied them appropriately. A handful of other
'unknowns' have also been included, even though no official record
of their disappearance or death has been traced. This applies to
cases where credible IRA accounts report the killing of unnamed
individuals, usually strangers to a district, shot as suspected spies
whose bodies were then disposed of.

   The importance of 'unknowns' is confirmed by Gerard Murphy
in a recent study of 'political killings' in Cork.[24] In addition to well
documented kidnaps or disappearances of soldiers, policemen and
civilians who are known to have been subsequently killed, Murphy
maintains that the Cork IRA captured and killed others whose fate
and identity was never publicly or officially acknowledged. These
included soldiers classed by the army as deserters and therefore
excluded from official returns of fatalities and of men missing in
action. Desertion was sufficiently widespread by June 1921 for the
IRA's GHQ to issue a directive to units on how to deal with them,
as 'some have recently turned out to be spies'. Although aspects of
Murphy's work have been strongly criticized as merely speculative,
evidence shortly to reach the public domain appears to support the
broad thrust of his argument even where he may be inaccurate in

particulars. Murphy states that in the area covered by E Company (Knockraha), 4th Battalion, 1st Cork Brigade, the OC (Martin Corry) claimed that thirty-five spies were killed and buried, of whom only three have ever been identified. The Military Service Pension records include a handwritten statement on Dáil letterhead (probably submitted by Corry), that 'some 27 ennemy [*sic*.] spies & Intelligence officers were captured by the Co[mpan]y and put to death'. Detailed returns in the Military Service Pension records submitted by other Cork IRA units also speak of the killing and disposal through secret burial of unidentified soldiers and civilians whom the IRA believed to be spies.[25]

The project used the historic county (as distinct from administrative counties such as Tipperary South Riding or Belfast County Borough) as the geographic unit by which fatalities are counted. This has several limitations. Since the population of counties varied widely, comparison of fatalities between counties such as Leitrim (15) and Limerick (121) is misleading without reference to population size. Furthermore, aggregating fatalities within counties such as Cork or Antrim obscures the distinction between urban and rural killings. In Cork, fatalities were not confined to the city but spread across the county, particularly in the east and south-west. In Antrim, almost all of the 224 reported fatalities occurred within the city of Belfast or its environs. People wounded elsewhere were often sent for treatment to hospitals outside their own counties, producing 'bonus' fatalities. For example, Joseph O'Neill, a 23-year-old labourer belonging to a nationalist fife band, shot by an off-duty special constable while marching in Coalisland, Co. Tyrone, on 16 August 1921, died in the Royal Victoria Hospital in Belfast and is therefore listed under Antrim. Likewise, Constable Albert Moore, RIC, died in Dr Steevens's hospital in Dublin on 19 June 1921 from wounds accidentally inflicted in Kilnaleck RIC barracks, Co. Cavan, so becoming a Dublin fatality.[26] Moreover, none of the groups of combatants responsible for fatalities adopted the historic county as the basis for its organization or operations. Despite the prevalence of localism in Irish political culture, this applied to republican bodies as well as the Crown forces.

IV

Between January 1917 and December 1921, 2141 fatalities have
been recorded. That number may be broken down by the historic
county (or country outside Ireland) where each death occurred:

FATALITIES BY COUNTY OR COUNTRY OF DEATH, 1917–1921

County	No.	County	No.
Cork	495	Wexford	23
Dublin	309	King's Co. (Offaly)	21
Antrim	224	Donegal	20
Tipperary	152	Kilkenny	19
Kerry	136	Westmeath	18
Limerick	121	Sligo	18
Clare	95	Meath	17
Galway	58	Tyrone	16
Roscommon	58	Leitrim	15
Mayo	43	Carlow	13
Londonderry	41	Kildare	12
Waterford	35	Great Britain	11
Armagh	28	Queen's Co. (Laois)	10
Down	28	Cavan	9
Longford	26	Fermanagh	9
Louth	26	Wicklow	7
Monaghan	25	India	3

The number of fatalities in each county is, of course, a very
crude index of the intensity of disruption experienced by people and
communities during the Irish revolution. This may explain why the
conflict and its aftermath seems to have left as distinct a memory,
and as deep a political imprint, in 'quiet' counties such as Cavan
or Queen's as in Cork, by far the most violent county in terms of
deaths. In Cavan, only nine people died including four members
of the IRA, two policemen, two civilians and one soldier (Private
Frank Catchpole of the Norfolk Regiment, shot by a comrade in
suspicious circumstances in September 1920).[27] In Queen's, one of
ten counties in which the British military suffered no fatalities and

the only one without police fatalities, just ten deaths were reported.

Assigning responsibility for the 2141 fatalities reported is not a matter of simply splitting the total between rebels and government forces. The IRA were definitely responsible for 46% of these fatalities, and Crown forces for 42%. A further 6% were the work of undenominated snipers or rioters, almost all in sectarian clashes in Belfast. 2% occurred in cross-fire between Crown forces and separatists, 1% were killed by loyalists, 1% by civilians, and the killers of the remaining 2% are unknown.[28]

Within the aggregate of 2141 deaths, 898 (48%) were civilian and 1243 (52%) combatant. The civilian proportion rose from 39% in 1920 to 45% in 1921. This confirms Peter Hart's finding that the proportion of civilian fatalities grew in 1921, which was also the most violent year accounting for 61% of all deaths between 1917 and 1921. However, Hart's estimate that 64% of deaths in 1921 were civilian is clearly excessive.[29] The discrepancy cannot be explained simply by methodological differences, such as our inclusion of deaths in motor traffic accidents involving police and military vehicles, which some might find problematic. Rather, it arises mainly from the restricted range of sources available when Hart conducted his research.

Of the 1243 combatant fatalities, 467 (38%) were IRA, 514 (41%) police and 262 (21%) British military. Within these categories, 9% of IRA fatalities were inflicted by the victim or his comrades, as were 14% of police fatalities and no less than 26% of British military fatalities. Accidental shootings were mainly responsible, along with premature explosions in the case of the IRA and motor vehicle accidents in the case of the police. It seems remarkable that a professional army should lose so many men in this manner, particularly by comparison with the hastily expanded police and the part-time, under-trained IRA. This may partly reflect the inexperience of many young soldiers in the new post-war army, and perhaps readier access to lethal weapons and armaments.

Determining responsibility for the 898 civilian fatalities is quite challenging, particularly in Antrim. For the 194 civilians killed there during riots and sectarian clashes, it is often impossible to determine who fired a particular shot, and we can be fairly sure of responsibility in only 91 cases. Across the country, many civilians died at the hands of mixed groups of soldiers and police. Consequently, those forces have been banded together in assigning responsibility. The IRA may confidently be held responsible for 281 (31%) of civilian fatalities, compared with 381 (42%) attributable to Crown forces. A miscellany of rather vague categories (loyalists, snipers, civilians, either IRA or Crown forces) accounts for the remaining 236 (27%).

Only 92 (10%) of all civilian fatalities were female. The majority of these were untargeted killings in riots, or traffic accidents involving Crown forces. The IRA abducted and shot at least three women as spies in 1921 (Bridget Noble and Mary Lindsay in Cork, and Kate Carroll in Monaghan). Two of the victims had a reputation for social deviance: Kate Carroll kept an illicit still and Bridget Noble, although married, was held to be too friendly with a number of RIC men on the Beara peninsula. These killings caused acute embarrassment locally and at GHQ.[30]

The project elucidates another vexed question, the experience of ex-servicemen during the War of Independence. Between 1919 and 1921, 420 ex-servicemen were killed, constituting 19.6% of all deaths. Of these, 227 (54%) were serving policemen, so their fates cannot be ascribed to their previous military service. Of the remaining 193 cases, 16 (4%) died as IRA men, leaving 177 (42%) who were civilians. Of these, the IRA clearly killed 99 (56%) and Crown forces 46 (26%). In the remaining 32 cases, including 13 in Antrim, it is impossible to determine responsibility.

What is more telling is the distribution of responsibility for civilian ex-servicemen's deaths across the country. In Antrim, 26 civilian ex-servicemen were killed, mainly during riots or sniping in Belfast. In all 13 cases where responsibility can reliably be assigned, Crown forces were to blame. In Dublin, the IRA killed 14 of the 25 civilian ex-servicemen who died. Even there, it is dangerous to assume that all were singled out on account of their backgrounds: for example Frank Davis, caretaker in the Custom House, was shot because he supposedly went towards a telephone, not because he was a Boer War veteran. In Cork, the most violent county, 49 civilian ex-servicemen were killed. Of these, 32 were definitely victims of the IRA, while Crown forces killed 15, including one shot when caught in the act of raping a young girl (meaning that Cork accounted for almost a third of all civilian ex-servicemen killed by the IRA and likewise by Crown forces). Though the evidence that ex-servicemen were systematically targeted by the IRA is strongest in Cork, more than half of all civilian casualties in two relatively 'quiet' counties were ex-servicemen, all killed by the IRA. In King's (Offaly), the figure was 6 (60%), and in Meath 5 (50%).

The 35 fatalities occurring on Bloody Sunday reflect the diversity of circumstances, often contested, associated with revolutionary killings in general. As noted above, members of the IRA (3), Crown forces (16) and civilians (16) were all represented, the civilian proportion approximating that for all fatalities (48%). All died after being shot, the predominant means by which death was inflicted throughout the War of Independence. All fatalities were investigated in an expeditious but cursory manner through military courts of inquiry. What sets Bloody Sunday apart is the three spectacular events for which it became notorious: the co-ordinated assassinations in the morning, the indiscriminate shooting of civilian spectators in the afternoon, and the killings in custody of three prisoners during the night. None of these three episodes, however, was truly representative of the conduct of either the IRA or its enemies during the Irish War of Independence. To that extent, the events of Bloody Sunday were *sui generis*.

NOTES

1. Funding for this project from the Irish Research Council for the Humanities and Social Sciences is gratefully acknowledged, as is the work of IRCHSS postdoctoral fellow, Dr Daithí Ó Corráin, from 2003 to 2007. I must also particularly thank Dr John Gibney, Dr Eve Morrison, Dr Ciaran Wallace and Robert Towers for invaluable help and advice. The overall findings of the study will be published by Yale University Press as *The Dead of the Irish Revolution*.

2. *The Times*, 22, 23 Nov. 1920.

3. *The Times*, 27 Nov. 1920. On Spenle, see NAL, WO 35/159B; Anne Dolan, 'Killing and Bloody Sunday, November 1920', *Historical Journal*, 49 (2006), 789–810 (792); *IT* and *The Times*, 26 Nov. 1920; David Neligan, *The Spy in the Castle* (London 1968), p. 123.

4. MS account by John Fitzpatrick, 25 Jan. 1922 (private collection).

5. Oscar Traynor, MAD, BMH, WS 340; David Neligan, WS 380; Patrick McCrae, WS 413; Joseph Leonard, WS 547; Bernard C. Byrne, WS 631; Frank Henderson, WS 821; Jack Stafford, WS 818; Joseph McDonough, WS 1119; Thomas Francis Meagher, WS 1156; Harry Colley, WS 1687; *FJ*, 24, 27 Nov. 1920; *II*, 24, 26 Nov. 1920; *Saturday Record*, 27 Nov. 1920; Charles Dalton, *With the Dublin Brigade, 1917–1921* (London 1929), pp. 57–8; Neligan, *Spy*, p. 124.

6. Statement of Maj. E. Mills, 22 Nov. 1920, NAL, WO 35/88B.

7. *II*, 29 June 1921.

8. Summary of police reports, Nov. 1920, NAL, CO 904/143; HO 184/36; WO 35/152; Stephen Holland, WS 649.

9. Summary of police reports, Nov. 1920, CO 904/143; WO 35/153A; *Kerry News* and *Connaught Telegraph*, 27 Nov. 1920.

10. WO 35/148; *Meath Chronicle*, 27 Nov. 1920. Cowley was one of 7 deaf men and a woman, Kate Bray of Belfast, whose deaths were attributed to their inability to hear commands to halt.

11. Alan F. Parkinson, *Belfast's Unholy War: The Troubles of the 1920s* (Dublin 2004), p. 334. Boundary is not listed in the Commonwealth War Graves Commission's 'Debt of Honour' register (see below, n. 13).

12. WO 35/146A; *FJ*, 22 Nov. 1920; *II*, 23, 26 Nov. 1920.

13. The Commonwealth War Graves Commission 'Debt of Honour' register (accessible at www.cwgc.org) is not comprehensive as regards military fatalities, mainly because the Commission catered for deaths attributed to the two world wars. It also contains anomalies: the Connaught Rangers mutineers James Joseph Daly and Patrick Sears are listed without reference to the circumstances of their deaths at army hands in 1920. Daly, regarded as the leader of the mutiny, is also commemorated on a 1914–18 war memorial at Kirkee in India. Richard Abbott's pioneering *Police Casualties in Ireland, 1919–1922* (Dublin 2000) is invaluable. There are no comparably robust studies of military, civilian or IRA casualties.

14. Eunan O'Halpin, 'The Military Service Pensions Project and Irish history: a personal perspective' in Patrick Brennan and Catriona Crowe (eds), *A Guide to the Military Service Pensions Project* (Dublin, forthcoming).

15. CILI records, WO 35.

16. Wimberley memoir, p. 152, National Library of Scotland, Acc. 6119. The only unknown infant in Co. Cork recorded in the General Register of Deaths for 1921 was a girl (1st quarter, 5/49). The adult death may be that of John O'Connell, a civilian accosted and shot in Queenstown by an unknown gunman: *IT*, 29 May 1921.

17. WO 35/155B; *Anglo-Celt*, 1 Jan., 23 July 1921; *Nenagh Guardian*, 1 Jan., 26 July 1921.

18. WO 32/1498; *II*, 5 Feb. 1921.

19. Summary of police reports, Jan. 1921, CO 904/144; WO 35/155B; Morgan Portley, WS 1559, p. 25.

20. Fearghal McGarry, *Eoin O'Duffy: A Self-Made Hero* (Oxford 2005), pp. 54–5. I am grateful to Roy Garland for telling me of his kinswoman's death.

21. Patrick P. Fitzgerald, WS 1079; Michael O'Leary, WS 1167; *FJ*, *IT*, *II*, 8 Mar. 1921.

22. *Irish News*, 23 Nov. 1921, 14 Jan. 1922; *Northern Whig*, 26 Nov. 1921.

23. WO 35/161A; *FJ*, 5 July 1921. This death was registered under 'Unknown' on 15 July 1921.

24. Gerard Murphy, *The Year of Disappearances: Political Killings in Cork, 1921–1922* (Dublin 2010).

25. *Ibid.* pp. 2–9; IRA, GHQ , General Orders, no. 27 (22 June 1921), Thomas Brennan Papers (private collection); unsigned, undated list on Dáil Éireann letterhead of activities of E Co. (Knockraha), 4th Battalion, Cork no. 1 Brigade, quoted in O'Halpin, 'Military Service Pensions Project'.

26. CI, MCR (Tyrone), Aug. 1921, CO 904/116; *II*, 16, 18 Aug. 1921; HO 184/40; WO 35/155B; *II*, 21 June 1921; *Anglo-Celt*, 25 June 1921.

27. Summary of police reports, Sept. 1920, CO 904/142; WO 35/120; Commonwealth War Graves Commission, 'Debt of Honour' register; *Anglo-Celt*, 18 Sept. 1920.

28. I use the umbrella term 'IRA' as short-hand for all militant separatists from 1917 onwards, including the handful of killings attributable to or fatalities incurred by the Irish Volunteers, Fianna Éireann and the Irish Citizen Army. Similarly, the term 'police' embraces the RIC, DMP, Auxiliary Division, Belfast Harbour Police and Ulster Special Constabulary.

29. Peter Hart, *The I.R.A. at War, 1916–1923* (Oxford 2003), p. 79.

30. Alexander Noble to President de Valera, 8 Sept. 1921, and OC, Cork no. 5 Brigade to Adjutant, 1st Southern Division, 22 Oct. 1921: MAD, A/0649; *IT*, 22 Aug. 1921 (where Bridget Noble appears on a list of missing persons presented to the House of Commons as 'Nogle'). On Kate Carroll, see Summary of police reports, Apr. 1921, CO 904/145, and WO 35/147B; Statements of Patrick McGrory and of Paddy Moran, Paddy McCluskey, Harry Lavery and Francie McKenna: Monaghan Co. Library, Marron Papers, 2G1, 3F; Notebook marked 'IRA', Thomas Brennan Papers; John McConnell, WS 574; James McKenna, WS 1028; *II*, 20 Apr. 1921; *Northern Standard*, 22 Apr., 24 June 1921; *Dundalk Democrat*, 23 Apr. 1921; McGarry, *O'Duffy*, pp. 65–6. GHQ ordered the release of Mrs Lindsay and her chauffeur on 9 July 1921, when they had been dead four months: Mrs Benson to de Valera, 6 July, Director of Publicity to Minister for Defence, 7 July, and OC, Cork no. 1 Brigade to GHQ, 11 July 1921: UCDA, Mulcahy Papers, P7/A/21.

9. Kilmichael Revisited: Tom Barry and the 'False Surrender'

Eve Morrison

I

In *The I.R.A. and Its Enemies*, Peter Hart suggested that Tom Barry, OC of the West Cork flying column responsible for the Kilmichael ambush on 28 November 1920, had systematically lied about the circumstances in which several Auxiliary police were killed during the attack.[1] Barry's account in *Guerilla Days in Ireland* was widely acknowledged (at least in public) as authoritative.[2] Sixteen died during the ambush itself. One Auxiliary, C. J. Guthrie, escaped but was later caught and executed. Another, H. F. Forde, was seriously wounded but survived. According to Barry, he and the other men in the command post, supported by a fusillade from no. 1 Section, killed the Auxiliaries in the first lorry in a matter of minutes, but a number from the second lorry held out longer:[3]

> Now that we had finished with the first lot, we could see the second lorry stopped thirty yards at our side of No. 2 Section. The Auxiliaries were lying in small groups on the road firing back at No. 2 Section, at about twenty-five yards' range. Some men of No. 2 were engaging them. Waiting only to reload revolvers and pick up an Auxiliary's rifle and some clips of ammunition, the three riflemen from the Command Post, Murphy, Nyhan and O'Herlihy, were called on to attack the second party from the rear. In single file, we ran crouched up the side of the road. We had gone about fifty yards when we heard the Auxiliaries shout 'We surrender.' We kept running along the grass edge of the road as they repeated the surrender cry, and actually saw some Auxiliaries throw away their rifles. Firing stopped, but we continued, still unobserved, to jog towards them. Then we saw three of our comrades on No. 2 Section

stand up, one crouched and two upright. Suddenly the Auxiliaries were firing again with revolvers. One of our three men spun around before he fell, and Pat Deasy staggered before he, too, went down.

When this occurred, we had reached a point about twenty-five yards behind the enemy party and we dropped down as I gave the order, 'Rapid fire and do not stop until I tell you.' The four rifles opened a rapid fire and several of the enemy were hit before they realised they were being attacked from the rear. Two got to their feet and commenced to run back past No. 2 Section, but both were knocked down. Some of the survivors of our No. 2 Section had again joined in and the enemy, sandwiched between the two fires, were again shouting, 'We surrender.'

Having seen more than enough of their surrender tactics, I shouted the order, 'Keep firing on them. Keep firing, No. 2 Section. Everybody keep firing on them until the Cease Fire.' The small I.R.A. group on the road was now standing up, firing as they advanced to within ten yards of the Auxiliaries. Then the 'Cease Fire' was given and there was an uncanny silence as the sound of the last shot died away.

I ran the short distance to where I had seen our men fall and scrambled up the rocky height. Michael McCarthy, Dunmanway, and Jim O'Sullivan, Knockawaddra, Rossmore, lay dead and, a few yards away, Pat Deasy was dying.

The 'false surrender' story recounted in Barry's memoir had been circulating since 1921. Even the former commander of the Auxiliary Division in Ireland, Brigadier-General Frank P. Crozier, had accepted it.[4] Yet Hart claimed that it was a fiction concocted by Barry to save his reputation, and that a number of the Auxiliaries had been killed after surrendering legitimately. What made his conclusions so damning was that they relied primarily not on British accusations or 'black' propaganda but on oral accounts from other Kilmichael veterans. It was an Irish separatist counter-narrative every bit as credible as Barry's own.

Hart's arguments prompted extensive conspiracy-laden controversy and disputation that has continued even since his death in July 2010.[5] He did not name his Kilmichael interviewees, and Barry's partisans implied that he had fabricated evidence. They also maintained that he had relied on a forged record reproduced in internal British army documents, purporting to be Barry's after-action report of the ambush. This article revisits the Kilmichael controversy, reassessing Hart's sources and arguments in the light of newly available sources.

II

Accounts from Kilmichael participants were collected by individuals and institutions at different times with various purposes. Some interviewees featured in several collections, and some veterans also wrote articles for newspapers or books. In the 1940s and 1950s, the Bureau of Military History compiled 1773 testimonies from separatist veterans of Ireland's revolutionary decade, including six accounts of Kilmichael.[6] Ernie O'Malley interviewed another Kilmichael veteran, Stephen O'Neill.[7] Fr John Chisholm spoke to several veterans about the ambush in 1969, while conducting research for what would become Liam Deasy's history of the West Cork Brigade, *Towards Ireland Free*. Deasy's papers contain an earlier draft of Paddy O'Brien's account of the ambush, considerably longer and less flowery than that in Deasy's book.[8] Meda Ryan cited interviews with eight Kilmichael veterans in her biography of Tom Barry.[9] In addition, a long-forgotten account, apparently by H. F. Forde, was published by the *Irish Independent* in January 1921.[10]

While Hart never identified his interviewees, an unfinished and unpublished riposte to his critics, entitled 'The truth about Kilmichael' (2004), suggests he was considering it.[11] By then, the Bureau's witness statements were available and he had heard or read ten separate unpublished accounts (five witness statements and five other interviews) from seven Kilmichael veterans. Apart from his own interviews, two were by Chisholm and one had been conducted by a 'son of one of the veterans'. All seven veterans, apart from one scout, were named in his draft riposte: Paddy O'Brien, Jim 'Spud' Murphy, Jack Hennessy, Ned Young, Michael O'Driscoll and Jack O'Sullivan.

As the interviewees are now long dead, and in response to the unwarranted attacks on Hart, Fr Chisholm has kindly made his tapes available to me. Chisholm recorded four Kilmichael veterans: O'Sullivan, Young, O'Brien and Jack Aherne. Of these, only O'Sullivan and Young discussed Kilmichael on tape, but Chisholm queried Young about what O'Brien had told him and also referred to a discussion with Barry, whom he met once in 1969.[12] In his book, Hart quoted excerpts from the Chisholm interviews with Young and O'Sullivan. In one case his transcription is not word-perfect, but the meaning is not compromised. Another quotation from the interview with O'Sullivan – stating that when O'Sullivan came across a wounded Auxiliary in the road he was ordered by Barry to 'finish him' – is wrongly attributed to an unidentified scout whom Hart interviewed on 19 November 1989. Two further quotations remain unattributable.[13]

None of the Bureau testimonies or interviews by Chisholm and Hart confirm Barry's version of events. Ever more evidence is becoming available to suggest that Barry's memoir was never as widely accepted as has been suggested, even in West Cork. When asked how Barry succeeded in persuading so many veterans to go along with the false surrender story, Liam Deasy's nephew and namesake replied simply: 'He didn't succeed.'[14]

Deasy's papers and Bureau records indicate that the reaction to *Guerilla Days in Ireland* among Cork veterans was mixed. When the book appeared, Barry claimed that no-one, apart from his wife and his solicitor, had seen it before submission to the publisher. He failed to mention that it had been substantially revised in 1947 with the help of Florrie O'Donoghue, who privately recorded his shock at the inaccuracies that he found in the initial draft.[15] Barry was clearly uncomfortable at the idea of fellow veterans providing accounts over which he would have no control, and displayed a particular animus against the Bureau because it took confidential testimony. In July 1948, he accused Michael McDunphy, the Bureau director, of providing a platform for malicious IRA veterans who had 'developed a mental kink about other men and matters which have no foundation in fact'.[16] Barry was doubtless aware of the stirrings of dissatisfaction in West Cork, over a host of issues, prompted by serialization of his memoir in *The Irish Press* in May and June 1948.[17] In 1949, Sean Collins (brother of Michael) informed McDunphy that he and several other veterans had met and decided to defer giving witness statements pending publication of Barry's book, as it was 'their intention to examine it critically and to record their comments on it, and to present a copy to the Bureau'.[18]

When interviewing veterans about Kilmichael, the Bureau concentrated on those who could give accurate details about the Volunteer fatalities. They interviewed five well-known column members
and two previously unknown witnesses.[19] Four of the seven accounts
were from men in no. 2 Section. Michael O'Driscoll was near Jim
O'Sullivan, Jack Hennessy was next to McCarthy, Timothy Keohane
fought beside Deasy, and Ned Young was across from them on the
south side of the road.[20] 'Spud Murphy' was in the command post
beside Barry, and Paddy O'Brien was south of the road facing them.
Keohane, lieutenant of the Timoleague Company, was omitted
from previously compiled lists of Kilmichael participants though he
fought there and also at Crossbarry.[21] The other previously unknown
Bureau witness was Cornelius Kelleher, Kilmichael Company, who
carried a dispatch for Barry from Sean Hegarty, OC Cork no. 1
Brigade. He did not reach the column before the ambush began but
saw the burning lorries in the distance, and later escorted a priest to
Buttimer's farmhouse to give Pat Deasy the last rites.[22]

Bureau records also show that its investigators actively sought
observations on controversial issues and published accounts. Bureau
investigators were instructed to familiarize themselves with all available information about every witness and the events in which they
were involved, including Military Service Pensions records, and to
question witnesses closely.[23] Ryan maintains that Barry's attacks on
the Bureau challenge the validity of the statements. However, as
questions were not included in the typed statements, there is no
evidence to substantiate her claims that Bureau investigators asked
'leading questions' and failed to query individuals on 'omissions
and inaccuracies'.[24] The suggestion that the veterans were unaware
of their deviation from Barry's account is also untenable. References
to the memoir, mostly positive, crop up regularly in the West Cork
statements. A few even supply page references to his descriptions
of ambushes.[25] Both Young and O'Brien made specific reference
to Barry's memoir, and the Bureau Chronology that investigators
carried with them when collecting statements was, if anything, too
reliant on Barry's account. It recounted the 'feign surrender' and
gave the same inaccurate figure for Auxiliary fatalities (eighteen)
as did *Guerilla Days in Ireland*.[26] Yet not a single witness state-

ment by a Kilmichael veteran mentioned the false surrender. This greatly weakens Ryan's case against Hart, though both she and Niall Meehan have argued otherwise, claiming that Jack Hennessy's statement supports Barry's account of the ambush.[27] As shown below, this is not the case.

Deasy and O'Brien were prepared to challenge Barry more openly. O'Brien's account of the ambush in *Towards Ireland Free*, published in 1973, sparked the first public confrontation over Kilmichael:[28]

> The opening fusillade killed the driver instantaneously, and the tender came to a halt. Barry appeared on the road and threw a hand grenade into the back of the tender, and all was over so far as that one was concerned. When Stephen O'Neill and I came out on to the road from the opposite side, we found 'Flyer' and 'Spud' were at the first tender; all the occupants had been killed.
>
> Meanwhile, the second tender was about one hundred and fifty yards behind, and had become stuck at the side of the road where the driver had tried unsuccessfully to turn it. The Auxiliaries had jumped out, threw themselves on the road and were firing from the cover of the tender. We then opened fire from their rear and when they realised that they were caught between two fires, they knew they were doomed.
>
> It was then realised that three of our men had been killed in Michael McCarthy's section; he himself had been shot through the head, Jim O'Sullivan through the jaw, and Pat Deasy had two bullet wounds through the body. Two others had been wounded, Jack Hennessy and John Lordan, but though they had lost a great deal of blood, their wounds were not serious. It had been a short but grim fight.

This account did not explicitly contradict Barry's, but he was outraged. A few months after Deasy's death in August 1974, he published a scathing attack on it, claiming that O'Brien had depicted him as a 'bloody-minded commander who exterminated the Auxiliaries without reason'.[29] There was no mention of a false surrender, which Barry had always explicitly blamed for the deaths of some of his men and consequent shooting of all the Auxiliaries. Barry also insisted that, contrary to O'Brien's account, only men in the command post and the Auxiliaries were on the road during the fighting, and that no other members of the column moved onto the road until all the Auxiliaries were dead.[30] Fourteen West Cork veterans, including O'Brien, later publicly disassociated themselves from Barry's pamphlet.[31]

It is clear that, over four decades, a sub-set of Kilmichael veterans consistently contradicted or ignored the false surrender story. O'Brien's account in *Towards Ireland Free* had been identified as controversial even before publication. Dan Nolan, publisher of *The Kerryman*, to whom the manuscript was sent initially, refused to publish it unless Barry was cited as a source.[32] Deasy's response leaves little doubt that the Kilmichael account was a deliberate challenge to Barry's version: 'The main details were corroborated by two living members of the Column who also fought there. Perhaps if Pat [the internal reviewer] enquired more closely into the full details of the fight he might come to appreciate that I have been more discreet than he would seem to credit me.'[33] The storm over Hart's claims was in fact the second time that trouble had erupted over rival accounts of the ambush. The controversy surrounding the anonymity of those interviewed by Chisholm and Hart, and the delay until 2003 in releasing the Bureau's collection, have obscured the fact that it is Barry's story that does not fit the generally agreed narrative. Only one other Kilmichael participant apart from Barry has ever confirmed the occurrence of a false surrender in print.[34] There are no grounds for treating Barry's account of Kilmichael (or any other incident recounted in his book) as holy writ. Even *The Wild Heather Glen*, which faithfully reproduced passages from *Guerilla Days in Ireland*, silently corrected some of Barry's claims.[35] Some Kilmichael veterans gave several interviews to various combinations of Ryan, Chisholm, Hart and the Bureau. Ryan states that her interviewees recounted the false surrender story, but the other available testimonies follow the general pattern of O'Brien's account rather than Barry's and provide much additional detail.

III

Collectively, this counter-narrative of Kilmichael is strikingly accurate, being confirmed by two important contemporary records. The report of the British army's court of inquiry includes details of Dr Jeremiah Kelleher's autopsy and the wounds inflicted on the bodies of the Auxiliaries.[36] A map, drawn up by a member of the Auxiliary patrol that located the ambush site, marks where each of the lorries and the dead or wounded Auxiliaries were found, and the positions taken by the column. This invaluable record, annotated and signed by Tom Barry himself, hangs on the wall of Barrett's pub in Coppeen, West Cork.[37] The interviews and testimonies by veterans other than Barry can be linked closely to the descriptions of wounds and positions in these sources.

COPY OF MAP SHOWING LOCATION OF CASUALTIES AND POSITIONS AT KILMICHAEL AMBUSH[38]

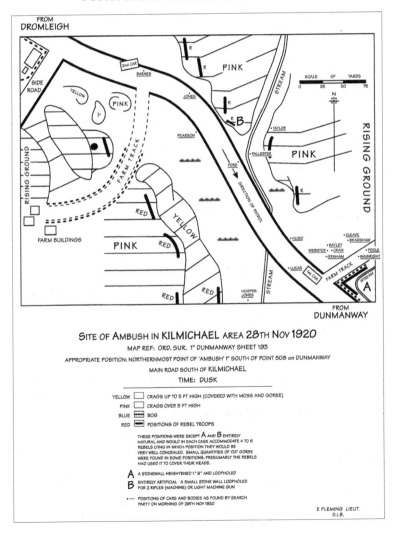

SITE OF AMBUSH IN KILMICHAEL AREA 28TH NOV 1920

MAP REF: ORD. SUR. 1" DUNMANWAY SHEET 193

APPROPRIATE POSITION: NORTHERNMOST POINT OF 'AMBUSH' 1" SOUTH OF POINT 503 on DUNMANWAY

MAIN ROAD SOUTH OF KILMICHAEL

TIME: DUSK

YELLOW ☐ CRAGS UP TO 5 FT HIGH (COVERED WITH MOSS AND GORSE)
PINK ☐ CRAGS OVER 5 FT HIGH
BLUE ▨ BOG
RED ▬ POSITIONS OF REBEL TROOPS

THESE POSITIONS WERE EXCEPT A AND B ENTIRELY
NATURAL AND WOULD IN EACH CASE ACCOMMODATE 4 TO 6
REBELS LYING IN WHICH POSITION THEY WOULD BE
VERY WELL CONCEALED. SMALL QUANTITIES OF CUT GORSE
WERE FOUND IN SOME POSITIONS. PRESUMABLY THE REBELS
HAD USED IT TO COVER THEIR HEADS.

A A STONEWALL HEIGHTENED 1" 6" AND LOOPHOLED
B ENTIRELY ARTIFICIAL A SMALL STONE WALL LOOPHOLED
FOR 2 RIFLES (MACHINE) OR LIGHT MACHINE GUN

•— POSITIONS OF CARS AND BODIES AS FOUND BY SEARCH
PARTY ON MORNING OF 29TH NOV 1920

E FLEMING LIEUT.
D.I.B.

As is always the case in individual testimony, some of the details vary.[39] Not every veteran saw the same incidents, and the circumstances in which the information was given influenced what was said. Thus Michael O'Driscoll was the only veteran to say that the Auxiliaries were singing as they approached. Hennessy failed to mention the sidecar of Volunteers who drove into the ambush site just before it began. All agreed that they left for the ambush site very early in the morning and waited in position until early evening, but they gave different times for when the column set out and arrived. The same basic positioning was reported in all testimonies, but the Bureau's witness statements gave more detail, terminology varied, and some denied that the men on the south side of the road constituted a third section.

A recent study of Kilmichael by W. H. Kautt benefits greatly from his knowledge of the US army's experience in assessing combat interviews (collected regularly since the Second World War). Kautt points out that such details always vary and that often, when several veterans give identical information, this indicates that something is being covered up.[40] Unlike most combat interviews, however, the Kilmichael testimonies were given long after the event. Such retrospective narratives ('retellings') tend to be more consciously structured than more immediate testimony.[41] Individuals involved in events that have become part of 'public memory' (through news reports, published memoirs, commemoration or political debate) tend to frame their personal memories in terms of well-known narratives, contrasting or confirming their own experience with the story that everyone knows.[42] This does not necessarily render them inaccurate or invalid, but makes it essential to relate each version to the allegiances of those involved and the specific controversies that arose during and after the revolutionary period.[43] The dominant public narrative of the Kilmichael ambush was Barry's. Deviations in other testimonies concerning the 'false surrender' cannot by attributed to faulty questioning by Bureau investigators or to lapses of memory.

As Barry's reaction to O'Brien's account in 1974 proved, veterans did not have to say explicitly that 'there was no false surrender' to undermine his claims. It was quite sufficient to deviate from his account of how and when the three Volunteers were fatally wounded. All testimonies from men in no. 2 Section confirm that the three IRA fatalities – McCarthy, O'Sullivan and Deasy – were shot in the initial exchanges of fire with the second lorry; while men by the first lorry (O'Brien and Murphy) became aware of the column's losses only after the ambush. O'Sullivan and McCarthy suffered head wounds. Deasy was fatally shot in the stomach. In their witness statements, both Murphy (right next to Barry during the ambush) and Young also stated explicitly that Barry and his men began firing on the Auxiliaries from the second lorry as soon as all those from the first were dead, leaving no interval for a false surrender.[44] Jack O'Sullivan categorically denied to Chisholm that there had been a false surrender.[45] Young, as shown below, was reluctant to discuss the question.

Both Hennessy's and Keohane's witness statements bear out the subsequent assertion in *Towards Ireland Free* that Hennessy and John Lordan received minor wounds during the ambush, and explain how it happened. Hennessy and Lordan were the Volunteers from no. 2 Section who stood up and were fired on by Auxiliaries whom Barry had called on to surrender, *after* O'Sullivan, McCarthy and Deasy had been shot.[46] As Keohane recalled:[47]

> The survivors from the second lorry continued to fight for about 20/30 minutes. At this stage Tom Barry blew a blast on his whistle as a signal that all men should get on to the road. At the same time he moved with his section along the road from the east to take the survivors in the rear. Tom Barry then called on the enemy to surrender and some of them put up their hands, but when our party were moving on to the road the Auxiliaries again opened fire. Two of our men (John Lordan and Jack Hennessy, I think) were wounded by this fire.

Hennessy's statement confirmed that he had stood up, though already wounded. He told the Bureau:[48]

> I had fired about ten rounds and had got five bullets through the hat when the sixth bullet wounded me in the scalp. Vice Comdt. McCarthy had got a bullet through the head and lay dead. I continued to load and fire but the blood dripping from my forehead fouled the breech of my rifle. I dropped my rifle and took Ml.

McCarthy's. Many of the Auxies lay on the road dead or dying. Our orders were to fix bayonets and charge on to the road when we heard three blasts of the O/C's whistle. I heard the three blasts and got up from my position, shouting 'hands up'. At the same time one of the Auxies about five yards from me drew his revolver. He had thrown down his rifle. I pulled on him and shot him dead. I got back to cover, where I remained for a few minutes firing at living and dead Auxies on the road.

At no stage in his witness statement did Hennessy say, as Ryan reports, that he 'almost' got up around the same time as McCarthy when 'the Auxies shouted'.[49]

What Hennessy's and Keohane's statements describe is the panic and confusion among the Auxiliaries when, as O'Brien recounted in *Towards Ireland Free*, they were 'caught between two fires' and 'knew they were doomed'.[50] Hennessy's depiction of what happened next is one of the most graphic accounts of a killing in the entire Bureau collection:[51]

The Column O/C sounded his whistle again. Nearly all the Auxies had been wiped out. When I reached the road a wounded Auxie moved his hand towards his revolver. I put my bayonet through him under the ribs. Another Auxie tried to pull on John Lordan, who was too near to use his bayonet and he struck the Auxie with the butt of his rifle. The butt broke on the Auxie's skull.

According to the report of the court of inquiry, the bodies of William Pallester and F. Taylor were found off the road alongside a stream near the second position. Pallester had a fractured skull 'through which the brains protruded'. Not far from Pallester was Taylor, who, amongst other injuries, had a 'perforating wound upper right chest'.[52] Young told Chisholm that he had seen Lordan bayonet an Auxiliary, and that after the ambush members of the column had informed him that this Auxiliary had surrendered falsely. When pressed by Chisholm, Young said that he had not heard any cries of surrender himself, and he could not recall which Volunteers said there had been one, but he was sure that the story had not come from Lordan.[53]

This testimony clarifies the remark by one of Hart's interviewees that there had been a 'sort of false surrender, but that no I.R.A. men died as a result'.[54] The false surrender story was afterwards associated with the deaths of these two Auxiliaries; yet Hennessy and Lordan, who had done the killing, never said this themselves. There is no indication in Hennessy's statement that he and Lordan believed they had been tricked: the Auxiliary might have thrown down his rifle because it was out of ammunition. The claim that they were on the road at all contradicts Barry's account. Hennessy and Lordan might have acted in response to being fired on, or because of the casualties inflicted on their section. It is significant that the two men reportedly stood up during a lull in the fighting when called on to the road by their OC, not because they heard the Auxiliaries surrendering. Keohane stated explicitly that Barry called them on to the road *before* demanding that the Auxiliaries surrender. Barry might indeed have blown his whistle because he saw some of the Auxiliaries throw down their rifles, but there is no corroborative evidence to support his account of a false surrender. These testimonies suggest that Barry himself, not trickery by Auxiliaries, was responsible for the exposure of Hennessy and Lordan to a still dangerous enemy. Far from supporting Barry's account, on close inspection the statements of Hennessy and Keohane undermine it.

Perhaps, as Kautt has suggested, historians have underestimated how confusing and bewildering and frightening war can be, even for seasoned veterans like Barry.[55] The sun was setting as the ambush began. Barry might not have been sure who had stood up, merely assuming them to have been the fatally wounded Volunteers from no. 2 Section. He was clearly sensitive to any suggestion that he had put his men in danger, as suggested by his declaration in 1974 that 'O'Brien has Lordan wounded when he was not even scratched'.[56]

IV

Collectively, the testimonies from the other Kilmichael participants also undermine the 'false surrender' story in a broader sense. O'Sullivan, Young, Hennessy and O'Brien all said that the men who were not in Barry's section were on the road during the fight, which Barry denied. There are several descriptions of surrendering Auxiliaries, some wounded and begging for their lives, being killed throughout the ambush, thus providing chilling confirmation that there had never been any intention to take prisoners. As Young told Chisholm: 'Barry told us before we went in to the fight that it was a fight to a finish (Chisholm: Yes) and if we were to fight it to a finish we were to fix bayonets and come out on the road and fight them.'[57]

O'Brien and Young both stated that men from south of the road took part in the attack on the first lorry. Young, who witnessed it, had a vivid memory of the chaos:

> Young: I saw the first lorry now below, at a, when the first lorry went down I saw the Tans running, you know, to the left and to the right.
>
> Chisholm: To the right, yes.
>
> Young: I saw the fellows that were on the left, Paddy O'Brien and a couple more of them, coming down towards them, and [whispers] shooting them at the bottom of the ... well, I suppose I shouldn't be saying things like that too, but coming down.[58]

Later in his interview there was an even more explicit exchange:

> Chisholm: Paddy O'Brien was telling me about one of the Auxiliaries in the first lorry when they were lifting him down and putting them on the bank he said 'I'm a Catholic, don't shoot me,' did he ever tell you that?
>
> Young: He did.
>
> Chisholm: Now, I take it that they did shoot him off too because –
>
> Young: Oh he was shot off.
>
> Chisholm: They shot him off? They shot the whole lot of them off?
>
> Young: They did.

O'Brien does not relate this story in any of his accounts of the ambush, but he does say he was on the road. There were eleven bodies found in the vicinity of the first lorry of whom five had been shot in the head or neck, two in the back and one in the chest at point blank range. According to an annotation by Barry on the map, most were 'in one heap'.[59]

Young and O'Sullivan each remembered disarming an Auxiliary who was subsequently shot out of hand. O'Sullivan told Ryan that a surrendered Auxiliary whom he was 'walking up the road' had been shot dead at his feet. Young, in an interview quoted by Hart, describing a similar incident in which the disarmed Auxiliary asked him: 'What am I going to do?' Young had advised him to 'go down the road to the others and they'll tell you.'[60] The body closest to the second lorry, probably that of the Auxiliary disarmed by Young, was W. T. Barnes. He was shot six times, once in the axilla (armpit), which is consistent with Young's description of him walking down the road with his hands in the air. Another Auxiliary, W. Hooper-Jones, was found on the south bank across from the first lorry. He was shot twice, once in the groin and once in the axilla, suggesting that he was also 'shot off' while running towards the Volunteers in O'Brien's position with his hands in the air.[61]

Jack O'Sullivan described to Chisholm other Auxiliaries being shot down after surrendering:

> Chisholm: And you saw the two men standing up with their hands above their heads, and throwing their rifles?
>
> O'Sullivan: They left the rifles where they were.
>
> Chisholm: Left them where they were, and they stood up?
>
> O'Sullivan: Stood up.
>
> Chisholm: And then one of them, they were shot at?
>
> O'Sullivan: Shot at, yeah.

H. F. Forde, shot and clubbed in the head, taken for dead but still alive, lay in the road between the two lorries.[62] He could easily have witnessed the deaths of several of the Auxiliaries from the second lorry. The Kilmichael testimonies confirm and are confirmed by his account published in January 1921 which, given its provenance, might otherwise be dismissed as atrocity propaganda. Forde's testimony suggests that the surrendering Auxiliaries described by O'Sullivan may not have been the same individuals as those killed by Lordan and Hennessy:

> I suddenly heard a whistle blown loudly, and a cry to cease fire. ... After knocking us about, they called on us all to stand up and hold our hands up. There was no response for a time, but after about two minutes two of the party were able to stagger to their feet, and were immediately shot down again at very close range by

the 'Shinners'. Then one of the Cadets quite near to me, who had been lying on his back, groaned heavily and turned over. One of the civilians, who had a rifle and bayonet, immediately walked up to him and plunged the bayonet into his back as near as I could see between the shoulder blades. [63]

The bodies of A. G. Jones and H. D. Pearson were also found near no. 2 Section's position. Jones was shot seven times, once in the armpit. Not far from Jones and at the edge of the road was Pearson, shot three times. Later, O'Sullivan shot another wounded Auxiliary in the head who was 'be-crying after' him. [64]

After the ambush, crown forces and officials gathered information about what had occurred from Forde, from locals, and from a report from Colonel Buxton Smith, the commander of the Auxiliaries stationed at Macroom who was evidently so traumatized that he killed himself a year a later. [65] Official claims that unsuspecting Auxiliaries had been lured into the ambush by men wearing British army uniforms, who later robbed and mutilated the bodies, were certainly exaggerated but not outright fabrications. Jack Hennessy was wearing a steel helmet. He, Lordan and Young were armed with bayonets. Dr Kelleher's autopsy confirmed that three of the Auxiliaries had wounds inflicted after death, one of them 'by an axe or some similar heavy weapon'. [66] Kilmichael participant Jack McCarthy afterwards wore a gold ring taken from a dead Auxiliary, and Forde remembered someone trying (unsuccessfully) to pull one from his finger. [67]

Hart maintained that Barry had changed his story, citing two earlier accounts in which the false surrender was not mentioned. In the case of an article written for *The Irish Press* in 1932, Ryan has conclusively established that Barry had in fact protested at the editor's omission of the relevant passage. [68] Less convincing is the contention by Ryan and Murphy that an after-action report on the ambush from 'oc Flying Column', [69] captured and reproduced in two internal British army publications in 1921–2, was a forgery. [70] This report is more in line with oral testimony than they suggest. It does not contradict 'all other accounts of the ambush' in stating that the column had left their positions when the Auxiliaries arrived. Young recalled that, just before the ambush, McCarthy and Barry discussed changing positions because the Auxiliaries were late, and they were no longer sure from which direction they would come. Likewise, the report's statement that the IRA lost one killed, and two who died of wounds, is hardly the 'most telling sentence in the report' in exposing its falsity. There is no consensus among the veterans about the timing of McCarthy's death. Hennessy stated that he died during the ambush; Young, who came across McCarthy when he moved from the road into no. 2 Section, told Chisholm that McCarthy 'wasn't dead, but he was finished anyway'.[71] O'Brien told the Bureau that O'Sullivan died instantly, McCarthy died shortly afterwards and Deasy survived for only a few hours.[72] This chronology is also consistent with local tradition. A monument erected in 2007 at Buttimer's farm, where the IRA's dead and wounded were brought after the ambush, confirms the account given by Young, O'Brien and other Kilmichael veterans such as Tim O'Connell.[73]

Meehan, Ryan, Murphy, Ruan O'Donnell and the Aubane Society are not the custodians of uncontested 'popular memory' or 'local history.'[74] They have taken sides in a long-standing disagreement between veterans of the West Cork flying column. Hart muddled a handful of citations. Such errors should be noted, but they do not undermine the authenticity of what he uncovered. It is sad that he died before he could fully vindicate himself and the men whose narratives he championed. It was Fr Chisholm's determination to get to the truth that provided Hart with much of his evidence. Chisholm and the Deasys never credited the false surrender story and they, like Hart, suffered considerable abuse over the years. It is high time to put an end to this.

Why were the other Kilmichael veterans so determined not to corroborate Barry's account? Some were unwilling to diminish their adversaries through accusations of treachery, and anxious to counter the suggestion that Barry and three others had done almost all the fighting. O'Sullivan told Chisholm that it had been a 'clean' fight on both sides.[75] He and several others make a point of saying that 'Sonny' Dave Crowley, vice-commandant of the Dunmanway Battalion, was in the command post with Barry, something unmentioned in *Guerilla Days in Ireland*.[76] Murphy, who was with Barry at the command post, added two more men – 'Denis O'Brien,

Newcestown and one other'.[77] O'Brien's witness statement explicitly noted that Barry's memoir had ignored Crowley. Some interviewees wanted to restore the reputation of the dead Volunteers who, according to Barry, had stood up because of inexperience.[78] Jack O'Sullivan described the memoir as a 'wild west story', reflecting that 'another thing which I think is very wrong and I, it weren't up to me because his own pals from Dunmanway should have taken care of it, it was the wrong thing to say, that Michael McCarthy got up out of his position'.[79] He was presumably one of Hart's two interviewees who 'considered Barry's account to be an insult to the memory' of McCarthy and Jim O'Sullivan.[80]

Most Kilmichael veterans who gave testimony were reluctant to employ the 'false surrender' to justify their actions. Yet several acquiesced in the story and recounted it to Ryan and others. Understanding the aftermath of Kilmichael involves consideration of how silence and omission can function in local communities and groups, allowing those who disagree to live side by side, to attend the same churches and commemorative functions, and to get on with their lives. The priority for many veterans, in later years, was preserving harmony. The controversy in 1973–4 demonstrates how difficult that could be. In a passage in her first biography omitted from later versions, Ryan remarked on the consequences of the trouble over Deasy's memoir: 'Memory began to play tricks on many of the old men, and strangely enough I found that some of them whom I had interviewed previous to the event, who had thought Barry one of the greatest men who ever walked Irish soil, had altered their attitudes.'[81]

Why was the story necessary? Barry himself indicated that if there was no 'false surrender', he had broken the rules of war.[82] All of the veterans knew how troubling the reality of violence was to the public, and so it remains. As Deasy's nephew said to me: 'People want heroes, not human beings.'[83] The veterans were intensely aware of their families, and the families of the men who had died. The conflict between the heroic public narrative and private memory so evident in their testimony, including Barry's, suggests that in remembering Kilmichael they resembled the men they fought and veterans of other wars. As Antoine Prost observed about French veterans of the Great War:[84]

Above all, the soldiers were the prisoners of civilian expectations: they could only say what civilians allowed them to say. Lies or silence became the only alternative. They lied sometimes for the wrong reasons: to flatter the militaristic patriotism which turned them into heroes. ... But there were other good reasons for lying: the wish to reassure one's nearest and dearest.

The available testimony reveals that sometimes they also told the truth, for the sake of their families, the fallen, and each other.

Rest in peace, all the boys of Kilmichael – Volunteers, Auxiliaries, and Peter Hart.

NOTES

1. Peter Hart, *The I.R.A. and Its Enemies: Violence and Community in Cork, 1916–1923* (Oxford 1998), pp. 21–38.

2. Meda Ryan, *Tom Barry: IRA Freedom Fighter* (Cork 2005; 1st edn 2003), pp. 70–1.

3. Tom Barry, *Guerilla Days in Ireland* (Dublin 1989; 1st edn 1949), pp. 44–5.

4. F. P. Crozier, *Ireland for Ever* (London 1932), p. 128.

5. See Eoghan Harris in *Sunday Independent*, 25 July 2010; Niall Meehan, 'Distorting Irish History, the stubborn facts of Kilmichael: Peter Hart and Irish historiography' (www.spinwatch.org, 24 Oct. 2010); Niall Meehan and Brian P. Murphy, *Troubled History: A 10th Anniversary Critique of Peter Hart's 'The IRA and Its Enemies'* (Millstreet, Co. Cork 2008); Ryan, *Tom Barry*, passim; Jack Lane and Brendan Clifford, *Kilmichael: The False Surrender* (Millstreet 1999); Kevin Myers in *IT*, 7 July, 26 Sept. 1998. Restrained and fair-minded assessments of the Kilmichael controversy appear in Ryan's first biography, *The Tom Barry Story* (Dublin 1982); D. M. Leeson, *The Black and Tans: British Police and Auxiliaries in the Irish War of Independence, 1920–1921* (Oxford 2011); William H. Kautt, *Ambushes and Armour: The Irish Rebellion, 1919–1921* (Dublin 2010); John Dorney, 'Peter Hart – A legacy', (www.theirishstory.com, 9 Aug. 2010); Seamus Fox 'The Kilmichael ambush – a review of background, controversies and effects' (www.dcu.ie/~foxs/irhist, version 5, 2005).

6. Timothy Keohane, MAD, BMH, WS 1295; Patrick O'Brien, WS 812; Edward Young, WS 1402; James 'Spud' Murphy, WS 1684; Jack Hennessy, WS 1234; Michael O'Driscoll, WS 1297 (copies of all witness statements are also in NAD).

7. Stephen O'Neill, UCDA, OMN, P17b–112, pp. 103–8. He recounted his arrest after the ambush, but not the ambush itself.

8. Liam Deasy (ed. John E. Chisholm), *Towards Ireland Free: The West Cork Brigade in the War of Independence, 1917–1921* (Cork 1992; 1st edn 1973), pp. 170–2; Paddy O'Brien, 'Kilmichael ambush 28 November 1920' (undated), NLI, Deasy papers, MS 43,554/13. I conducted four interviews with Fr Chisholm, on three occasions taking notes only (15, 29 Mar., 8 Apr. 2010) and recording the fourth on 25 Oct. 2010. We also exchanged numerous emails. Chisholm is adamant that the account reproduced in *Towards Ireland Free* was exactly as given to him by Deasy, and was distressed to discover (in 2011) that it was not the original.

9. Ryan's interviewees were Tom Barry, Dan Hourihane, Paddy O'Brien, Tim O'Connell, Pat O'Donovan, James O'Mahony, Jack O'Sullivan and Ned Young: Ryan, *Tom Barry*, p. 428 (n. 90).

10. *II*, 17 Jan. 1921. See also the account by Bill Munro, a member of the Auxiliary patrol that investigated the ambush site, in James Gleeson, *Bloody Sunday* (London 1962), pp. 61–80.

11. I am very grateful to Robin Whitaker for making this available to me.

12. Chisholm tapes, *c.* 1969 (private collection). Chisholm states that he did not, as reported by Ryan, unsuccessfully invite Barry to read *Towards Ireland Free* before publication: Ryan, *Tom Barry*, p. 372.

13. Out of the five extracts attributed to Chisholm's interviews, the second is by O'Sullivan and the remainder are by Young: cf. Hart, *The I.R.A. and Its Enemies*, pp. 34–5.

14. Notes of interview with Liam Deasy (nephew), 20 Apr. 2010. I interviewed him further on 19 Dec. 2010, 26 Feb. and 1 July 2011.

15. Barry, *Guerilla Days*, author's note and p. ix; Bureau Journal, vol. 2, 24–5 Sept., 23 [May 1947] and vol. 4, 28 Apr., 1 May [1948]: NLI, Florence O'Donoghue Papers, MSS 31,355/1–2.

16. Barry to McDunphy (extract), 4 July 1948, BMH S 1030; Tom Barry, *The Reality of the Anglo–Irish War, 1920–21, in West Cork: Refutations, Corrections and Comments on Liam Deasy's 'Towards Ireland Free'* (Tralee and Dublin 1974), p. 9; Ryan, *Tom Barry*, pp. 323–4. The Bureau asked Barry for a statement on several occasions, filing his final refusal as WS 1743.

17. Flor [Begley] to Deasy, 22 May 1948, NLI, Deasy Papers, MS 43,554/23.

18. Note by McDunphy, 'Conversation between the Director and Mr. Sean Collins, 11 May 1949', BMH, S 1355.

19. Ryan, *Tom Barry*, pp. 67–8.

20. O'Driscoll, WS 1297, p. 5; Hennessy, WS 1234, p. 6; Keohane, WS 1295, p. 7; Young, WS 1402, p. 14.

21. Keohane was recommended to the Bureau by Dan Holland (QM, Bandon Battalion) and Liam Deasy. His involvement in Kilmichael is confirmed by John O'Driscoll, his company captain: Keohane, WS 1295, pp. 5–7 and investigator's notes; O'Driscoll, WS 1250, p. 15; Deasy, *Towards Ireland Free*, p. 351.

22. Kelleher, WS 1654, pp. 10–14. Don Wood, a local journalist, recently pointed out that Michael O'Dwyer, named as a section commander by Barry himself in 1974, was also left off earlier lists: *Southern Star*, 27 Nov. 2010; Barry, *Reality*, p. 14 (reference to 'Mick Dwyer').

23. Military Service Pension files were consulted in one case, and Deasy read over O'Brien's draft statement at his request: 'Military service pensions files received in Bureau, 14 Feb. 1950 to 6 June 1958', BMH, S 655; investigator's notes for O'Brien (WS 812), BMH (uncatalogued); 'Taking of evidence: instructions to representatives of the Bureau, 10 May 1948', BMH, S 851.

24. Ryan, *Tom Barry*, p. 59.

25. For example, Patrick O'Sullivan, WS 1481, p. 8; Cornelius Connolly, WS 602, p. 2; Sean O'Driscoll WS 1518, pp. 12–13. The only overtly negative references to Barry are in Donal Hales, WS 292, p. 5.

26. '1913–1921: Chronology, pt. iii, secn. 2, for 1920', p. 274, BMH (uncatalogued); O'Brien, WS 812, p. 15; Young, WS 1402, p. 17.

27. Meehan, 'Distorting Irish History'; Meda Ryan, 'The Kilmichael ambush, 1920: exploring the provocative chapters', *History*, 92, no. 306 (2007), 235–49 (242).

28. Deasy, *Towards Ireland Free*, pp. 171–2.

29. *II*, 3 Oct. 1973; Barry, *Reality*, p. 14.

30. Barry, *Guerilla Days*, pp. 44–5; Barry, *Reality*, pp. 16–17.

31. *IT*, 12, 13 Dec. 1974.

32. Nolan to Deasy, 4 Aug. 1971, Pat Lynch to Chisholm, undated, and Nolan, quoted in Brennan to Deasy, 22 July 1972: NLI, Deasy Papers, MS 43,554/22.

33. [Deasy] to Nolan, undated [Oct. 1971], *idem*.

34. Stephen O'Neill, 'Auxiliaries annihilated at Kilmichael' in *Rebel Cork's Fighting Story, 1916–1921* (Tralee 1947), pp. 83–5 and 'The ambush at Kilmichael', *The Kerryman* (Christmas Number), 1937.

35. It stated that Paddy O'Brien 'held the rank of Commandant in Barry's column' (which Barry denied in *Reality*, p. 14) and confirmed that 'Sonny' Dave Crowley took part in the ambush: Louis Whyte, *The Wild Heather Glen: The Kilmichael Story of Grief and Glory* (Co. Cork 1995), pp. 61–4, 89–91.

36. CILI, 30 Nov. 1920, NAL, WO 35/152.

37. 'Site of Ambush in Kilmichael area 28th Nov. 1920', signed by 'E. FLEMING, LIEUT. D.I.3 "C." COY. AUX. DIV. R.I.C. 25. i. 21' ('D.I.3'

signifies that Fleming held the temporary rank of District Inspector, 3rd Class, in the Auxiliary Division). According to an explanatory note under the map in Barrett's, it was used by the family of Cadet H. F. Forde when claiming compensation for his injuries. It was retained by a law firm in Macroom until the 1960s when it was given to the O'Mahony family of Ballymichael, personal friends of Tom Barry, who passed it on to Sean Crowley. The original map, and the tidier copy reproduced in the text, were kindly made available by Sean Crowley and Colum Cronin.

38. Comparison of this copy with the much scrawled over and scarcely reproducible original map reveals only minor discrepancies, such as the misdescription of Fleming as 'LIEUT. D.I.B.' (see previous note). For 'rebels lying in which position they would be very well concealed', read 'riflemen lying in which position they would be fairly well concealed'. For '2 rifles (machine)', read '2 rifles (kneeling)'.

39. Anthony Seldon and Joanna Pappworth, *By Word of Mouth: 'Elite' Oral History* (London 1983), p. 17; Michael Conway, *Autobiographical Memory: An Introduction* (Milton Keynes 1990), pp. 10–11.

40. Kautt, *Ambushes*, p. 114.

41. Samuel Schrager, 'What is social in oral history?' in Robert Perks and Alistair Thomson (eds), *The Oral History Reader* (London 1998), pp. 284–99 (284).

42. Popular Memory Group, 'Popular memory: theory, politics and method' and Alistair Thomson, 'Anzac memories: putting popular memory theory into practice in Australia' in Perks and Thomson, *Reader*, pp. 75–86, 244–54; T. G. Ashplant, Graham Dawson and Michael Roper, *The Politics of War Memory and Commemoration* (London 2000), pp. 13, 18.

43. Seldon and Pappworth, *By Word of Mouth*, p. 25; Schrager, 'What is social?', p. 284.

44. Murphy, WS 1684, pp. 6–7; Young, WS 1402, pp. 15–16.

45. This denial was more emphatic in an untaped portion of the interview with O'Sullivan: telephone interview with Chisholm, 27 July 2011.

46. Hennessy, WS 1234, pp. 5–6; Keohane, WS 1295, pp. 6–7; O'Brien, 'Kilmichael ambush'; Deasy, *Towards Ireland Free*, p. 172.

47. Keohane, WS 1295, pp. 6–7.

48. Hennessy, WS 1234, p. 6.

49. Ryan, Tom Barry, p. 67, citing Whyte, *The Wild Heather Glen*, p. 71 (with excerpts from Hennessy's witness statement) and an interview with Dan Hourihane. Her information probably came from Hourihane's account of what Hennessy had said to him.

50. Deasy, *Towards Ireland Free*, p. 172.

51. Hennessy, WS 1234, p. 6.

52. CILI, 30 Nov. 1920, WO 35/152.

53. Taped interview with Young.

54. 'AF' (a scout), paraphrased in Hart, *The I.R.A. and Its Enemies*, p. 35 (n. 61).

55. Kautt, *Ambushes*, pp. 116–17.

56. Barry, *Reality*, p. 17.

57. Taped interview with Young.

58. Taped interview with Young. Peter Hart slightly mistranscribed part of the interview as 'I saw the first lorry below and men shooting Tans (and added 'I suppose I shouldn't be saying that now').' Hart, *The I.R.A. and Its Enemies*, p. 35.

59. See map.

60. Ryan, *Barry Story*, p. 32 and Tom Barry, p. 56; Hart, *The I.R.A. and Its Enemies*, p. 34; taped interview with Young. Ryan quoted O'Sullivan anonymously in 1982, with the result that Hart misattributed the story to Young.

61. CILI, 30 Nov. 1920, WO 35/152.

62. See map.

63. *II*, 17 Jan. 1921.

64. Taped interview with Jack O'Sullivan.

65. Gleeson, *Bloody Sunday*, p. 74; *II*, 17 Jan. 1921; Clarke to Street, 1 Dec. 1920, CO 904/127; Hart, *The I.R.A. and Its Enemies*, pp. 35–6.

66. See information relating to W. Pallister, W. T. Barnes and A. F. Poole: CILI, 30 Nov. 1920, WO 35/152; Ryan, *Tom Barry*, p. 66; Hennessy, WS 1234, pp. 5–6; taped interview with Young.

67. *II*, 17 Jan. 1921; Whyte, *The Wild Heather Glen*, p. 77.

68. Hart, *The I.R.A. and Its Enemies*, p. 26; Ryan, *Tom Barry*, pp. 87–8; *Irish Press*, 26 Nov. 1932.

69. 'Extracts from seized documents', June 1921, WO 141/40; Record of the Rebellion in Ireland 1920–21, vols 1, 4, WO 141/93.

70. Ryan, *Tom Barry*, pp. 73–84; Brian Murphy, 'Poisoning the well or publishing the truth? From Peter Hart's *The I.R.A. and Its Enemies* to RTÉ's *Hidden History* Film on Coolacrease' in Meehan and Murphy, *Troubled History*, pp. 34–6.

71. Ryan, *Tom Barry*, pp. 79, 77; taped interview with Young.

72. Ryan, *Tom Barry*, pp. 79, 77; O'Brien, WS 812, p. 16.

73. Notes of interviews with Liam Deasy (nephew), 1 July 2011 and Sean Crowley, 12 Aug. 2011; Corkman.ie, 23 Aug. 2007.

74. Niall Meehan, 'Troubles in Irish history: a 10th anniversary critique of *The I.R.A. and Its Enemies*' in Meehan and Murphy, *Troubled History*, p. 9.

75. Telephone interview with Chisholm, 29 July 2011.

76. Taped interviews with Young and O'Sullivan; O'Brien, WS 812

p. 15, Young, WS 1402, p. 14; O'Brien, 'Kilmichael ambush'.

77. Murphy, WS 1684, p. 5.

78. See Barry's description of the dead Volunteers as 'green', quoted in Ryan, *Tom Barry*, p. 65.

79. Taped interview with O'Sullivan.

80. Hart, *The I.R.A. and Its Enemies*, p. 35 (n. 58).

81. Ryan, *Barry Story*, p. 181 (cf. Ryan, *Tom Barry*, p. 375).

82. Barry observed that *Towards Ireland Free* 'suggests I broke the rules of war, but that is not so': *II*, 3 Oct. 1973.

83. Interview with Liam Deasy (nephew), 26 Feb. 2011.

84. Antoine Prost (tr. Helen McPhail), *In the Wake of War: Les Anciens Combattants and French Society, 1914–1939* (Oxford 1992), p. 12.

10. The Execution of 'Spies and Informers' in West Cork, 1921

Thomas Earls FitzGerald

I

On 24 March 1936, at around 9.30 p.m., retired Vice-Admiral Henry Boyle Townshend Somerville was shot and killed by the IRA on the doorstep of his home at the Point, Castletownshend. He was seventy-two years old. The murder of Somerville was widely condemned by nearly all sections of Irish society. The Fianna Fáil government took the opportunity to denounce its former allies, and in June the IRA was proscribed as an illegal organization. According to Fianna Fáil propagandists, the contemporary IRA were no better than criminals whose actions were not rooted in the patriotism displayed in 1916–23.[1] A clear distinction was drawn between the 'old IRA' and the impostors of the 'new IRA'. Yet the men who executed Somerville were under the command of Tom Barry, then the IRA's commandant in Cork and previously the most successful guerrilla leader in the War of Independence.

Somerville was condemned as a 'British agent' by the IRA because he had given references to local men who wanted to join the Royal Navy.[2] His murder revived awkward issues concerning the killing of civilians in the War of Independence. Were the alleged 'spies' and 'informers' executed on account of who they were rather than what they had done? Were they in fact spies or informers? IRA veterans of the 'glorious' years who went on to write best-selling memoirs usually denied or ignored the killing of unarmed men. 'My countrymen know well that I would never aim at a gun at an unarmed opponent,'[3] wrote Dan Breen in *My Fight For Irish Freedom*. Ernie O'Malley's more cerebral *On Another Man's Wound* portrayed such killings as unpleasant and uncommon. Having supervised the execution of three British army officers in Tipperary in May 1921, O'Malley reflected that 'it seemed easier to face one's own execution than to have to shoot others'.[4]

Richard Mulcahy, as Chief of Staff, insisted that no civilians should be liable for punishment by the IRA unless they were active enemies of the national cause. On 14 May 1921, he wrote to the Minister for Defence (Cathal Brugha) that 'no one shall be regarded as as an Enemy of Ireland, whether they may be described locally as Unionist, Orangeman etc., except that they are actively anti-Irish in their outlook and in their actions'.[5] All civilian targets, according to GHQ orders, were to be given a fair trial and sentenced only if proven beyond doubt to have acted against the republic.[6] Yet GHQ had limited influence beyond Dublin, and Tom Barry stated that the West Cork Brigade never sought sanction for any execution.[7] By 1921, many jittery local Volunteers were launching unauthorized attacks on civilians belonging to suspect groups. Of the eighty-two ex-servicemen reported to have been killed by the IRA, most were attacked in spring or summer 1921.[8]

In the first two months of 1921, the 3rd (West) Cork Brigade was responsible for the murder of at least ten civilians labelled as 'spies' or 'informers'. Two more civilians, both Protestants, were killed in late March.[9] Opinion on the nature, purpose and morality of these killings differs greatly. Barry himself made no apology for the executions. He wrote that extreme action was needed in early 1921 to counter the increasing success of the Crown forces, which he attributed to assistance from anti-national civilians. Barry identified the 'spies' and 'informers' as being made up of three groups: degraded Irishmen who sold out their country for British gold; ex-servicemen whose allegiance still lay with Britain; and wealthy landowners with a vested interest in British domination of Ireland.[10] Liam Deasy, the Brigade's OC, wrote in his memoir, *Towards Ireland Free*, that the policy of executions was a necessity because an anti-Sinn Féin society intent on destroying the IRA had developed in the Bandon valley: 'That it was an unpleasant duty is obvious; that it was a necessary duty becomes evident when one thinks of the many noble efforts made down the ages to secure our freedom that were defeated by English gold and Irish greed.'[11] According to John Bor-gonovo, the 1st Cork (City) and the 2nd (North) Cork Brigades also detected 'loyalist civilian spy rings in their areas'.[12] Meda Ryan's biography of Barry supported Barry's and Deasy's version of events, claiming that Barry was known for his capacity for 'sizing up facts and motives' in an 'extremely accurate' manner.[13]

Less positively, Michael Hopkinson concluded that the failures of the Cork IRA and recent setbacks in early 1921 'emphasised the need to root out informers and led to a big rise in the execution of so-called spies', leading to something of a 'vendetta'.[14] The late Peter Hart took an even more jaundiced view of the executions. He wrote that 'many suspects were guilty only by association. ... Almost all victims were officially described as spies or informers but in practice this could mean anything.' Though genuine informers were occasionally killed, 'such "definite cases" were still excep-tional. In reality on the run and afraid for their lives, the guerrillas usually acted on their own suspicions.' Hart believed that the Cork IRA generally selected civilians for execution on the basis of their affiliations rather than their actions. Protestants, ex-servicemen and vagrants, three groups particularly at risk, were seldom in a posi-tion to know anything that could damage the IRA. The most telling evidence cited in support of his claim is a passage concerning the West Cork killings in the army's official 'Record of the Rebellion in Ireland', which stated that 'in every case but one the person mur-dered had given no information'.[15]

The most recent work on political killings in Cork, by Gerard Murphy, presents an inconsistent account of what happened in West Cork in early 1921. Murphy maintains that these killings were 'of a sectarian nature' and set the scene for the slaughter in Dunmanway in April 1922. Yet Murphy also cites a statement in the 'Record of the Rebellion', which suggests that the victims were indeed informers, identifying 'the Bandon area' as the only part of Southern Ireland in which Protestants readily offered informa-tion to the Crown forces. Regrettably, 'it proved almost impos-sible to protect these brave men, many of whom were murdered'. According to Murphy: 'There can be little doubt that this refers to the half a dozen or so loyalist farmers who were shot as informers by members of Tom Barry's column and others who were driven out in fear of their lives.'[16] As shown below, only three of the eight Protestants reportedly killed in the Bandon area in 1921 were farmers. Were these victims in fact active informers or innocent victims of circumstance? In *Guerilla Days in Ireland*, Barry refused to name the executed 'informers' on the grounds that it could upset their living relatives. He did, however, advise curious readers that the names had been recorded in 'the daily press of the first six months of 1921'.[17] Through examination of the local papers, and statements collected by the Bureau of Military History, this chapter seeks to identify the alleged 'informers' and establish why, and with what justification, they were killed.

II

The late winter of 1921 was the bleakest phase of the War of Independence for the West Cork Brigade. Between 17 January and 16 February, thirteen members of the Brigade were killed by the Crown forces, compared with one man in October 1920 (Lieutenant John Connolly) and five in December. After February the spate of killing subsided, with five deaths in March and three in May.[18] On 1 February, *The Cork Examiner* reported that there were at least 100 prisoners in the military barracks at Bandon as a result of recent searches by the Essex Regiment.[19] Both the RIC and the army had recently undertaken substantial and effective intelligence operations. According to Hugh McIvor, an Antrim Protestant deployed in Bandon with a rapid response unit of the RIC, a 'special squad' was organized in the district by a head constable in plain clothes with four or five men, 'dressed liked old farmers', who 'gathered information'.[20]

On occasion, such information was misused when barbarous attacks were made on relatives of revolutionaries. On 5 February, Dan Moloney of Barryroe, who had three sons imprisoned for membership of the IRA, was shot and 'severely wounded in circumstances not yet made clear' according to a local press report.[21] Three days later, 'armed and masked men' raided the house of John O'Brien of Ballineen.[22] O'Brien, aged sixty-five, was shot and wounded by disguised Auxiliaries who also burned his home and stole his livestock.[23] His son Patrick was adjutant of the Dunmanway Battalion.

On 14 February, Auxiliaries killed two brothers active in the IRA, Patrick and James Coffey, at home in their beds in Enniskeane. According to Barry, the Auxiliaries were led to the Coffeys by 'two masked civilians', though this claim cannot be corroborated.[24]

Undoubtedly, however, civilians were actively involved in helping the Crown forces. The County Inspector in West Cork reported at the end of January that information 'is being given freely and it is believed that it will still be given'.[25] This claim was confirmed by an episode following the execution of an alleged 'informer' by the West Cork flying column on 22 January. The body of Denis Dwyer, an ex-serviceman, was left on the road three miles outside Bandon, in the hope of ambushing any Crown forces attempting to retrieve the body. According to Charles O'Donoghue, a member of the flying column: 'A reliable farmer was told to call to the military Barracks in Bandon, three miles away, and to tell the officer in charge that the he saw a man dead on the road with a label marked "spy" on him. This he did and the officer's reply was "Yes, I know but what about the 300 men that are in ambush out there?" '[26]

It was in this context that the West Cork IRA undertook a concerted campaign against informers. Of the ten civilians killed in late January and February 1921, eight were Protestants. Does this imply, as some believe, that such killings were motivated by sectarianism rather than the pursuit of rough republican justice? As shown below, it appears that nine of the ten victims had in some way offended the IRA or made themselves suspect, and that in six cases they may well have provided information. Whether these actions merited capital punishment is another matter. Yet it cannot be denied that there was a sectarian strain in the West Cork IRA. In several cases, IRA men looking back on their past deeds could scarcely veil their contempt for Protestants. In *Rebel Cork's Fighting Story*, Tim O'Donoghue recalled that the people of Ireland were entirely sympathetic to the IRA except for the 'mixed breeds', who were 'openly hostile'.[27] Captain Timothy Warren of the Ballineen Volunteers described that town as 'the little Derry of the South', conjuring up horrific images of sectarian division.[28] Nevertheless, the West Cork IRA did not systematically kill Protestants simply because of their religious profession. Examination of the background of the victims, and the justifications offered for killing them, suggests four categories: (1) past misconduct towards the IRA; (2) association with the RIC; (3) simple suspicion; (4) proof that the victim had been an 'informer'.

Interestingly, the first three people to be killed in West Cork as 'informers' belong to the fourth group. In relation to Denis Dwyer, and two men both named Thomas Bradfield, all accounts identify them as informers. This is corroborated by the memoirs of Liam Deasy and Tom Barry and testimony by Denis Lordan and James 'Spud' Murphy of the Brigade's flying column. On 21 January, Catholic ex-serviceman Dennis Dwyer was found by members of the column at Mawbeg outside Bandon. Deceived by their uniforms, he mistook them for British army officers and tried to ingratiate himself by claiming that he had often delivered information on the IRA to the barracks in Bandon. He was subsequently shot and killed.[29]

Next day, a section of the column seeking a billet stumbled upon Thomas Bradfield, a Protestant farmer at Carhue outside Bandon who mistook the Volunteer uniforms for those of Auxiliary Cadets. Bradfield began to criticize the performance of the Crown forces and gave the names of local IRA men and an account of their activities. Shortly afterwards, he was killed.[30] According to Deasy and the historian Leon Ó Broin, however, it was Peter Monahan's Scottish accent that convinced Bradfield he was addressing an Auxiliary. In Deasy's account, the fact that the IRA had stumbled on these two spies suggested the necessity of removing all other informers in the Brigade area against whom 'conclusive' evidence could be procured.[31] On 1 February, Barry, dressed as an Auxiliary, was let into the home of a second Thomas Bradfield, a Protestant farmer from Desertserges. He too was deceived, revealed information concerning IRA activities, and was shot that night.[32] *The Cork Examiner* confirmed that both Bradfields were killed as a result of conversing with Republicans masquerading as members of the Crown forces.[33] If not actual informers, Dwyer and the Bradfields were certainly willing to be informers.

Other probable informers included two Protestant farmers who were shot dead in the Skibbereen district on 19 February, 65-year-old Matthew Sweetnam and 59-year-old William Connell.[34] The *Cork County Eagle* reported that 'they were killed merely because they gave evidence against a party recently for collecting for the IRA arms fund'.[35] Patrick O'Sullivan, brother of Gearóid and quartermaster of the Skibbereen Battalion, wrote that in autumn 1920 twenty Protestant farmers in the area refused to contribute to that fund. O'Sullivan stated that in early February 1921 the Battalion received orders from the Brigade HQ that 'Connell and Sweetnam should be executed and their lands forfeit. These farmers had informed the British of the names of the men who had called on them to collect the arms fund levy.'[36]

Other cases were less clear-cut. Alfred Cotter, an Episcopalian aged thirty-five in 1921, managed a bakery in Ballineen with his brother Frederick.[37] On 27 February, armed men entered his mother's house in Ballineen at around 2.30 a.m. and took him outside, where he was shot and killed.[38] The background to this attack was the initiation in early 1919 of a republican boycott of the RIC, to which all traders were expected to adhere. In Ballineen, all complied except the Cotters. Jack Hennessy, adjutant of the Ballineen Volunteer Company in 1919, claimed that the Cotters were 'anti-Irish' and that 'the RIC used visit their premises'. According to Hennessy, the Cotters noted all his movements for the benefit of the RIC, as well as those of Captain Tim Warren. In retaliation, the Ballineen company insisted that all local people boycott the Cotters' bakery.[39]

The boycott was effective, but costly for the organizers. In July 1920, according to both Hennessy and Warren, a detachment of the Essex Regiment visited Ballineen and burned both their homes, forcing Warren and Hennessy to live 'on the run'.[40] They claimed that Cotter continued to inform on the activities of the Ballineen IRA.[41] Hennessy, who became a section leader in the flying column, alleged that 'there appeared to be evidence to connect him with spying' when the Brigade was 'cleaning up the British spy ring in west Cork in the early days of 1921'.[42] Yet no such evidence has come to light for the period after 1920, and Cotter was probably killed for his past rather than present activities.

Two other cases indicate that the IRA sometimes killed civilians as 'informers and spies' on the basis of past suspicions. Frederick Stennings, a 57-year-old Episcopalian and native of England, lived in Innishannon. In his 1911 census return he proudly described himself as a pisciculturist (fish breeder).[43] He too was executed as a spy on 30 March 1921.[44] Richard Russell from Innishannon, in charge of signals in the Bandon Battalion, offered no clear justification for Stennings's execution in his statement for the Bureau of Military History. He stated that in August 1920 Stennings was observed watching members of the Battalion who had taken up ambush positions at Granure, on the road from Bandon to Ballineen, and then cycling off towards Innishannon. No other evidence was offered for the claim that he was executed for 'acting as a spy'. Was he killed simply because the IRA believed that he had passed on information in the previous August and was therefore liable to have repeated the offence? There is, however, another aspect to the case of Stennings. He had refused to let the executioners into his home and, before trying to escape, had opened fire with a revolver on his unwanted guests.[45] If Stennings was armed, willing to fire upon IRA men, and ready to attempt escape, he presumably expected to be interfered with. Whether this was because he had something to hide, or because his background made him a likely suspect, cannot be determined.

Thomas Cotter was executed on 1 March with a note pinned to his body proclaiming: 'Convicted Spy. Informers Beware. IRA.'[46] His story is similar to that of Stennings. Cotter, an Episcopalian farmer from Curraghlough, south Kilmurry, near Dunmanway, was fifty-five in 1921.[47] Sean Murphy, quartermaster of the Dunmanway Battalion in 1920, was in an ambush position on the road from Dunmanway to Ballineen. He stated that two men named Cotter were seen hunting rabbits in a nearby field. They were both placed under arrest as, according to Murphy, 'we did not want them to return to Ballineen to report to the military column'.[48] This is the only information I have been able to find concerning a Cotter from the Dunmanway district. If one of the Cotters mentioned by Murphy is Thomas Cotter, it seems probable that he too was killed because the IRA suspected that he had acted as an informer in the past. Like Alfred Cotter and Fred Stennings, he may have been a victim of the panic that overtook the West Cork Brigade in early 1921 when, as Barry maintained, the execution of all suspects was essential to ensure 'the continued existence of the Irish Republican Army'.[49]

Suspicion, of course, does not imply guilt. In the case of Robert Eady of Clonakilty, the IRA killed an innocent man, though more than any other West Cork victim he dug his own grave, having given the IRA every reason to believe he was informing. On the night of 10 February, Eady was executed as a spy, a mile from his home outside Clonakilty.[50] Eady was a 40-year-old Catholic.[51] He was also the father of four children, the youngest of whom was three years old. At his funeral on Sunday, 13 February, Monsignor O'Leary read out a letter he had received from District Inspector John Kearney on the circumstances of Eady's death. Three weeks earlier, Eady had arrived at the Clonakilty RIC barracks late at night, dressed in a woman's shawl. He told Kearney that he had recently lost his job, and asked for assistance in getting a passport so that he and his family could move to England. In response, Kearney said he would help but that Eady should not again come to the barracks in female dress. He emphasized that otherwise Eady had had no connection with the RIC in Clonakilty.[52] The Clonakilty IRA or a well-wisher must have identified Eady beneath the shawl as he either entered or left the barracks, leading to the reasonable but incorrect inference that he had something to hide and was in collusion with 'the enemy'. Like Stennings, he was clearly fearful of being attacked even though Eady was not supplying information.

In other cases, the threadbare available evidence suggests that civilians were killed on the basis of unsubstantiated suspicion. On the night of 9 February, William Johnston, a 22-year-old Protestant, was shot dead at his home in Kilbrittain.[53] Johnston's deceased father had been a constable in the RIC.[54] In a joint statement for the Bureau of Military History by members of the Kilbrittain company, James O'Mahony, Denis Crowley and John FitzGerald stated that, in early March, 'B.1 Company executed a Spy'.[55] As only one civilian is known to have been executed as a 'spy' in Kilbrittain, they must have misremembered the date.[56] Not content with William's death, the IRA raided the family home in late October 1921. According to the RIC, 'the motive for the attack was to intimidate Mrs Johnston to force her to clear out of the area'. The widow and her four daughters subsequently moved to Bandon.[57] On 7 February Gilbert Fenton, a Methodist shopkeeper aged seventy-seven, and his son William, aged fifty-two, were both seriously (but not fatally) wounded trying to prevent armed men from entering their home in Gaggin outside Bandon.[58] I have found no reference to this attack in any testimony from the Bandon district. In such cases, the presumption must be that the victims were selected on the basis of mere suspicion rather than firm evidence of active informing or spying.

Various mitigating circumstances might be cited in defence of the conduct of Barry and his fellow executioners. The killing of unarmed men was commonplace in the Irish revolution, whether directed by Barry at Kilmichael, the Black and Tans or Auxiliaries at Balbriggan, Cork City and Croke Park, the Army Council during the Civil War, or Paddy O'Daly at Ballyseedy, Co. Kerry. Violence generated by unsubstantiated suspicion was not restricted to the various sections of the IRA. On the night of 7 February, Auxiliaries in Tralee shot and injured an RIC sergeant and a constable for refusing to halt when ordered.[59] Nor were all suspected informers actually punished: in at least one case a Protestant farmer was arrested and interrogated by the IRA yet, according to Charles O'Donoghue, he was given 'the benefit of the doubt and got away with a warning'.[60] The existence of informers was not confined to West Cork: by 1921, the flying column of the 2nd Tipperary Brigade was unable to operate in safety outside the desolate Galtee Mountains and Nire Valley (outside the Brigade area) because of the activity of informers elsewhere.[61] We should also remember that the perpetrators were often immature (Barry turned twenty-one in 1920), inexperienced, and perhaps prone to uncontrolled violence driven by fear. Unlike those affected by indiscriminate unofficial 'reprisals', the IRA's civilian targets were all carefully selected, in the sense that the killers had some reason, however tenuous, to believe that their victims were helping the enemy.

In some cases, the killers derived material benefits from the execution of informers. In October 1921, the District Inspector in Skibbereen reported that the farms of the late William Connell and Matthew Sweetnam were 'being used as training camps' by the IRA.[62] The legacy of the campaign against informers in West Cork lingered beyond the Civil War. In June 1923, the superintendent in Bandon informed the Commissioner of the Civic Guard that 'it is

true that this farm owned by the late Thomas Bradfield was confiscated and let into small plots by persons who had no authority to do
so', and that the IRA were responsible for this land seizure.[63] Three
months later, when a Mr FitzGerald attempted to purchase William
Connell's farm from his relatives, FitzGerald received a note from
the IRA:

> Mr Fitzgerald. Information has reached this headquarters that
> you are going to purchase, or have purchased the farm formerly
> owned by the late William Connell, Lissanhouigh, Skibbereen,
> now the property of the Republican Army. As you are going to, or
> have purchased the farm, without the authority of the Republican
> Army you must be prepared to take the responsibility. Bearer will
> forward any communication you desire with us. Signed O.C XX
> 2nd Battn.[64]

It seems unlikely, though not impossible, that at the height of a
guerrilla war the IRA would have killed farmers in order to seize
their land. But, as the military conflict died down, members of the
IRA set about helping themselves to what the supposed enemies of
the republic had left behind.

In later years, West Cork veterans such as Barry decided not to
name civilians they had killed.[65] Was this a considerate attempt to
avoid offending any surviving relatives, or a tacit admission of guilt
and shame? Or, possibly, both?

NOTES

1. Brian Hanley, *The IRA, 1926–1936* (Dublin 2002), p. 144.

2. *Ibid*. p. 83.

3. Dan Breen, *My Fight For Irish Freedom* (Dublin 1924), p. 175.

4. Ernie O'Malley, *On Another Man's Wound* (Dublin 1936), pp. 330,
332.

5. Quoted in Maryann Gialanella Valiulis, *Portrait of a Revolutionary:
General Richard Mulcahy and the Founding of the Irish Free State* (Dublin
1992), p. 53.

6. *Ibid*. p. 68.

7. Tom Barry, *Guerilla Days In Ireland* (Cork 1949), p. 106.

8. Jane Leonard, 'Getting them at last: the IRA and ex servicemen' in

David Fitzpatrick (ed.), *Revolution? Ireland, 1917–1923* (Dublin 1990), pp. 119–29 (120–1).

9. John and William Good: Report on Breach of Truce, Cork West Riding, 24 Aug. 1921, NAL, CO 904/152 (microfilm, TCD).

10. Barry, *Guerilla Days*, p. 106.

11. Liam Deasy (ed. John E. Chisholm), *Towards Ireland Free: The West Cork Brigade in the War of Independence, 1917–1921* (Cork 1973), p. 201.

12. John Borgonovo, *Spies, Informers and the 'Anti-Sinn Féin Society': The Intelligence War in Cork City, 1920–1921* (Dublin 2007), p. 25.

13. Meda Ryan, *Tom Barry: IRA Freedom Fighter* (Cork 2003), p. 127.

14. Michael Hopkinson, *The Irish War of Independence* (Dublin 2002), p. 111.

15. Peter Hart, *The I.R.A. and Its Enemies: Violence and Community in Cork, 1916–1923* (Oxford 1998), pp. 298, 300, 306, 300.

16. Gerard Murphy, *The Year of Disappearances: Political Killings in Cork, 1921–1922* (Dublin 2010), pp. 73, 77, 230.

17. Barry, *Guerilla Days*, p. 106.

18. *Ibid.* pp. 236–7.

19. *Cork Examiner,* 1 Feb. 1921.

20. John D. Brewer, *The Royal Irish Constabulary: An Oral History* (Belfast 1990), pp. 115, 21.

21. *Cork County Eagle and Munster Advertiser,* 12 Feb. 1921.

22. *Cork Examiner,* 9 Feb. 1921.

23. Patrick O'Brien, MAD, BMH Papers, WS 812, p. 27.

24. Barry, *Guerilla Days*, p. 98.

25. CI, MCR (Cork West Riding), Jan. 1921, CO 904/114.

26. Charles O'Donoghue, WS 1607, p. 6.

27. Tim O'Donoghue, 'Destruction of Rosscarbery Police Barracks' in *Rebel Cork's Fighting Story, 1916–1921: Told by the Men who Fought It* (Tralee 1947), p. 105.

28. Timothy J. Warren, WS 1275, p. 1.

29. Deasy, *Towards Ireland Free*, p. 200, Barry, *Guerilla Days*, p. 109; James 'Spud' Murphy, WS 1684, p. 9.

30. Dennis Lordan, WS 470, p. 16; James Murphy, WS 1684, p. 9.

31. Deasy, *Towards Ireland Free*, p. 200; Leon Ó Broin, *Protestants in Nationalist Ireland: The Stopford Connection* (Dublin 1985), p. 177. Monahan, a deserter from the Argyll and Sutherland Highlanders, was killed at Crossbarry.

32. Murphy, WS 1684, p. 9; Ryan, *Tom Barry*, p. 127.

33. *Cork Examiner*, 26 Jan., 3 Feb. 1921.

34. Family schedules, Census of Ireland, 1911, DED Cloghdonnell, Lissanoohig (accessible online).

35. *Cork County Eagle*, 26 Feb. 1921.

36. Patrick O'Sullivan, WS 1481, p. 7.

37. Family schedule, Census of Ireland, 1911, DED Ballymoney, Ballymeen.

38. *Cork Examiner*, 28 Feb. 1921.

39. Jack Hennessy, WS 1234, pp. 1, 2.

40. *Ibid.* p. 6; Warren, WS 1275, p. 2.

41. Hennessy, WS 1234, p. 12; Warren, WS 1275, p. 7.

42. Hennessy, WS 1234, p. 12.

43. Family schedule, Census of Ireland, 1911, DED Innishannon, Innishannon.

44. Richard Russell, WS 1591, p. 21.

45. *Ibid.* pp. 10, 21.

46. *Cork Examiner*, 3 Mar. 1921.

47. Family schedule, Census of Ireland, 1911, DED Warrenscourt, Curraghclough.

48. Sean Murphy, WS 1445, p. 7.

49. Barry, *Guerilla Days*, p. 107.

50. *Cork Examiner*, 12 Feb. 1921.

51. Family schedule, Census of Ireland, 1911, DED Kilkeranmore, Knockaphorey.

52. *Cork County Eagle*, 12, 19 Feb. 1921.

53. *Cork Examiner*, 10 Feb. 1921.

54. Family schedule, Census of Ireland, 1911, DED Kilbrittain, Kilbrittain Town.

55. James O'Mahony, Dennis Crowley and John FitzGerald, WS 560, p. 54.

56. Barry, *Guerilla Days*, p. 106.

57. Report of Outrage, Bandon District, 3 Nov. 1921, CO 904/152.

58. *Cork Examiner*, 8 Feb. 1921.

59. T. Ryle Dwyer, *Tans, Terror and Troubles: Kerry's Real Fighting Story, 1913–1923* (Dublin 2001), p. 278.

60. O'Donoghue, WS 1607, p. 6.

61. Charles Townshend, 'The Irish Republican Army and the development of guerrilla warfare, 1916–1921', *English Historical Review*, 94, no. 371 (1979), 318–45 (328).

62. DI C. Bowles, Report on Breach of Truce, 30 Oct. 1921, CO 904/152.

63. E. O'Dubhthaigh (Eamon O'Duffy) to Eoin O'Duffy, 21 June 1923, NAD, Department of Justice, H5/800.

64. H5/969.

65. Ryan, *Tom Barry*, p. 128.

11. Revolution and Terror in Kildare, 1919–1923

Michael Murphy

I

This study of violence and terror in revolutionary Kildare will examine three propositions. First, that Kildare's reputation for acquiescence in British rule ran counter to a long-standing tradition of republican disaffection. Second, that the strong military presence in the county tended to impede rather than strengthen republican resistance. Third, that violent opposition to the Free State was surprisingly vigorous in Kildare, partly due to the ruthlessness of Jim Dunne, leader of a flying column in the Kill district. Fourth, that republican violence after the Treaty tended to erode rather than inspire public support for continued revolution.

Between 1912 and 1918, Kildare conformed to the familiar drift from constitutional to separatist nationalism, while remaining relatively peaceful. By January 1916, Kildare had twenty-five companies of Irish National Volunteers with 2615 members, yet only two Irish Volunteer companies with thirty-seven members.[1] In Kildare, and throughout nationalist Ireland, Redmond's Home Rule movement remained predominant. Nevertheless, a small party of Irish Volunteers from the county participated in the 1916 Rising under the command of Domhnall Ó Buachalla (Daniel Buckley), a prominent Gael and Maynooth shopkeeper. Fourteen men left Maynooth on Easter Monday and marched to Dublin along the railway line, and a few from other parts of Kildare also participated. Seventeen Kildare men were later interned at Frongoch camp, where Ó Buachalla (like Michael Collins) became a prominent personality.

Popular reaction in Kildare to the Rising was generally hostile and unsympathetic, partly because many had relatives who had answered the call to service since August 1914. The unionist *Kildare Observer* condemned the rebellion in an editorial titled 'The Dublin Horror': 'It collapsed within a week, leaving ruin, havoc and unnumbered graves to mark the madness of an attempt not alone to outrage the feelings of the vast majority of the Irish people, but also to defy the might of England. A more suicidal effort or one with less justification has never been made in the history of the world.'[2] As elsewhere, the repression that followed the Rising prompted a rapid radicalization of nationalist sentiment. Ó Buachalla recalled how attitudes had changed by the time the detainees were released: 'We were released from Frongoch a few days before Christmas 1916. We arrived back in Dublin in the morning. There was a notice-able change in the people, now, and I received a royal reception on reaching Maynooth.'[3] Sinn Féin clubs multiplied in early 1918, leading to an emphatic victory in the general election of December 1918. In North Kildare, Ó Buachalla defeated his constitution-alist opponent (John O'Connor) by 5979 votes to 2722. In South Kildare, Art O'Connor from Celbridge had an even more pro-nounced success, defeating Denis Kilbride by 7104 votes to 1545.[4]

Sinn Féin's electoral triumph was not merely the local reflection of a national transformation, but also the outcome of an unusu-ally robust tradition of revolutionary republicanism. It may even be argued that Kildare in 1798 was what Cork became during the War of Independence. Kildare, which had one of the strongest con-centrations of United Irishmen, was among the counties affected by the first outbreak of rebellion on 24 May 1798. In 1803, a sub-stantial force of Kildare rebels combined with men from Wexford and Meath to assist Robert Emmet's futile uprising in Dublin.[5] In the later nineteenth century, the IRB developed strongly throughout the county. John Devoy from Kill was the chief Kildare conspirator, subsequently dominating a sister organization in the United States (Clan na Gael).

The latent republican menace contributed to the location of an extensive military establishment in the county. Naas infantry bar-racks was opened in 1813, Newbridge cavalry barracks in 1819, the Curragh camp in 1855, and Kildare town artillery barracks in 1901.

The number of troops in the county averaged 10,000.[6] This notable
military concentration had contradictory political consequences.
While tending to provoke tension between soldiers and civilians,
it also created powerful economic and trading links, as the story of
Newbridge testifies. The building of the cavalry barracks in 1819
resulted in rapid development of the village, attracting many rural
inhabitants from the surrounding plains. Most civilian employees
at the Curragh camp also came from the Newbridge district, and
custom generated from the garrisons was vital in sustaining the local
economy. According to a report published on Christmas Eve, 1921,
in *The Irish Times*, the military presence on the Curragh alone generated over £90,000 per month. In Newbridge, nine-tenths of traders
depended on the military for their income.[7] Since many Irish Volunteers were also tradesmen, shopkeepers or labourers, any attempt to
translate republican sentiments into violent attacks on the Crown
forces amounted to biting the hand that fed. The Sheehans from
Newbridge were in the boot-making business and dealt with the
Curragh barracks on a daily basis, despite their avowed republicanism. Nevertheless, even before the Easter Rising, local Volunteers were able to secure arms and ammunition from sympathetic
civilian workers. Michael Smyth, commandant of the Athgarvan
Company, recalled that, after 1918, 'I procured a further supply of
arms and ammunition from British soldiers from the Curragh Camp
and Newbridge barracks.'[8]

II

Despite the constraint imposed by economic self-interest, Kildare's
Sinn Féiners and Volunteers contributed vociferously and sometimes violently to the campaign for independence after 1919. On
11 January 1919, the *Leinster Leader* reported a Sunday afternoon
meeting held in Naas to protest at the detention of Irish political
prisoners. The reporter cited the address delivered by Tom Harris,
one of the leading Volunteer organizers in the county and future
TD. Harris was aware of the importance of such rallies for the
republican campaign: 'To-day the Irish people are assembled to
voice a nation's demand for the release from English prisons of
Irishmen and Irishwomen who have been imprisoned by the mili-

tary government of England because they dared declare for Ireland the right that her people should self-determine the sovereignty under which they wished to live [applause].'[9] Harris was a veteran of 1916 whose foot had been injured by shrapnel as he evacuated the GPO. After spending a brief period in Dublin Castle hospital, he was sent to Frongoch where on one occasion he met Asquith, the Prime Minister, whom he described as 'sympathetic and friendly' to the Irish prisoners.[10]

Revolutionary violence in Kildare was initially sporadic. At 2 a.m. on 2 January 1919, the village hall in Kill was burnt down.[11] This act was attributed to the refusal of Lady Mayo to permit the Kill Sinn Féin club to use the hall.[12] Reports of cattle drives affecting Protestant large farmers and prominent loyalists later became widespread in the local press. Escalation in the Volunteers' campaign was apparent by early 1920.[13] At 10 p.m. on 21 February, Sergeant Hughes and five constables from Maynooth RIC barracks were patrolling the village when a band of local republicans began shooting at them near the junction of the Moyglare and Kilcock roads. The exchange of fire lasted for thirty minutes, until the Volunteers disbanded (having presumably exhausted their ammunition). Sergeant Hughes died the following morning from wounds sustained in the ambush. Constable Crean had a fortunate escape, as his leather ammunition pouch smothered a bullet.[14]

Hunger strikers were more effective than terrorists in arousing popular support and sympathy. Edward Malone from Athy was among those who abstained from food in Mountjoy with the aim of restoring political status for internees. In response to this crusade, the town of Naas shut down completely on 14 April 1920 in protest at the treatment of the Mountjoy inmates. On the previous evening, the signal operator at Sallins railway station had been accosted by a group of men who threatened to shoot him dead if he attempted to resist or raise the alarm. He was subsequently marched at gunpoint along the line while his workplace was burnt down.[15] Arms raids began in the Naas district. In mid May, a large Volunteer contingent cycled from Naas to Sallins, discharging shots and setting the barracks alight. On the same night, the residence of the excise officer for Naas was raided and official documents were taken away.

Claims for compensation indicate how destructive and costly the IRA's campaign became. Lord Frederick Fitzgerald made a claim of £2592 for the destruction of Maynooth's town hall and courthouse. In May, the RIC's Inspector General sought £300 for the burning of Donadea barracks. Further claims of £640 and £500 were made for damage caused to Leixlip and Sallins barracks respectively.[16] Newbridge and Kildare Town were traditionally regarded as 'safe havens' for loyalists. However, as Con Costello has suggested:

> The effects of some of the subversion of the I.R.A. was visible at the Kildare Quarter Sessions when awards were made to injured parties. At the end of November the authorities were granted compensation of £246 for damage done to a Crossley tender which had run into a trench on the road near Kildare, and £200 was awarded for the malicious burning of a military motor car. A soldier whose personal bicycle was destroyed was given £18 compensation.[17]

The Inspector General's report for June 1920 claimed that numerous attempts had been made by republicans to prevent members of the community from having contact with the police. This tactic was only partly effective.[18] In July, eighteen outrages were reported and all were attributed to the IRA. Further burnings of barracks and courthouses were reported in Athy, Castledermot and Ballymore Eustace. Naas post office was raided, there were regular attacks on mail trains at Sallins and Rathangan, and arms raids intensified. The Inspector General believed that 'the loyal element which is considerable was completely dominated by Sinn Féin'.[19] Kildare's campaign against the forces of 'law and order' involved few murders but much intimidation and arson. Eight policemen resigned in Kildare between January 1919 and the Truce. By the end of July 1920, twelve barracks and six courthouses had been burnt down.[20] Only six police stations were left standing, one-quarter of the number in operation before 1919.[21] As Michael Smyth recalled: 'The only RIC barracks which remained occupied in the battalion area were those at Naas, Newbridge and Hollywood.'[22]

As elsewhere, revolutionary violence intensified during the year before the Truce of 11 July 1921. In August 1920, one of Kildare's most notable ambushes took place at Greenhill's outside Naas. Jim Dunne took part in the operation and provided a detailed account:

About 10:30 p.m., a cycle patrol of four police appeared, riding singly about 20 yards apart, we let the last R.I.C. man pass and closed up about 100 yards behind when the first R.I.C. man, a sergeant neared the end of the main body, he was called on to halt. He said 'All right men.' When Tom and Pat Domican jumped from behind the ditch, he opened fire on them. General firing broke out along the main body of volunteers. Two of them attempted to escape back to barracks and were captured by myself and Sullivan. P. Brady, although unarmed rushed in and disarmed the two police whom we took prisoners. The other two R.I.C. men were killed in the first volley. All the arms and ammunition were collected and given to unarmed volunteers to dump. The whole operation was over in 20 minutes.[23]

The ambush gave rise that night to a series of reprisals. A motor convoy of military personnel arrived in Kill and caused extensive damage to Broughall's public house.[24] Between midnight and 1 a.m., two convoys of 'Black and Tans' numbering around twenty came into Naas from the Curragh. Boushell's tannery was set alight while shots were fired at randomly selected premises.[25] The *Leinster Leader* offered a grim assessment of the incident in an editorial article entitled 'The Naas Outrage'. The author was Michael O'Kelly, a founding member of the Kildare Volunteers and a staunch Sinn Féiner:

> On Thursday night or the early hours of Friday morning they were obliged to undergo an ordeal which although not quite so serious or severe as that experienced in other towns, yet was sufficient to enable them to more readily realise the terrorism practiced in the south and west of Ireland. Bullet marked houses and the burnt ruins of Mr. Boushell's boot and shoe establishment told their own tale when day dawned and people could with some [semblance] of safety venture forth again to inspect the damage and render assistance where required. But who can adequately picture the agonised hours of terror passed by families while volleys crashed in the streets and bullets flew in every direction, amid the sound of breaking glass and all culminating in the lurid glare from the houses given to the flames? Several of these families have since fled for safety elsewhere.[26]

III

If violence was relatively muted in pre-Truce Kildare, it became surprisingly widespread thereafter. Both Kildare TDs voted against the Treaty. When the military conflict commenced, Art O'Connor joined anti-Treaty republicans in Dublin who occupied buildings in the area of Sackville (O'Connell) Street. Domhnall O'Buachalla argued that the mandate he had received from the electorate in 1918 was to 'strive for freedom for the country'. He claimed that, with continued British control of the Treaty ports, Ireland was not an independent nation. He also emphasized the treacherous and oppressive symbolism of the Union flag, recalling a speech he had delivered in Kildare during the 1918 election campaign when a few 'khaki-clad warriors' hoisted a Union flag on the lamp post adjacent to the platform. Ó Buachalla had told the crowd he would not rest until 'every vestige of that rag was cleared out of the country'.[27]

For Jim Dunne and his comrades, plans for further fighting were taking shape before the Treaty was signed. After the Truce, Dunne recalled a visit by Eoin O'Duffy to Naas to 'put the Treaty position before the brigade and battalion officers'. Dunne refused to attend: 'I had made up my mind to take the anti-treaty side and had the whole Kill Company behind me.' While the meeting was in progress, Dunne and his company raided Naas RIC barracks and secured twenty shotguns, ammunition and revolvers. During the Treaty negotiations, Dunne occupied Kill barracks and held it until the outbreak of the Civil War. He remarked that 'at the outbreak of Civil War, I had a column of 36 men in the field from Naas and Kill Companies. We held Kill village and sent a section of men to reinforce the South Dublin Brigade holding Rathcoole.'[28]

In early 1922, opponents of the Treaty found themselves skirmishing on two fronts. In Kildare, Commandant Patrick Brennan took charge of pro-Treaty units. The 'Irregular' or anti-Treaty section, under Robert Brennan, was incorporated into the 1st Eastern Division. One of the first collisions occurred when republicans from the Leixlip column ambushed and burnt a National army ration truck on the road from Maynooth to Leixlip.[29] Meanwhile, the Truce was repeatedly flouted by attacks on British servicemen and police. On 13 February 1922, armed men murdered Lieutenant

Wogan-Browne as he was collecting wages for his regiment in Kildare town.[30] In March, six houses in Kill, belonging to former members of the RIC, were attacked. Huge stones were thrown through the windows. Many of these men had young families, which obviously meant nothing to the antagonists.[31]

Over a period of several months from the end of January, large convoys of British troops travelled through Naas *en route* for Dublin and departure from the country. The evacuation of Naas and New-bridge barracks coincided with that of the Curragh camp. Despite republican exultation at the end of British 'occupation', tradesmen and businessmen around Newbridge, Naas and Kildare town deplored the economic consequences of the military evacuation. The deadline for evacuation was set for 15 May. Costello notes that 'as the time of departure of the British forces approached the civilian residents of the Curragh area, and especially those of Newbridge became more apprehensive, fearing a great loss of employment and a decline in trade'.[32] 1000 garrison employees from the vicinity were made redundant and 3000 were put out of work in North Kildare.[33] J. J. Fitzgerald, a member of Kildare County Council, led a deputa-tion to meet Michael Collins and his colleagues. Collins informed them that the National army would recruit civilian workers when they moved into the Curragh. Recruitment started in August. Mean-while, the artillery barracks in Kildare town became a depot for the new police force, the Civic Guard. As British forces withdrew from depots and barracks, a race had developed to secure occupation. Tom Daly, a Cork IRA veteran, headed a group of dissidents who attempted to seize Kildare barracks, leading to the resignation of Michael Staines, first Commissioner of the Civic Guard.[34]

On 29 June 1922, the day after pro-Treaty forces deploying British artillery had finally bombarded Rory O'Connor's garrison in the Four Courts, three Kildare republicans (Tom Harris, Ó Buachalla and Patrick Mullaney) were arrested. Harris was among the first inmates of an internment camp in Newbridge barracks, opened in August and accommodating 1200 internees. Mean-while, anti-Treaty forces had taken up positions around the village of Blessington, Co. Wicklow. Liam Lynch, the anti-Treaty chief of staff, arrived with other officers at Newbridge railway station and took a number of hackney cars to Kilcullen to meet Commandant William Byrne. Lynch instructed Byrne to take his thirty-five men to Blessington. Ernie O'Malley, Lynch's assistant chief of staff, had appointed Seán Lemass as director of operations and Harry Boland as quartermaster.[35] The anti-Treatyites failed miserably to entrench their forces in Blessington and were soon routed.[36]

Within Kildare, Jim Dunne and his anti-Treaty comrades were busy building up their weaponry. Their most successful operation was an attack on Rathangan barracks: 'We captured 22 rifles, 20 shotguns, 70 bombs and a large supply of ammunition. Ten Free State troops were wounded. We suffered no casualties. We could only use seven riflemen during the attack, as there was no room for more from the only position available.'[37] On 4 August, while attempting to detonate explosives at a bridge near Sallins, Dunne and his column were arrested by the canal bank, but released within a few weeks. At that time he had fifteen men under his command, including nine from the Kilteel section of the Kill Company who were called upon for any big jobs. An ambush at Sallins railway station left one member of the National army dead and two wounded. Dunne co-ordinated many operations on the main road from Dublin to Naas, killing two army personnel and wounding several others. One soldier was shot dead on Dunne's home patch near Kill when a convoy was surrounded by republicans. Two more were injured.

During the last quarter of 1922, the conflict in Kildare remained intense. On 14 October, a private car was taken from a civilian by Leixlip anti-Treatyites at Louisa Bridge. This incident eventually led to the capture of twenty-two IRA men. On 24 October, a convoy of National army soldiers was held up near Castledermot. In December, the *Kildare Observer* reported an incident with momentous consequences:

> A small detachment of troops from the Curragh searching a farm-house at Moore's Bridge, about one and a half miles from the Curragh Camp, found the proprietress in possession of a fully loaded webley revolver. A subsequent search disclosed a dug-out underneath a floor containing 10 men, 10 rifles, a quantity of ammunition, 1 exploder, a cable and about 3 tons of food supplies.[38]

On 18 December, seven captured anti-Treatyites were executed in the 'Glass House', a glass-ceilinged room in the internment camp on the Curragh. These were the first official executions to occur outside Dublin. Durney's research indicates that these men had bought the weapons found in the dug-out from a National army soldier based in Naas barracks. Thomas Behan, who was in the dug-out, was shot dead on 13 December when allegedly attempting to escape.[39]

Republican attacks continued in 1923. Athy barracks was burnt down on 23 January. Six days later Palmerstown House near Naas, the home of the Earl of Mayo, was set on fire in retaliation for the Curragh executions. On 23 February, the home of Senator Sir Bryan Mahon at Mullaghboden, Ballymore-Eustace, was destroyed. Mahon had commanded the 10th (Irish) Division in the Great War. Regardless of the national credentials of men such as Mahon, the destruction of 'big houses' was easily rationalized as a symbolic repudiation of the legacy of British rule in Ireland.

IV

The final proposition under scrutiny is that the continuation of violence and terror after the Treaty had the effect of eroding public support for republicanism. The best available barometer of public opinion is the local press. Following the 1916 Rising, the attitude of the *Leinster Leader* had shifted from horror to guarded sympathy. During the War of Independence it avoided full commitment to the republican cause, though highly critical of the methods employed by the British government and its forces. In 1920, the paper praised the republican courts while denouncing the 'Black and Tans'. Though strongly hostile to partition, it backed the Treaty, in common with all local authorities in Kildare. It viewed the Civil War as a calamity. For the most part, the paper lived up to its motto of 'serving the common good'.[40] Its rival, the *Kildare Observer*, was closely associated with the landed gentry and Protestant community. During the War of Independence, it constantly condemned the IRA's campaign, and was no less scathing in its attitude to the 'Irregulars'. An editorial in December 1922, entitled 'The Dawn of a New Era', maintained that the forces of the Provisional government were not merely attempting to defeat opponents to the Treaty, but also contending with a 'criminal class taking advantage of the situation for the purpose of robbing and looting'.[41]

Inspection of the local press suggests that most civilians passively supported the IRA's military campaign before the Truce, but tolerated the National army's policy of repression during the Civil War. Popular rejection of militant republicanism was confirmed at the general elections held on 16 June 1922 and 27 August 1923. In 1922, the only anti-Treatyite elected for the five-seat constituency of Kildare–Wicklow was Robert Barton, the remaining seats being secured by two Labour candidates, one representative of the Farmers' Party, and one Treatyite. Both Art O'Connor and Donal Ó Buachalla, Kildare's TDs in the First and Second Dáils, were soundly trounced as anti-Treaty 'Pact' candidates. They were again defeated in 1923, when Labour, the Farmers' Party and Cumann na nGaedheal each secured one of Kildare's three seats.[42] Having sustained a bloody and costly struggle against British rule, ordinary citizens craved a lasting peace and demanded an end to terrorism when directed against an Irish state.

NOTES

1. CI, MCR, Jan. 1916, NAL, CO 904/99 (microfilm, TCD).
2. *Kildare Observer*, 6 May 1916, 4.
3. Domhnall Ó Buachalla, MAD, BMH Papers, WS 194.
4. *Leinster Leader*, 4 Jan. 1919, 3.
5. Interview with James Durney, Kildare historian (3 Nov. 2010).
6. James Durney, 'The War of Independence, 1916–21: did County Kildare play its part?' in *Irish Sword*, 27, no. 108 (2010), 217–32 (217).
7. Con Costello, *A Most Delightful Station: The British Army on the Curragh of Kildare, Ireland, 1855–1922* (Cork 1996), p. 326.
8. Michael Smyth, WS 1551.
9. *Leinster Leader*, 11 Jan. 1919, 3.
10. Tom Harris, OMN, UCDA, p17b/120.
11. *Leinster Leader*, 4 Jan. 1919, 3.
12. James Durney, *On the One Road: Political Unrest in Kildare, 1913–1994* (Naas 2001), p. 46.
13. CI, MCR, Feb. 1920, CO 906/112.
14. Terence Dooley, 'IRA activity in Kildare during the War of Independence' in William Nolan and Thomas McGrath (eds), *Kildare: History and*

Society: Interdisciplinary Essays on the History of an Irish County (Dublin 2006), p. 627.

15. *Leinster Leader*, 17 Apr. 1920, 3.

16. *Ibid.* 22 May 1920, 2.

17. Costello, *Most Delightful Station*, p. 324.

18. IG, MCR, June 1920, CO 906/112.

19. *Ibid.*

20. Dooley, 'IRA activity', p. 629.

21. IG, MCR, Aug. 1920, CO 906/112.

22. Michael Smyth, 'Kildare Battalions – 1920', 565, in *Capuchin Annual*, 37 (1970), 564–73 (565).

23. Jim Dunne, WS 1571.

24. *Leinster Leader*, 28 Aug. 1920, 5.

25. Durney, *On the One Road*, p. 66.

26. *Leinster Leader*, 4 Sept. 1920, 2.

27. DÉ, *Official Report: Debate on the Treaty between Great Britain and Ireland*, p. 213 (4 Jan. 1922).

28. Dunne, WS 1571.

29. Padraic O'Farrell, *A History of County Kildare* (Dublin 2003), p. 106.

30. Durney, *On the One Road*, p. 96.

31. *Kildare Observer*, 11 Mar. 1922, 3.

32. Costello, *Most Delightful Station*, p. 335.

33. Durney, *On the One Road*, p. 101.

34. *Ibid.* p. 102.

35. Ernie O'Malley, *The Singing Flame* (Dublin 1978), p. 129.

36. Hopkinson, *Green Against Green*, p. 143.

37. Dunne, WS 1571.

38. Durney, *On the One Road*, pp. 121–2.

39. *Ibid.* p. 127. For a fuller account, see James Durney, *The Civil War in Kildare* (Cork 2011).

40. For more on the *Leinster Leader*'s policy on 'serving the common good', see centennial special supplement (1980), 4.

41. *Kildare Observer*, 16 Dec. 1922, 2.

42. Brian M. Walker (ed.), *Parliamentary Election Results in Ireland, 1918–92* (Dublin and Belfast 1992), pp. 7, 102, 106, 112.

12. Persecuting the Peelers

Brian Hughes

In June 1920, Constable Daniel O'Sullivan resigned from the RIC. O'Sullivan was a 31-year-old native of Limerick and had joined the force in 1908. He had spent his career stationed in Kerry.[1] O'Sullivan had not been shot at, had not been held up and disarmed, had not been ambushed while on patrol, and had not defended his barracks against a late-night attack. He was at home on leave in Abbeyfeale, Co. Limerick, when, at 12.50 a.m. on 11 April 1920, a gang of masked men entered the family home. Finding O'Sullivan, they told him to resign from the RIC or he would be shot. O'Sullivan refused. As the gang attempted to drag O'Sullivan outside, his mother intervened, declaring that she would also have to be shot, then fainting. At this point O'Sullivan agreed to resign and signed a declaration that he would not return to his station 'on account of his mother's health'.[2] O'Sullivan's reason for resignation in the RIC Register is simple: 'Intimidation by SF.'

When Daniel O'Sullivan joined the RIC, it was a respected – even popular – civil police force; the vast majority were Irish Catholics. When O'Sullivan resigned in June 1920, however, the RIC was widely reviled as the most obvious instrument of British oppression in Ireland, the eyes and ears of the enemy, spies and traitors to their country. Terror took many guises during the Irish revolution, and O'Sullivan's case exemplifies a variety of terror quite different to the ambushes and assassinations of popular folklore. Some policemen were shot and killed or wounded, but most were not. More often they were shunned in public, refused supplies and transport, denied information and forced to endure an isolated and dangerous existence. This essay will focus less on violence than the threat of violence: the attempts by the IRA to intimidate and humiliate RIC men, their families, their suppliers and friends.

This form of terror, involving a general boycott regularly enforced by intimidation and aggression, was not new to Ireland. Its most common features were sending anonymous threatening letters, posting proclamations, administering oaths by force, raiding homes and damaging property. These were all prominent aspects of the agrarian agitation that was endemic in rural Ireland throughout the nineteenth and early twentieth centuries. The aim was simple: to induce policemen to resign and make it impossible for those who remained to carry out their duty. The first signs of a movement aimed directly against the police were noted by the Inspector General in June 1917: 'The attitude of the Sinn Feiners towards the police has also undergone a change. They will now scarcely salute them and especially if two or three of them are together.'[3] Next month, it was reported that 'a spirit of hostility towards the Police has arisen, particularly in the provinces of Connaught and Munster where the defiant attitude of the people towards law and authority has made the duties of the police extremely difficult'. County Inspectors in Clare, Galway and Tipperary all noted a hostile reception from 'Sinn Feiners'.[4] In October, the County Inspector for Clare reported that 'the people appear to regard the police as their enemies and have ceased all friendly intercourse with them. Shops continue to supply provisions but in many cases they would prefer that the police did not come to them. No opportunity is lost to try and bring discredit on the Force.'[5]

Despite the enmity observed in certain southern and western counties, actual attacks or attempts to threaten police remained rare and much of the country continued in a relatively peaceful state. Levels of activity and hostility varied and fluctuated, with the Inspector General optimistically reporting a general improvement in the public attitude towards the police on a number of occasions in 1917 and 1918.[6] In 1918, attempts were made to deprive the RIC of food, turf and transport in some small rural communities in Clare, Galway and Cork. It is not surprising that the counties most affected at this early stage had a persistent tradition of agrarian agitation and violence. Their inhabitants were very familiar with the concept of boycotting and ostracism. Old methods were applied to a new cause. Interestingly, the RIC believed that much of the emphasis behind this early boycotting came from local clergymen.[7] Away from these 'disturbed areas', however, the police suffered relatively little. Early boycotting was confined to local communities and depended on local initiative for its success. Yet in 1917, as Peter Hart has pointed out: 'For the first time since the 1880s, violence, or the threat of violence, became a constant feature of regular police work. ... No longer could constables walk their districts without fear of challenge.'[8]

Just after Constables McDonnell and O'Connell were killed in Soloheadbeg on 21 January 1919, the County Inspector reported: 'There was no improvement in the attitude of the people towards the R.I.C. who, in the disaffected counties, are treated with bitter hostility and are boycotted in various ways.'[9] In March 1919, the Sinn Féin TD for Mid Tipperary (Séamus Aloysius Bourke) reportedly declared that 'the way to deal with the police was not to shoot them ... but to make their life unbearable, treat them as outcasts of society, as we cannot be in any place that some of these vipers are not in our midst'.[10] Other speakers claimed that the RIC were the 'greatest enemies' of Ireland, the last great obstacle in the way of Irish freedom, 'spies', 'traitors' and worse.[11] The public were urged not to acknowledge the RIC and to avoid saluting them in the street. Traders were asked not to sell them goods and the public were even asked not to sit beside them at Mass. Boycotting of the RIC grew slowly and sporadically throughout 1919, the most affected counties being Clare, Galway, Tipperary and Cork. The County Inspector for Dublin summed up the situation in many areas:

> There is no boycotting but intimidation in a great way exists owing to the malign influences of Sinn Fein. ... People are afraid to offend the extremists and comply with their wishes fearing injury if they did not do so. Also there is no doubt a general scheme on the part of Sinn Fein to intimidate and cow the police to prevent them from doing their duty and to deter young men from joining the Police.[12]

As the year continued a shift in relations with the public and serious difficulties in obtaining information became noticeable, particularly in Kerry and Limerick. By the turn of 1920, police in Donegal, Sligo, Roscommon and Longford were also remarking on an atmosphere of increased hostility. Reports indicate a dramatic surge in crime against the police in the first half of 1920 with the number of reported incidents peaking in July. In a single week in that month, there were 78 outrages aimed directly against the police, including 6 threats to policemen and 29 to their suppliers and tradesmen. In March 1920, the RIC began to compile statistics and abstracts of attacks against the police, including their families, candidates for the force, pensioners, tradesmen and suppliers, and magistrates.[13] These reports give a vivid picture of the experience of the individuals who became victims of the IRA campaign. They help recreate a more common experience of the revolution: one where the consequences of association with the RIC were made clear by threatening letters and 'proclamations', compellingly reinforced by shootings, assaults and destruction of property.

The most common method of threatening a policeman was an age-old device: the threatening letter. Anonymous death threats were posted – with little or no risk to the sender – usually with a view to forcing the recipient's resignation. Letters varied in length and detail, but invariably threatened death or warned of impending violence. Some letters contained drawings, often of a coffin or a revolver.[14] Letters sometimes made reference to recent acts of violence: the recipient was to meet the same fate as colleagues killed by the IRA. A letter received by a sergeant in Brosna, Co. Kerry, contained a list of RIC men who had been killed or wounded by 'our brother Volunteers during the week'.[15] A common theme that emerges in a number of the letters reported to the RIC is revenge for the Lord Mayor of Cork, Tomás MacCurtain, murdered in March 1920, reputedly by members of the RIC.[16] Policemen faced raids on their houses when they were forced, often at gunpoint, to agree to leave the force. These raids usually took place when a member was at home on leave and away from the comparative protection of his barracks. Such raids had the additional advantage of intimidating family members, as in the case of Daniel O'Sullivan. This was also a method favoured by the IRA to dissuade men whom they believed had decided to join the force. Raids of this nature met with mixed results and success often depended on the individual target. For every man who was compelled to resign there was another who brushed off the threat and reported back to his barracks for duty.[17]

RIC members and candidates were often targeted through their families. Parents who had sons in the RIC were subjected to threats of violence – usually by letter or armed raid – unless they brought their sons home from the force. The idea of writing to parents of policemen to induce them to resign and take up a job in civil life had been advocated in 1919. Initially, this strategy was ineffectual; but, by 1920, parents were targeted with much greater belligerence, and ultimately more success. This more aggressive approach in part stemmed from necessity. By mid 1920, those men who were going to be easily intimidated out of their jobs had left. Those who remained were men who had decided to 'stick it out' in the force for the duration, or recruits who had joined in 1919 and 1920. The minority of recent recruits who had enlisted in Ireland were well aware of the perils of service in the RIC, and were unlikely to resign on the basis of a nasty letter or warning.

Between 1919 and 1921, the RIC Registers record at least 105 resignations from the force as a direct result of intimidation and boycotting of – or pressure from – wives, parents and family. Sixty-one of these men had joined the force after January 1920.[18] Hugh Cunniffe from Co. Roscommon joined the RIC on 5 April 1920. On 9 April, a group of masked and armed men entered the house of Cunniffe's 65-year-old father and made him swear he would bring his son home. Cunniffe resigned on 11 April, having spent less than a week in the Phoenix Park Depot.[19] Most of the men who joined in 1920, and resigned under similar circumstances, were still in training and had not yet been transferred to a station. A policeman could feel assured that he was able to protect his own person, and may have felt safe in the training depot or armed in a heavily fortified barracks; but he could do nothing to protect his family who, due to RIC regulations, were unlikely to be living in the same county. Peter Hart has described how defensive measures introduced to barracks in late 1919 – steel shutters, sandbags, barbed wire – 'did nothing to offset their occupants' sense of helplessness'.[20] Their helplessness in protecting family members was even more acute.

Boycotting and intimidation brought much hardship and difficulty to the wives and children of serving members of the RIC.

As the County Inspector for Galway West Riding reported: 'Their wives are miserable, and their children suffer in schools, and nobody cares.'[21] Policemen's relatives endured not only humiliation and social exclusion, but also direct intimidation. Threatening letters were sent directly to the wives of policemen. These letters usually warned the wife to force her husband to resign or leave the locality. The accommodation of many RIC families was also targeted, wives and children being put out of lodgings while furniture and other possessions were burned. Landlords received letters warning them not to let property to police and their families or to evict those already lodged. It was initially deemed safe to allow police families to live in vacated barracks.

However, in December 1919, the family of a sergeant in Clare was turned out of a vacated hut and refused shelter in neighbouring houses.[22] There were several similar incidents over the following eighteen months. Mrs Donnellan, an RIC widow, received the following letter in April 1920 from self-styled 'Competent Military Authority' in Kerry, following the IRA's eviction of a Constable Murphy from the local barracks: 'Mrs Donnellan. The rumour has it that Mrs Murphy is to reside in your home. If so your house will be burned. We regret this action, but we must comply with a general order.' Mrs Murphy went to reside with the wife of another policeman, Mrs Sullivan, who subsequently also received a threatening letter. Mrs Sullivan's house was then raided and both women were told to leave the area. When they complained to the local priest, 'he said he could do nothing, that they were strangers and must go'.[23] A few days later Mrs Sullivan and her children were forcibly removed from her house. When she sought refuge in the local post office 'the raiders informed her she would not be allowed to remain in the parish another night and she was forced to cycle to Castleisland, 'wet through and in deplorable condition', to seek shelter.[24] Most did not suffer the horrific treatment experienced by Mrs Sullivan, but other RIC families suffered severely from the retailers' boycott. James Goulden, son of an RIC man, has described conditions for his family around Easter 1920: 'For some time before we had found difficulty in getting milk and had to use condensed milk.' Even the fear that necessities would be denied could cause huge strain, though

Goulden noted that 'on occasions on which any child was ill we always managed to get supplies'.[25] For its part, GHQ was willing to allow wives and children be supplied with food and milk.[26]

The most common victims of IRA intimidation were those who provided services to the RIC – labour, supplies and information. From 16 March 1920 to the 'cessation of hostilities' on 11 July 1921, there were 160 reported cases of threats to policemen. For the same period there were about 500 threats against tradesmen and suppliers. In a rural community where everybody knew everybody and an embattled police force could not adequately protect them, those considered 'friendly' to the RIC were highly susceptible to violence, and many had no reason to doubt the validity of threats. If the IRA could convince the community to deny the RIC transport, necessities and information, as well as social interaction, they would effectively cease to function. For example, the RIC normally relied on privately owned carts and motor vehicles to convey everything from turf to prisoners. The owners of carts and cars used by the police were regularly threatened, some had their carts destroyed, and a motor car hired by the police in Leitrim had its wheels removed.[27] Lack of information and willing witnesses inhibited the arrest and prosecution of offenders. Those who cut turf for the RIC, or provided them with milk, butter, labour and other necessities, were sent threatening letters; notices were posted up in towns warning the public of the consequences of dealing with 'the enemy'. The punishment for women who kept company or were friendly with Crown forces was often to have their hair cut off, a grim visual reminder of the consequences of transgression.[28]

Though de Valera and Sinn Féin had long advocated a non-violent police boycott, Dáil Éireann did not endorse 'social ostracism' of the RIC until 10 April 1919.[29] An official order from GHQ followed on 4 June 1920:

> Volunteers shall have no intercourse with the R.I.C., and shall stimulate and support in every [way] the boycott of this force ordered by the Dail. Those persons who associate with the R.I.C. shall be subjected to the same boycott, and the fact of their association with and tolerance of this infamous force shall be kept in public in every possible way. Definite lists of such persons in the area of

his command, shall be prepared and retained by each Company Battalion and Brigade Commander.'[30]

It was up to individual companies of Volunteers to implement the boycott and ensure others did likewise. This, however, had always been the case. Local boycotts against the RIC had waxed and waned ever since 1917, and the new policy did little more than attempt to centralize and control local practice.

How effective was the campaign of persecution against the police? This depended to a large extent on the willingness of local IRA members to carry out boycotting and intimidation in a zealous and energetic way, and their ability to whip up fear of violence and to maintain it. Financial concerns were often paramount. Many had joined the RIC in the hope of a steady, if not vast, income when other prospects were limited. Men who resigned from the force would often be left without an alternative livelihood. There was no guarantee that these men would be accepted back into their home communities. David Neligan, a DMP detective who worked for IRA Intelligence, wrote that 'no effort was made by anybody to provide an alternative lifestyle. ... The result was that they could see nothing ahead but starvation. So literally they stuck to their guns and fought their own countrymen.'[31] This logic must have convinced many men to tough it out for the duration of the conflict, or at least until they could retire with a pension. Cecil King's father, a member of the RIC in Sligo, was one of five brothers from a poor family. King recalled that 'the I.R.A. made repeated overtures to my father to resign from the force, but he refused, preferring fear of death by bullet to the alternative – a life of abject penury and a brand of cowardice'.[32] Women who worked for the RIC as barrack servants were regularly threatened, often successfully, in a bid to force them to leave their employment. Some women, however, simply refused to resign. The financial implications of losing their employment were too great. In Adare, Co. Limerick, the house of a barrack servant was entered by two armed and masked men who attempted to force her to leave her employment. This she refused as 'it was her sole means of earning a livelihood and had six children to support'. No harm was done to her by the raiders.[33] On the other hand, a majority of Justices of the Peace were easily induced to resign their commissions. Theirs was an unpaid post.

By refusing to work for or trade with the RIC, members of the community would inevitably suffer a loss of income. Conversely, IRA orders stated that those who continued to serve the RIC would be subject to a boycott themselves, with lists of persons to be boycotted posted in towns. Therefore, where political affiliation did not discourage trade with police, the fear of personal injury had to outweigh potential economic loss. In Donaghmore, Co. Cork, a notice was posted on the church gate stating that, as Philip and Thomas Barrett continued to trade with 'Enemy forces', anyone seen to be interacting with them would be 'shot at sight'. The following month a notice was posted claiming that, as the Barrett brothers had 'apologised to the Irish Republican Government', the previous proclamation against them was withdrawn.[34] According to Donal O'Sullivan, most people were willing to serve RIC members, if clandestinely, as they were considered good customers.[35] In many localities, policemen would take for themselves what was needed and leave payment behind, though this consumed considerable time and manpower for an already stretched force.

Eventually, some traders decided that it was time to end the boycott. Already, in January 1920, the County Inspector for Roscommon had commented 'that the majority of the people are not in favour of the criminal campaign and realise it is not good for them to boycott or display hostility to the Crown Forces'.[36] In August, at a meeting of traders in Castlerea, it was decided to lift the police boycott: 'The Volunteers are strongly opposed to the decision of the traders' meeting.'[37] Thomas Crawley, a Volunteer from Roscommon, recalled that the boycott was not very effective in Castlerea, as the traders had continued to supply the RIC under the pretence that the goods had been commandeered.[38] Reports noted that boycotts were collapsing around the country by the end of 1920, at least in part for the same reasons seen in Castlerea.[39] Where the IRA was unable to maintain the pressure against suppliers, many seem to have been willing to return to supplying the police. Additionally, as pointed out by W. J. Lowe, reprisals by Crown Forces may have persuaded traders to abandon boycotting in order to protect their property from damage.[40]

Some accounts by IRA men indicate that the boycott against

the RIC could have a negative effect. According to Martin Fallon, a Roscommon Volunteer:

> The effects of this boycott were a doubtful gain. While it did help to drive a wedge between the R.I.C. and the people, very few of them resigned as a result. Instead, it seemed to make them stubborn and arrogant and, in this way, I am afraid we antagonised some of them who would be good friends of ours. We forgot they were Irishmen, and there is an old saying that you can lead an Irishman, but you can't drive him.[41]

Similarly, Patrick Cassidy from Mayo reflected that 'we did not succeed in making any substantial number of the police resign; rather, I think the boycott had the opposite effect and only hardened them and made them sullen and arrogant towards the people'. Cassidy did, however, add that the 'deep void' created between police and public was very useful for what was to follow later.[42] Clearly, some RIC men who may have had political sympathies with the rebels were turned away by the tactics employed against them, including men who might have been useful. As Seán Gibbons noted: 'I feel now we could have made more use of the Royal Irish Constabulary, but it was too difficult to break the unapproachability that had grown up around them and, further, we regarded them as enemies.'[43]

W. J. Lowe has concluded that, 'like the burning of vacant police stations, by 1921 the work of intimidation had been largely accomplished'.[44] The outrage statistics indicate a large drop in the number of cases of intimidation in December 1920 and January 1921. These figures began to steadily rise again in the months before the Truce, but never reached the peak of spring 1920. Does this mean that the campaign of intimidation had been a success and was no longer necessary? Police reports indicate otherwise. In January and February 1921, County Inspectors across the country were reporting that while there was still much violence and unrest, relations between the police and public were improving and there was a greater willingness to come forward with information in certain areas. The RIC also believed that the majority of civilians had become sick of the present state of the country and desired peace.[45] This would suggest that in many areas the attempts to effectively neutralize the RIC by boycotting and intimidation had either failed or began to wane. The increased threat

of Crown reprisals was an important element, the effectiveness of the
campaign against the RIC often depending on which fear was greater
– fear of the IRA or the 'Tans'. Nor should one neglect the force of
loyalty to the Crown and revulsion towards the Republican campaign, from both policemen and civilians, in restricting the impact
of intimidation. Such a campaign was extremely difficult to maintain
indefinitely: by 1921, war-weariness, affecting both combatants and
civilians, and an increasingly entrenched enemy had greatly reduced
the effectiveness of boycotting and intimidation. Even more ruthless
techniques of terror were now required.

The persecution of 'peelers' during the Irish revolution had much
in common with nineteenth-century agrarian agitation. It was comprised mainly of low-level, local activity. It was sporadic in intensity
and effectiveness. While there was some belated central direction, it
depended for its impetus on local leadership. Results were mixed.
By 1921, an important shift can be seen. With increasing frequency,
those suspected of informing the enemy were taken from their
homes, shot dead and labelled with messages such as 'Spies and
Informers Beware IRA'. These cards provided a chilling substitute
for the traditional threatening letters and notices. Anything that
might lead to such a fate was to be avoided. This, perhaps, was a
more effective means of keeping the public in line than the psychological warfare of 1920.

NOTES

1. RIC, General Personnel Register, NAL, HO 184/33 (microfilm, Dublin
City Archives).

2. RIC, Weekly Summaries of Outrages against the Police and Returns
of Recruitment, Retirement and Dismissal, June 1920, NAL, CO 904/148
(microfilm, TCD).

3. IG, MCR, June 1917, CO 904/103.

4. *Ibid.* July 1917.

5. CI, MCR, Clare, Oct. 1917, CO 904/104.

6. IG, MCR, Dec. 1917, June, Sept. 1918, CO 904/104–6.

7. CI, MCR, Galway East Riding, June 1918; IG, MCR, Dec. 1918, CO
904/106–7.

8. Peter Hart, *The I.R.A. and Its Enemies: Violence and Community in Cork, 1916–1923* (Oxford 1998), p. 54.

9. IG, MCR, Jan. 1919, CO 904/108.

10. IG, MCR, Mar. 1919, CO 904/108.

11. IG and CI, MCRs, Jan.–Aug. 1919, CO 904/108–9.

12. CI, MCR, Dublin, Jan. 1919, CO 904/108.

13. Weekly Summaries, CO 904/148–50.

14. *Ibid.*

15. Weekly Summaries, May 1920, CO 904/148.

16. Weekly Summaries, Apr. 1920, CO 904/148.

17. For successful and failed raids respectively, see reports by Constables Calnan and Drury, in Weekly Summaries, July, Aug. 1920, CO 904/149.

18. RIC Registers, HO 184/33–7. For more detailed statistics and analysis of RIC resignations, see David Fitzpatrick, *Politics and Irish Life, 1913–1921: Provincial Experience of War and Revolution* (Cork 1998; 1st edn 1977), pp. 34–9.

19. RIC Register, HO 184/36; Weekly Summaries, Apr. 1920, CO 904/148.

20. Hart, *The I.R.A. and Its Enemies*, p. 64.

21. CI, MCR, Galway W. R., Aug. 1920, CO 904/112.

22. W. J. Lowe, 'The war against the R.I.C., 1919–21', *Éire-Ireland*, 37, nos. 3–4 (2002), 79–117 (84); CI, MCR, Kerry, Apr. 1920, CO 904/111.

23. Weekly Summaries, Jun. 1920, CO 904/148.

24. *Ibid.*

25. J. R. W. Goulden, MAD, BMH Papers, WS 1340.

26. Response to query from IRA officer, Dingle, Co. Kerry, NLI, P911/AO495 (microfilm).

27. Weekly Summaries, Apr. 1920, CO 904/148.

28. Weekly Summaries, CO 904/148–9.

29. A circular from Diarmuid O'Hegarty stated that as 'persons who, having been adjudged guilty of treason to their country', the RIC were 'unworthy to enjoy any of the privileges or comforts which arise from cordial relations with the public': Arthur Mitchell, *Revolutionary Government in Ireland: Dáil Éireann, 1919–22* (Dublin 1995), p. 69.

30. UCDA, Mulcahy Papers, P7/A/45.

31. David Neligan, *The Spy in the Castle* (London 1968), pp. 80–1.

32. Elizabeth Malcolm, *The Irish Policeman, 1822–1922: A Life* (Dublin 2006), p. 227.

33. Weekly Summaries, May 1920, CO 904/148.

34. Weekly Summaries, Mar. 1920, CO 904/148.

35. Donal O'Sullivan, *The Irish Constabularies, 1822–1922: A Century of Policing in Ireland* (Dingle 1999), pp. 313–14.

36. CI, MCR, Roscommon, Jan. 1920, CO 904/114.

37. *IT*, 18 Aug. 1920.

38. Thomas Crawley, WS 718.

39. IG and CI, MCRs, Oct.–Dec. 1920, CO 904/113.

40. Lowe, 'War', p. 105.

41. Martin Fallon, WS 1121.

42. Patrick Cassidy, WS 1017.

43. Sean Gibbons, WS 927.

44. Lowe, 'War', p. 101.

45. IG and CI, MCRS, CO 904/113–14.

13. Terror Confined? Prison Violence in Ireland, 1919–1921

Justin Dolan Stover

In June 1920, the governor of Belfast prison responded to a questionnaire regarding the extent to which warders and prison officers had suffered, physically and mentally, under the stress of guarding Irish political prisoners. Major Edward Shewell, an army veteran with ten years' experience in the prison service, painted a sombre picture in his response to the General Prisons Board (GPB) in Dublin Castle:

> During the last three years, an entirely new element has been introduced into the Irish Prisons Service by the committal of a large number of men who (in furtherance of their desire to establish an independent Irish Republic) are acting on a concerted plan to make His Majesty's Government in Ireland impossible. Having been committed to prison the only public officials against whom their efforts can be directed become the Governors and Staff of H.M. Prisons.[1]

What governors, warders and medical officers encountered between 1919 and 1921 was much more than agitation for political status or improved treatment – it was a campaign of systematic, persistent and violent terror aimed against the Irish prison system as a symbol of British rule. Though insulated from the guerrilla warfare that affected much of Ireland during this period, prisons were, in Seán McConville's phrase, 'theatres of war'.[2] As Piaras Béaslaí testified, the prison experience was capable of evoking 'deeper emotions than a thrilling narrative of dangerous exploits of war'.[3] This was due, in part, to the continuous state of rebellion in Irish prisons, creating an environment of incessant physical and psychological terror. Imprisonment therefore failed in its objective of curbing

revolutionary violence. This chapter will explore Irish prisons as
theatres of republican terror during the Anglo–Irish War. In tribute
to the late Peter Hart, it will investigate themes close to his interests:
the varieties of revolutionary violence, the motives and actions of
its perpetrators, and the resultant camaraderie. The record testifies
to the indomitable temperament of many Irish revolutionary prisoners, and the boldness with which they pursued their campaign of
terror against the prison service.

While some republicans cited the creation of Dáil Éireann in
moral justification of revolutionary violence, prior to 1919 many
republican prisoners had felt no need for any official legitimation
when undertaking prison protests.[4] These involved co-ordinated
disruptions and organized 'outbreaks', 'smash-ups', riots, or (the
term preferred by the GPB) *émeutes*. General agitation amongst prisoners for political classification and ameliorative treatment developed after the Easter Rising in both convict prisons and internment
camps, persisting throughout 1917. This process culminated in an
organized outbreak at Mountjoy prison in late September 1917,
following a series of disruptions. Prisoners convicted of breaching
various regulations under the Defence of the Realm Act (DORA)
broke up their cells and remained disruptive for several days.[5]
This was followed by a prolonged hunger strike resulting in the
forcible feeding of about forty prisoners. The prisoners gave up
hunger-striking after gaining certain concessions, but not before
inexperience and panic by the medical staff had claimed the life of
Thomas Ashe.[6]

Ashe's death prompted the formulation of a charter of rights
and privileges for political prisoners in Ireland.[7] This was balanced by reintroduction of the Prisoners (Temporary Discharge for
Ill-Health) Act, 1913, commonly known as the 'Cat and Mouse
Act'.[8] Originally devised to cope with hunger-striking suffragettes,
this statute allowed prisoners to voluntarily abstain from food until
death seemed imminent. At that point they were to be released,
allowed to recuperate, then re-arrested to serve out the remainder
of their sentences.

Prison populations in Ireland swelled in 1918 with the widespread
implementation of DORA Regulation 9AA, which prohibited the

wearing of military-style uniforms, drilling and unlawful assembly.[9] As B. Rudden complained from Belfast prison in late October: 'There are men here doing twelve months for answering their name in Irish.'[10] Men were transferred from other prisons throughout Ireland to Belfast in order to consolidate the 'political' offenders.[11] As another prisoner observed: 'They are shifting the prisoners from every Prison in Ireland on to Belfast. I believe it will be the only Political Prison in Ireland. That is some crowd.'[12] The expansion of Belfast's population of political prisoners, peaking in autumn 1918, may be illustrated in the form of a chart:

POLITICAL INMATES IN BELFAST PRISON,
1 MAY–31 DECEMBER 1918[13]

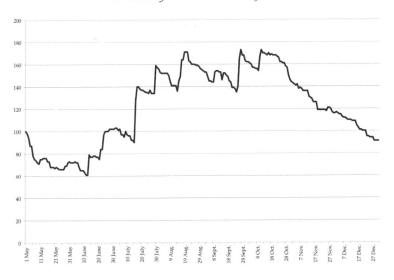

Imprisonment in connection with the Irish independence movement created pride among the inmates, promoted camaraderie and strengthened the spirit of resistance. Writing to his mother in August 1918, Kevin O'Higgins, the future Minister for Home Affairs, explained this outlook:

> Remember <u>no</u> sacrifice counts whether a man does his duty to his country – to be persecuted for doing so is the purest pleasure, for the past three months I have been absolutely content and will be

so for the next two. If it were years instead of months it would
be the same. ... The clan Ó h-Uigín takes its stand against the
government![14]

A relaxed prison atmosphere, coupled with a growing and
hostile political population, contributed to two violent outbreaks
in Belfast prison in 1918. The first occurred in late June, following
a perceived deterioration in the quality of food and efforts by the
prison staff to affix shutters to cells so as to prevent prisoners from
shouting to passers-by on the Crumlin Road. Prisoners removed the
windows and smashed them in protest, whereupon some were sent
to basement cells.[15] They again shattered the windows of their cells,
broke the spy-holes of their cell doors, destroyed dividing walls and
barricaded themselves behind any available furniture. 'Altogether
the din was considerable', recounted O'Higgins. 'Actuated by rage
and disgust at the treatment I had received, I was determined to do
as much damage as possible.'[16]

Warders were supplemented on this occasion by about fifty
policemen, who forcibly handcuffed and removed offenders to
basement cells. Several prisoners received blows to the head, had
their neckties twisted around their necks, or were dragged down
the stairs.[17] Once corralled, the prisoners remained handcuffed
and in discomfort. 'Calls of nature' were ignored by warders. John
McKenna only managed to relieve himself after a prolonged struggle
with buttons and undergarments: 'I managed eventually however to
tear down my pants, and then utilized a corner of my cell as a w.c.
for the remainder of the night; and the cell, as a result, was in a
pretty condition in the morning – quite a considerable lake being in
one part of the floor.'[18]

The second outbreak of violence was even more severe. Earlier
disputes over prison diet, and the prisoner commandant's decision
not to accept outside parcels of food, resulted in fifty-five prisoners
shedding (on average) more than one stone over a four-to-six week
period.[19] Coupled with the threat of 'Spanish flu' from July through
December, this induced prison officers to relax discipline in order
to aid recovery and prevent further infections. Cells were unlocked
day and night, allowing freedom of movement and association,
and a special diet was provided.[20] These ameliorations facilitated

further collusion to subvert the prison system, with encouragement from Sinn Féin's success in the 1918 general election. J. McCree considered that the electoral victory vindicated the prisoners' demand for political recognition: 'If they try to keep us any longer we will make it hot for them', he wrote to his parents.[21] Another Belfast prisoner, Timothy Brestone, also saw the election as pivotal: 'I think we are near the end of our holiday, and I dare say the beginning of our war.'[22]

On 23 December, prisoners barricaded the ends of three wards with bed planks and tables removed from cells, and doors and gratings wrenched from walls. The prisoners had taken up defensive positions on the first and second floors for two purposes: first, to prevent the reinstatement of normal prison discipline as it had existed prior to the influenza outbreak;[23] second, to protect their comrade John Doran, who had been 'rescued' from the company of 'ordinary criminals' in the adjacent wing.[24] Between thirty and forty prisoners climbed atop the roof of the laundry building, stripped roofing slates and displayed a menacing attitude,[25] 'shouting, singing, speechmaking and waving a Sinn Féin flag'. The prisoners were opposed by a crowd, 'so dense as to impede the progress of Tramway cars', who had gathered on the Crumlin Road and waved Union flags.[26] John Hassett observed that 'the Orange crowd of Belfast are thoroughly sick of us. They even went so far as to beat one of our fellows on the streets yesterday after he was released.'[27] Following the outbreak, it was reported that between twenty and forty nationalists, after visiting some DORA prisoners, had stood outside the prison singing 'Wrap the green flag round me'. One passer-by could scarcely articulate his indignation: 'Go on, you bloody Sinn Féin bastards.' In an effort to prevent bloodshed (and the expected loss of twenty lives should the prisoners have to be physically dislodged), Edward Shortt as Chief Secretary allowed the prisoners the privileges they had held prior to the influenza outbreak.[28] This decision was taken in the absence of Lord French, the Viceroy. Doran was granted political status, which, as French later explained, was sanctioned 'as a purely exceptional measure'.[29] An official estimate stated that £3000 would be required to repair the damage done to Belfast prison over Christmas 1918.[30]

By 1919 it had become clear to prison authorities in Ireland
that efforts to curtail disorder, or enforce discipline, only embold-
ened republican prisoners. These problems were recognized at the
highest levels of administration. Horatio J. Chippendall, the governor of Maryborough prison, noted that political prisoners were
organized and no longer accepted their situation. With few exceptions, they were 'filled with a dangerous, sullen antagonistic disposition towards Crown Officials which may at any time be fired into
open conflict without any provocation. ... What in June last [1918]
appeared to be pronounced dislike has now developed into hatred
which spreads to fresh committals.'[31] Max Green, chairman of the
GPB, concurred: 'They claim to be soldiers of the Irish Republic
taken prisoners of war and that they are illegally and unlawfully
retained in a Civil Prison. ... They look on this as a question of
principle and are determined to fight for it.'[32] The precedents of disorder in Irish prisons throughout 1917–18 strengthened the resolve
of many republican prisoners. 'Death fighting for Ireland's freedom
as they put it, they court,' remarked Chippendall, 'to die a martyr
being apparently their ambition.'[33]

Violence committed within Irish prisons during the Anglo–
Irish War created a sense of solidarity amongst prisoners, based
on loyalty to the Irish republic, which united those who fought in
its name. Numerous episodes between 1919 and 1921 exemplify
cohesion, co-operation and camaraderie among prisoners, in some
ways reflecting the wider terror campaign. Prolonged disturbances
at Cork, Galway, Limerick and Mountjoy prisons began almost
simultaneously in January 1919, though it is not clear that these
were co-ordinated in advance by the Volunteer executive. A secret
directive from Volunteer GHQ, however, retrospectively sanctioned
the disturbances, testifying to the success of previous disruptions
despite the decentralized leadership of the prisoners. A copy of the
order was discovered in a loaf of bread, left at the gate of Maryborough prison, by a Miss Walsh:[34]

> Every Irish Volunteer at present in jail as the result of any
> activity connected with the movement is instructed to immedi-
> ately demand and strike for treatment as a political prisoner. The
> strike should take the form of refusal to work, to wear the prison

garb, to obey any prison regulation whatever, generally subvert prison discipline.[35]

A minor outbreak in Cork on 1 January involving four prisoners who had been denied political status – John Sharry, Humphrey O'Sullivan, Thomas Reidy and Edward Moynihan – inspired sympathy and support among their comrades. On 22 January, eighteen DORA prisoners of the political class destroyed their cells and caused general uproar after being removed from the exercise yard. The men explained to the Cork governor that their behaviour was 'a protest against certain of their number whom they allege should not be treated as criminals'.[36] The next day the outbreak had grown to include thirty-four prisoners of both political and non-political classes. As punishment for their involvement, ameliorations were suspended in all cases, attendance at Mass was denied in the absence of a written undertaking to behave, and men were confined to their cells. Despite corrective measures, the outbreak continued to grow and by 17 February forty-one prisoners had joined in. As outside Belfast prison in the previous year, demonstrators gathered outside Cork prison after word of the disturbance was leaked by *The Cork Examiner*. Warders entering and leaving the prison required police protection from the incensed crowd, constantly primed by the *Irish Independent* since early February.[37] Prolonged inactivity, restraint, thrashing, shouting and refusal to bathe caused the men's bodies to deteriorate at an accelerated rate.[38] Governor King was informed that the prisoners wished to 'see it out', and that men were 'prepared to meet death rather than submit'.[39]

By 17 April, there were forty-six belligerents in Cork prison. Philip Lennon, a spokesman for the prisoners, insisted a few weeks later that ameliorations must be granted before order could be restored.[40] Six more political-class prisoners joined the revolt on 16 May, forfeiting their privileges in support of their comrades and raising the number of offenders to about fifty-seven. This state of affairs persisted until September, when, despite instructions from Volunteer headquarters, twenty-six prisoners resorted to hunger strikes, including prominent IRA officers such as Gearóid O'Sullivan and Maurice Crowe. Twenty more prisoners joined the hunger strikers shortly thereafter, causing great alarm in government circles.

Unable to resolve the issue without resorting to violence or forcible feeding, the twenty-six initial hunger strikers – all untried or
convicted by courts martial – were removed to Mountjoy. The
remaining twenty took food shortly thereafter, and order returned
to Cork prison on 30 September.

An even more noteworthy example of the solidarity engendered
by violence is the outbreak at Mountjoy in early October 1919.
Forty-four prisoners of various ages, sentences, backgrounds and
native counties took part in what was described by Mountjoy's governor, Charles Munro, as 'an evidently pre-concerted and organized
outbreak of cell-wrecking'.[41] This disturbance was the outcome of
a recent campaign for political treatment, intensified by the influx
of the twenty-six prisoners from Cork. It is interesting to note that,
in this instance, violence was not restricted to seasoned inmates, a
point which may be illustrated in the form of a chart (see opposite).

Recently committed inmates were as likely to support their
comrades in violence as those with longer prison experience. Furthermore, there is no evidence of reluctance to fight by those nearing
release: several men with less than a month remaining on their sentences participated in the outbreak. These included Patrick Griffin
and Bryan Shanahan, due for release on the morning of 6 October.[43]

Though the timing and location of violence was varied and
unpredictable, most damage was caused by synchronized outbreaks. That in Mountjoy on 6 October 1919 not only destroyed
much of the prison, but resulted in injury for several warders who
faced a barrage of bricks and pieces of woodwork while attempting
to dismantle barricades. Prisoners, some armed with iron bars, 'sav-
agely attacked the warders' once the barricades had been breached.
Michael O'Hehir, an experienced inmate, wielded two bricks in
defence of his cell. When tackled by two warders and deprived of
his weapons, he 'fought furiously with his fists' and barked that
Governor Munro would 'suffer in … turn like others'. Extracts
from the medical officer's journal indicate the extent of warders'
injuries. Contusions to the head, arms and legs were most common,
all warders sustaining abrasions to the hands. Warder Perry suffered a broken tooth, and the unfortunate Clerk Warder Gannon
received a debilitating blow to the testicles.[44] 'Dirty protests'

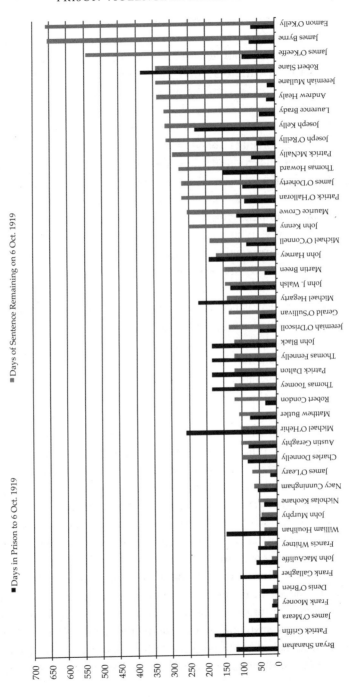

NUMBER OF DAYS SERVED BY MOUNTJOY PRISON RIOTERS, OCTOBER 1919[2]

■ Days in Prison to 6 Oct. 1919   ■ Days of Sentence Remaining on 6 Oct. 1919

extended beyond the taboo zones of the male body, anticipating
the tactics of a later generation of 'freedom fighters' in Northern
Ireland. Patrick Gaffney emptied the contents of his chamber-pot
over Warder Griffith at Belfast in early March 1919. The volume in
the pot was so great that it spilled on to Warder Brophy.[45] Thomas
Fitzpatrick surpassed this feat a few weeks later, covering or spat-
tering two warders and two constables with what was delicately
described in reports as 'nuisance'.[46]

Between 1919 and 1921, the focus of prison violence and disorder shifted from attacks against the prison and its staff to self-
abuse. By 1920, the hunger strike had eclipsed all other forms of
prison protest combined, as the following table shows:

NUMBER OF DISORDERLY ACTS REPORTED
IN IRISH PRISONS, 1919–20[47]

Type	Examples	1919	1920	Change, 1919–20
Disobedience	Singing, Shouting	534	58	−89%
Impersonal	Destruction of Cells	52	24	−54%
Personal	Assaults, Outbreaks	19	5	−74%
Self-Abuse	Hunger Strikes	289	439	+52%

By 1921, violence of all varieties was confined to a few prisons. As
with the IRA, the capacity of political prisoners to wage war was
curtailed over the months preceding the Truce of 11 July, mainly
by the prompt deportation of unruly prisoners to Britain.[48] This
practice expanded between 1918 and 1920, becoming the default
solution for the overcrowding that resulted from mass arrests and
internment.[49] Those at home kept close tabs on comrades deported
to British prisons, as did their captors. Art Ó Briain, an envoy in
London throughout the Anglo–Irish War, ensured through his correspondence with TDs that friends and relatives of prisoners were
informed of their situation.[50]

Far from halting outbreaks and hunger strikes within Irish
prisons, the Truce encouraged further protest by conveying the
impression that victory was imminent.[51] Requests for concessions

and special treatment, framed within the 'spirit of the Truce', were constantly submitted to prison governors, who sometimes relaxed discipline with often dire consequences. For instance, forty-four prisoners escaped from Kilkenny prison through a narrow tunnel on 22 November after weeks of unobserved preparation.[52] Despite significant police and military intervention throughout summer and autumn 1921, Irish prisons remained bastions of defiance.[53]

Although many prisoners were driven by republican ideals, group solidarity and militant leaders to commit violence, these factors did not ensure universal participation. Just as the Cork *émeute* of February 1919 was reaching its climax, Daniel Connell requested the restoration of his privileges and promised to conform to prison rules. Another Cork prisoner, John Conroy, also apologized for his misconduct.[54] In Dublin, M. J. Farrell told the governor of Mountjoy that, while not in favour of breaking up his cell, he had done so on 27 February as he 'had to fall-in with the others'.[55] Felix Connolly's tone was even more abject in a letter to Governor Munro of Cork prison, explaining his behaviour in early 1920:

> Well sir I apologise sincerely to His Majesty's Government for my conduct as I didn't understand it, and you may be sure if I went on strike it was completely against my will. ... [A]nd as I'm young in the world, if I was out of prison now I would be the most law-abiding citizen of His Majesty's Government.[56]

In other cases, communal and peer pressure may have induced men to participate in prison violence or hunger strikes against their conscience.

Acts of terror were nevertheless committed in abundance between 1919 and 1921, contributing to the physical and psychological breakdown of many prison staff. Chief Warder Moran was driven to insanity by the virtually incessant disruption at Belfast prison between June and December 1918, being committed to Richmond Lunatic Asylum. Requests for sick leave by Belfast's warders increased in this period, though this was presumably partly due to the outbreak of 'Spanish flu'.[57] Hitherto authoritative warders became noticeably 'nervy' or robotic. Chippendall reported in early 1919 that warders 'have become mere machines and report events in place of acting on their own initiative'.[58] Intimidation, compounded by overwork, was naturally a major factor in breaking the spirit of many prison officers. For instance, Warder J. Lyster was separately threatened by three DORA prisoners at Belfast in late March 1919:

> J. McMahon has threatened to assault me with an iron bar at first opportunity he can get. Prisoner McCarthy stated I was the means of putting on restrictions on them in their cells since I came here and that they would cut the bloody head off me. Prisoner Noonan threatened me by saying that if he could get out of his cell he would smash my big head that it was my fault for keeping them locked up.[59]

Threatening letters also reached Ireland's prisons, most often in connection with hunger strikes or outbreaks involving the restraint of prisoners. Some were quaintly addressed to the prison itself, pitting the author's grievance against the system represented by the faceless house of captivity. Other letters targeted specific officers, such as the chief warder of Mountjoy:

> Patrick J. Ryan. This is to give you notice that unless you resign from position as Warder of Mountjoy Prison within 14 days from this date your hour of judgement will have come. THIS IS FINAL. Failing your resignation, you will receive the just reward of your treatment of the Political Prisoners who were under your mercy. There will be no mercy for a dog like you – we shoot straight and sure! So clear out or prepare your soul. [signed] Vengeance.[60]

Medical officers attracted special attention from letter-writers, as they had authority to determine when a prisoner had reached the 'danger point' in a hunger strike, or whether he was fit for deportation or release under the 'Cat and Mouse Act'. In September 1920, amidst a lengthy and lethal hunger strike in Cork, the newly appointed medical officer received a peremptory communication purportedly from the Cork IRA:

> As your professional attendance upon the eleven hunger strikers in Cork Gaol gives a tinge of legality to the slow murder being perpetrated upon them, you are hereby ordered to leave the Gaol at once, and the country within 24 hours of this date – 3 o'clock p.m. Sept. 6th 1920. Failure to comply with this order will incur drastic punishment.[61]

Dr Alan Pearson hypothesized that this threat had been generated by the mistaken belief that he had failed to recommend the
release of the eleven hunger strikers.[62] He remained at Cork prison
until the end of the strike in early November, whereupon he hur-
riedly returned to England citing 'urgent private matters'.[63] Another
medical officer called to attend the Cork hunger strikers, D. J. Flynn,
refused to do his duty after learning of the IRA's threat to Pearson.[64]

Not all intimidation occurred within the prison, for warders
were increasingly intimidated and assaulted within their own communities. Warder John Comerford reported that as he and Thomas
Griffin were going off duty in early October 1920, they were
accosted by several men outside the gates of Cork prison. Griffin
was abducted while Comerford was held at bay by two men with
revolvers. 'During the evening,' Comerford stated, 'my house was
watched by three men who were parading up and down the foot-
path on the opposite side of the street. These three men wore fawn
or grey trench coats and were each about 22 to 24 years of age ...
and wore Trilby hats.'[65] In Dublin next spring, the medical officer
at Mountjoy reported that a mob of 'hooligans and guttersnipes'
had destroyed his garden, broken open his tool-house, smashed pictures and china within his home, and 'stole[n] and damaged every
scrap of property that could be stolen or damaged'. Dr B. J. Hackett
declared that the assault was the tenth instance in which his property
had been injured.[66] Like the police, prison officers were subjected to
communal ostracism. Two Cork warders requested increased pay
in the summer of 1920 to meet their rising costs of living as a result
of being rebuffed by local shopkeepers. On occasion, they had been
obliged to 'try a number of shops before they would be served and
then having to pay high rates'.[67] In and out of the prisons, the pro-
phetic words of Eoin MacNeill had been realized:

> In prison we are their jailers;
> On trial their judges,
> Persecuted their punishers,
> Dead their conquerors.[68]

Imprisonment tested both the bodies and minds of all who
endured it. Many Irishmen entered prison as mild dissidents,

incarcerated for minor infringements of the 'Defence of the Realm', only to be transformed into revolutionaries by their imprisonment. By 1919, the 'university of revolution', established at Frongoch in 1916, had incorporated several regional colleges. Imprisonment ultimately failed to restrict the expression of defiance against 'British' authority in the name of the Irish republic. These collective protests, coupled with a repressive and sometimes brutal environment, reinforced camaraderie among political prisoners. They destroyed cells, attacked warders, starved themselves, and otherwise irritated their minders, with extraordinary persistence and intensity. Prison violence may justly be categorized as a form of systematic and preconcerted terror against the 'British garrison' in Ireland. And, up to a point, it worked.

NOTES

1. Edward Shewell to Horatio J. Chippendall, 5 June 1920, NAD, GPB 1920/7224.

2. Seán McConville, *Irish Political Prisoners, 1848–1922: Theatres of War* (London 2003). Accounts illuminating the mentality of republican prisoners include Darrell Figgis, *A Second Chronicle of Jails* (Dublin 1919); Frank Gallagher, *Days of Fear* (London 1928); Brian O'Higgins, *The Soldier's Story of Easter Week; Poems of 1916; Prison Letters, 1917–20* (Dublin 1966); Íosold Ó Derig, '"Oh! Lord the unrest of the soul": the jail journal of Michael Collins', *Studia Hibernica*, 28 (1994), 7–34.

3. An Irish Priest, *In Maryboro' and Mountjoy: The Prison Experiences and Prison-Breaking of an Irish Volunteer (Padraic Fleming)* (no provenance, 1919), foreword.

4. 'Without Dáil Éireann there would, most likely, have been no sustained fight, with moral force behind it': Tom Barry, *Guerilla Days in Ireland* (Dublin 1989; 1st edn 1949), p. 11.

5. Extract from governor's report, Mountjoy prison, for 1917; evening guard report (Warder D. Finucane) and special night report (Warder R. Donohue), 22 Sept. 1917, GPB, DORA 1917–20, Box 1.

6. 'Examination of Raymond Dowdall', MO (Mountjoy), NLI, MS 31,734; Finian Lynch Papers, NLI, MS 33,008; 'Austin Stack's account of the forced-feeding of Thomas Ashe', NLI, MS 44,612; *Irish Nation*, 6 Oct. 1917.

7. 'Belfast prison: ill-treatment of republican prisoners, 1918', c. July 1918, NAD, DÉ 2/519; 'Ameliorations of prison treatment granted under

Rules of 29th September 1917 to prisoners sentenced for offences under DORA', 26 Feb. 1919, GPB 1919/1402; 'Rules for prisoners committed under the Defence of the Realm Act and Regulations', 8 Mar. 1918, GPB 1921/10909.

8. Prisoners (Temporary Discharge for Ill-health) Act, 1913, 3 Geo. V, c. 4 (25 Apr. 1913).

9. Colin Campbell, *Emergency Law in Ireland, 1918–1925* (Oxford 1994), esp. pp. 8–38.

10. B. Rudden to P. J. Brady, 18 Oct. 1918, GPB DORA 1917–20, Box 7.

11. 'Lists of prisoners awaiting removal to Belfast prison', 20 Sept., 8, 15 Oct. 1918, GPB 1918/8339.

12. James Talty to John Joe, *c.* 1918, GPB DORA 1917–20, Box 7 (1918/4611).

13. 'Return of the number of political prisoners in custody at lock-up on each day of the period of twelve months ended on 30 April 1919', submitted by William Barrows, governor of Belfast prison, 26 May 1919, GPB 1919/3991.

14. Kevin O'Higgins to his mother, 21 Aug. 1918, GPB DORA 1917–20, Box 7 (1918/5359).

15. Austin Stack, 'Belfast prison: ill-treatment of republican prisoners, 1918', undated, NAD, DÉ 2/519.

16. Statement of Kevin O'Higgins, 30 July 1918, DÉ 2/519.

17. Statements (undated) of John Gascoygne, Patrick McCarthy, DÉ 2/519.

18. Statement (undated) of John McKenna, DÉ 2/519.

19. Acording to Padraig Ó Cirgeareaig, 'Decreases in weight' (covering 31 July–*c.* Sept. 1918), the mean loss of weight was 14.78 lb.: NAD, DÉ 2/519. Austin Stack deemed it the government's responsibility to feed its prisoners, while others were willing to live off the food parcels sent in from friends. A majority of prisoners voted in favour of receiving parcels. See Michael Brennan and Austin Stack, correspondence, 10–11 Aug. 1918, NAD, DÉ 2/519; Michael Leahy, MAD, BMH, WS 1421.

20. 'Existing conditions at Belfast prison', 31 Dec. 1918, GPB 1919/46; anon. to J. W. Reid, 1 Nov. 1918, GPB DORA 1917–20, Box 7 (1918/6972); 'Outbreak of influenza October 1918, notation of papers received', GPB 1918/8338; Ernest Blythe, WS 939.

21. J. McCree to his parents, *c.* 28 Nov. 1918, GPB DORA 1917–20, Box 7 (1918/7435).

22. Timothy Brestone to Michael O'Donnell, 9 Dec. 1918, GPB DORA 1917–20, Box 7; *Irish Independent*, 30 Dec. 1918.

23. Max Green to MacMahon, 30 Dec. 1918, GPB DORA 1917–20, Box 8 (1919/138).

24. Barrows to Max Green, 24 Dec. 1918, GPB 1918/8192; statement of H. J. Chippendall, 9 Jan. 1919, GPB 1919/268.

25. Extract from Visiting Justices, Minute Book (29 Dec. 1918), GPB 1919/8251.

26. Telephone message, Barrows to Green, 27 Dec. 1918, GPB 1919/8227.

27. John Hassett to unknown, 3 Jan. 1919, GPB DORA 1917–20, Box 7 (1919/163).

28. Horatio J. Chippendall, 'Statement of occurrences in the prison recently', 4 Jan. 1919, GPB 1919/164.

29. MacMahon to French, 13 Jan. 1919, GPB 1919/382.

30. 'Outbreak of DORA prisoners', undated, GPB 1919/115.

31. Chippendall to Green, 2, 4 Jan. 1919, GPB 1919/133, 164.

32. Green to MacMahon, c. Jan. 1919, GPB 1919/115.

33. Green to MacMahon, 18 Dec. 1918, GPB (number lost); Green to MacMahon, c. Jan. 1919, GPB 1919/115; Green to MacMahon, 15 Jan. 1919, GPB 1919/382; W. E. Montgomery, 'Report for the year 1919, of the committee of visiting justices of H.M. prison Belfast', 7 Jan. 1920, GPB 1920/296.

34. L. J. Blake to Green, 29 Jan. 1919, GPB DORA 1917–20, Box 7 (1919/826).

35. 'Oglach na h-Éireann, special general orders, G.H.Q., Dublin', 13 Jan. 1919, GPB DORA 1917–20, Box 7 (1919/2026).

36. King to Green, 3 Feb. 1919, GPB 1919/1037.

37. *II*, 3, 6, 10, 14 Feb. 1919.

38. Extract from Flynn, MO, Journal, 17 Feb. 1919, GPB 1919/1464.

39. J. King to Green, 17 Feb. 1919, GPB 1919/1464.

40. Philip Lennon to King, 13 May 1919, GPB 1919/3780.

41. Munro to Green, 6 Oct. 1919, GPB 1919/7074.

42. 'List of DORA prisoners concerned in the organised outbreak of cell-wrecking on nights of 5th–6th October, 1919', GPB 1919/7139.

43. Munro to Green, 6 Oct. 1919, GPB 1919/7139.

44. *Ibid.*; [W.A. Cooke], 'Extract from medical officer's journal', 7 Oct. 1919, GPB 1919/7074.

45. Barrows to Green, 7 Mar. 1919, GPB 1919/1961.

46. Barrows to Green, 31 Mar. 1919, GPB 1919/2611.

47. Data compiled from GPB files, supplemented by documents in MAD and NAD, government publications and newspapers.

48. 'List of 40 convicted prisoners recommended for removal to England from Mountjoy prison', 27 Apr. 1921, GPB 1921/3386; 'Removal of prisoners to England', 10 May 1921, GPB 1921/3635; 'List of convicts for removal', 26 May 1921, GPB 1921/4078.

49. 'Weekly summary of arrests, courts martial and convictions, 7 Aug. 1920–1 Jan. 1921', MAD, Collins Papers, A/0410, Group VIII.

50. Ó Briain, correspondence with both British and Irish officials (particularly Collins), NAD, DÉ 2/453, 135; NAL, HO 144/1496/362269.

51. Governor, Waterford prison, to Green, 9 Oct. 1921, GPB 1921/8119 (with 8184); Waterford, GPB 1921/9824; Galway, GPB 1921/9785; Mountjoy, GPB 1921/9287; Limerick, GPB 1921/3516, 3437.

52. 'Sworn inquiry into escapes at Kilkenny on 22 Nov. 1921', in Green to MacMahon, 20 Dec. 1921, GPB 1921/9687.

53. 'Strength of police and military at various Irish prisons, 1921', GPB 1921/3727.

54. GPB 1919/1747, 2819.

55. Munro to Green, 28 Feb. 1919, GPB 1919/1751.

56. Felix Connolly to Munro, 26 Jan. 1920, GPB 1920/652 (with 987).

57. Green to MacMahon, 18 Dec. 1918, GPB 1919 (number lost).

58. Chippendall to Green, 2 Jan. 1919, GPB 1919/133; cf. 'Extract from MO's journal', 14 May 1920, GPB 1920/4410; Chippendall to Green, 29 Dec. 1920, GPB 1920/9573.

59. J. Lyster to Barrows, 26 Mar. 1919; Barrows to Green, 27, 31 Mar. 1919, GPB 1919/2523, 2611.

60. 'Threatening letter received by Chief Warder Ryan', 25 Aug. 1920, GPB 1920/7075.

61. OC, Cork no. 1 Brigade, IRA, to Alan Pearson, 6 Sept. 1920, GPB 1920/7486.

62. MO's reports, 4, 9 Sept., 16 Nov. 1920, GPB 1920/7441, 7615, 10,276.

63. MO's report, 16 Nov. 1920, GPB 1920/10276.

64. D. J. Flynn to J. King, 6 Sept. 1920, GPB 1920/7491.

65. 'Warder Comerford's report', 11 Oct. 1920, GPB 1920/8709.

66. B. J. Hackett to Munro, 15 Mar. 1921, GPB 1921/2303.

67. [Chippendall], 'Extract from inspector's report', 19 July 1920, GPB 1920/5979.

68. Quoted in Tim Pat Coogan, *Michael Collins: A Biography* (London 1990), p. 156.

14. Republican Terrorism in Britain, 1920–1923

Gerard Noonan

The beginning of the War of Independence is usually traced to
21 January 1919, when members of the Tipperary IRA killed two
RIC men near the village of Soloheadbeg. However, it was only
in the following year that the Volunteers' campaign of terrorism
against British rule in Ireland began in earnest. In November 1920,
that campaign was extended to Britain with attacks in Liverpool.
Over the subsequent seven and a half months preceding the Truce
of July 1921, reports of 'Sinn Fein Outrages', as they were termed,
became regular features of British newspapers. Throughout Britain,
farms suffered arson attacks; railway, telegraph and telephone net-
works were disrupted; and relatives of soldiers and policemen were
terrorized. As one Volunteer declared in April 1921, while firing
shots over the heads of workers in a Manchester café as a comrade
sprinkled the premises with paraffin: 'We are doing this because you
are doing it in Ireland.'[1] The campaign in Britain did not resume
after the Truce, though the anti-Treaty IRA planned further attacks
during the Civil War until thwarted by mass arrests.

The activities of Irish republicans in Britain in the nineteenth
and late twentieth centuries have been the subject of significant
scholarly attention. In contrast, very little has been written on the
activities of the IRA there during the War of Independence and Civil
War. The most significant publication is a 37-page article by the
late Peter Hart entitled 'Operations abroad: the I.R.A. in Britain',
first published in the *English Historical Review* in 2000. 'Man for
man, and operation for operation,' noted Hart, 'the Liverpool,
Manchester, Tyneside, and London I.R.A. outperformed many Irish

brigades.'[2] In an article published in 1993, however, Iain Patterson had demonstrated that in Scotland IRA terrorist attacks were 'isolated and infrequent', dubiously inferring that republicans in Scotland (and by implication in England and Wales) made only a 'slight' contribution to the IRA's campaign.[3] In my opinion, this assessment is unduly dismissive of the restricted but essential rôle of activists in Britain, as defined by Michael Collins in June 1921: 'in a manner of speaking, our people in England are only the auxiliaries of our attacking forces'.[4] Through an examination of the character and impact of republican violence in Britain, I hope to show that republicans in Britain made a significant contribution to the struggle for Irish freedom.[5]

On 9 March 1921, a meeting of the Liverpool City company of the IRA took place. Hugh Early, OC, ordered his men to set fire to farms in the Little Crosby area. Two targets had been chosen at opposite sides of a country lane, Whitehouse Farm and Hill Farm.[6] As Paddy Daly, a Liverpool gun-runner, told his IRB superior Michael Collins: 'We are having some farm-work to-night, just to keep the local coy in practice.'[7] When he and his comrades reached the laneway, Volunteer John Pinkman asked if the farms they were about to attack were equidistant from the road, for, if they were not, the fire at the farm closer to the lane would illuminate the men on their way to the second farm, possibly alerting passers-by to their presence. He was assured that the farms were equidistant from the road. The IRA men then divided into two groups and set off to burn down hay barns and any other targets they could find. As Pinkman and his accomplices neared their target, however, a Volunteer from the second group ran across their path. They then found themselves up against a fence when flames from a fire at the second farm illuminated the sky. Pinkman's concern had proved prescient.

Panicking, they ran about frantically trying to escape. As they ran in the direction of the train station, they noticed people on the foot bridge. By now the two farms were on fire, sparks from the first having blown across the road and started a second conflagration. Convinced that they had been spotted, the men dived into a hollow in the ground beside a ditch. There, they debated what to do. Unable to run across the electric railway lines, the four decided to rush across the foot-bridge. Pinkman threw away his revolver, confident that its use would result in his comrades and himself being 'slaughtered'. With Pinkman in front, they made an attempt to cross the bridge but were apprehended by commuters.[8] 'I hope our next move will have more effective results and come off very shortly,' wrote Paddy Daly, reflecting on the arrest of six Volunteers of whom one had been shot by a sharp-eyed farmer.[9]

Republican terrorism in Britain was motivated partly by desire for revenge. In the summer of 1920, Ernie O'Malley, an IRA organizer, attended a meeting in Dublin of GHQ staff and senior Volunteer commanders from around Ireland. The country officers, he remembered, 'pressed for a campaign in England to counteract the destruction of creameries and houses by the military and police'.[10] When George Fitzgerald, an intelligence officer connected with GHQ, was sent to London to mount terrorist operations, he was told by Collins that such attacks were 'by way of reprisals for burnings that were carried out at home by the Military and the Black and Tans'.[11] There also existed a related desire to force the British people to confront and acknowledge the violence being perpetrated in their name across the Irish Sea. According to Paddy O'Donoghue, OC Manchester, the overall aim of the Volunteers' terrorist campaign was 'to bring home to the British people the sufferings and conditions to which the Irish people were being subjected by their police and soldiers'.[12] A terrorist campaign in Britain would allow the IRA to wreak revenge for the activities of Crown forces in Ireland, in the hope that a frightened or enlightened British public would put pressure on the government to rethink its Irish policy.

The campaign was to be mounted by the IRA in Britain, a force that, like its sister organization in Ireland, traced its genesis to the Home Rule crisis of 1912–14. By September 1914, the Irish Volunteer organization had spread throughout Britain, its membership consisting mainly of men born to Irish immigrants.[13] Eighteen months later, an estimated 200 republicans travelled from Britain to Dublin to fight in the Easter Rising, seven being killed.[14] In early 1919, GHQ sent Joseph Vize to reorganize the Volunteers in Scotland. Later that year, reorganization commenced in London and Manchester. Branches of the IRB, Cumann na mBan and Na Fianna

Éireann were also established.[15] Rory O'Connor was appointed as
OC Britain in August 1920, three months before the terrorist campaign began. By autumn 1921, the organization in England encom-
passed Liverpool, London, Manchester, Tyneside, Birmingham,
Sheffield and other districts, comprising thirty-one companies with
a combined membership of 682. This modest force was dwarfed by
the Scottish Brigade, consisting of five battalions with an estimated
membership of 2000.[16] At its peak, therefore, the IRA in Britain had
around 2500 members. The IRA in Britain was 'a very rare phenom-
enon', as Hart noted: 'a guerrilla movement arising from an immi-
grant population as part of a struggle against the host country's
rule of their "native" land'.[17] Prior to the commencement of the
terrorist campaign, the main activity of republicans in Britain was
gun-running: the acquisition and smuggling into Ireland of munitions for use by the IRA.[18] Gun-running continued in parallel to the
terrorist campaign and was accorded greater importance by GHQ.

The planning of terrorist operations in Britain from November
1920 onwards was undertaken by IRA officers in Britain and
members of Rory O'Connor's staff visiting from Dublin. From the
beginning, GHQ set down the parameters of the campaign. Firstly,
O'Connor was instructed to confine operations to England. No
outrages were to be mounted in Scotland or Wales. This was motivated by a romantic belief that the Scots and Welsh were fellow
'Celts' suffering tyranny at the hands of the Anglo-Saxon English.
Disregarding GHQ's ruling, the Volunteers in Scotland mounted ten
attacks during the War of Independence, one of which caused the
death of a policeman. Secondly, in mounting attacks every effort
was to be made to minimize civilian casualties. Moreover, unemployment amongst the Irish section of the population was to be
avoided as much as possible. Therefore, attacks on large enterprises,
such as factories and mines, were effectively prohibited.[19]

The IRA's terrorist campaign in Britain began on 27 November
1920 with arson attacks against warehouses on the Liverpool docks.
It ended on 10 July 1921, when furze and fern were set on fire on
Ham Common in London. In total, the police suspected or attributed
Irish political motives to 235 incidents (or attempted incidents) of
terrorism in Britain during this period. Lancashire saw 97 incidents

(41.3% of the total), metropolitan London 46 (19.6%), Durham 30
(12.8%), Northumberland 19 (8.1%), Cheshire 15 (6.4%), Kent 9
(3.8%), Yorkshire North Riding 6 (2.6%), Warwickshire 2, both in
Birmingham (0.9%), and Essex 1 (0.4%). Convictions were secured
in relation to only 57 (24.3%) of these 235 incidents.[20]

What explains the regional variation in the frequency of
attacks? Differences in the level of militancy of IRA units was an
important factor. In a tour of Volunteer units in autumn 1921,
Rory O'Connor sought to ascertain the 'military outlook' of the
officers, in the expectation that terrorist attacks would soon recom-
mence should the peace negotiations collapse. He was particularly
unimpressed by the officers in Birmingham, who lacked all initiative. His frustration was compounded by the fact that, being a great
manufacturing centre, Birmingham would have been an 'excellent'
place for mounting operations.[21] Historians of the IRA in Ireland
have emphasized the importance of local leadership in the willingness of Volunteer companies to fight. Leadership was the 'decisive
factor' in determining the level of IRA activity in Co. Limerick, for
example. 'The units that did most of the fighting were, quite simply,
the units that chose to create the opportunities to fight', argues
O'Callaghan.[22] The same applied to the IRA in Britain.

Of the 235 incidents, 48.1% involved arson attacks on farms,
in which haystacks, barns, and machinery were destroyed or
damaged. Attacks on communications, such as telephone and telegraph wires and poles, along with railway signal boxes, accounted
for 18.3% of incidents. Warehouses constituted another 12.8% of
targets attacked, factories 6.8%, dwellings of RIC men and their
relatives 3.8%, and timber-yards 3.8%. Miscellaneous targets
(6.4%) included a labour exchange and Ministry of Pensions huts in
London, three hotels and some park chairs in Manchester, an aero-
drome in Newcastle-upon-Tyne, a spy in London, a prison-van in
Glasgow, and the theft of money from a railway worker in Mount
Vernon, Scotland.

Farms were probably chosen as targets because of the relative
ease of setting fire to a haystack and making a successful getaway.
Following the failure of a group of London Volunteers to set fire to
an urban warehouse, George Fitzgerald instructed them to mount

attacks on farms as a means of building up their self-confidence.[23] Rory O'Connor described attacks on farms as one of a number of 'minor operations' that Volunteers in Britain were capable of mounting despite their lack of training.[24] Attacks on communications and railway infrastructure were viable for similar reasons. As the campaign proceeded, attacks on warehouses and timber yards declined, while those on farms, communications and railways increased significantly. These latter targets were easier to attack, requiring less planning and preparation. Paddy Daly claimed that, with no recourse to 'technical or scientific laboratories', Volunteers were perforce restricted to arson attacks on farms and hotels. He conceded that a critic might dismiss such operations as 'pin pricks', yet, equipped as it was, the IRA 'could not have done more'.[25]

There was wild fluctuation in the number of attacks mounted in each month between November 1920 and July 1921, ranging from sixty-two in March 1921 to two in the following July. Much of this variation is attributable to the police. The arson attacks on warehouses in November 1920 precipitated a major response by the Merseyside police and their colleagues in London and Glasgow. A number of Volunteers, including OC Tom Kerr, were arrested in Liverpool. Decapitated and under close police surveillance, the Liverpool IRA spent the subsequent few months lying 'quiet, very quiet'.[26] The arrest of a significant number of IRA men following arson attacks in the city centre on 2 April 1921 had a similar effect on Volunteer operations in Manchester.[27] Yet Rory O'Connor, reflecting on the campaign up to the end of May 1921, judged it to have been 'fairly successful', as 90% of attempted operations had been accomplished.[28]

According to the police, IRA terrorism in the period 27 November 1920–11 July 1921 inflicted damage to the value of £674,002 5s. 11d. Incidents in Lancashire accounted for 87% of this amount, Durham 6%, Northumberland 2.3% and London 1.9%. These disparities are partly explained by the choice of targets in each area. Warehouses constituted a far higher proportion of targets in Lancashire than elsewhere in Britain. Twenty-nine of the thirty IRA attacks on warehouses in Britain took place there, the resultant damage being valued at £501,589 7s. 7d. All nine attacks on British timber-yards were conducted in Lancashire, causing damage amounting to £79,099 10s. 1d. Lancashire also accounted for half of the £17,492 6s. 2d. worth of damage caused by the IRA's sixteen attacks on factories in Britain. On the other hand, Lancashire witnessed only 21 of the 113 attacks on farms in Britain that in total caused damage valued at £63,581 9s. 6d. The most expensive attacks were those on warehouses, followed (in descending order) by attacks on timber-yards, factories and farms. No less than £497,608 17s. 6d. (73.8%) of the total damage was attributable to the first episode of the campaign, when twenty-four warehouses in Liverpool and Bootle were gutted on 27 November 1920.[29] In 1925, the government of the Irish Free State agreed to pay compensation of £500,000, 'on account of damage done by Irish agency in Great Britain' between November 1920 and July 1921.[30]

The most famous terrorist attack mounted by the IRA in Britain occurred nearly a year after the 'cessation of hostilities'. On 22 June 1922, Sir Henry Wilson, a unionist MP born in Co. Longford, was assassinated by Reginald Dunne and Joseph O'Sullivan, London Volunteers who probably acted on their own initiative. Recently retired as Chief of the Imperial General Staff, the most senior professional office in the British army, Wilson had become military adviser to the government of Northern Ireland. As such, Dunne (OC London) held him responsible for the violence that Ulster Catholics were experiencing at the hands of Protestant mobs. Dunne also hoped unavailingly that the assassination would provoke the British into revoking the Treaty and renewing its war against the IRA. The Irish, divided over the merits of the Treaty, would then reunite in the face of the common enemy.[31]

During the Civil War, the anti-Treaty IRA made plans for further terrorist attacks in Britain. Liam Lynch, CS, stated that 'action' in Britain should take the form of 'a war on Political-leaders, and their leading Soldiers'. He also contemplated 'the carrying out of destructive operations in Cities'.[32] However, the anti-Treaty IRA in Britain numbered only about 430 and suffered organizational problems.[33] On 7 March 1923, Lynch's GHQ issued an order to the OC Britain 'to have operations carried out at once'.[34] Four days later, however, 110 IRA members and other republicans were arrested by the police in Britain at the request of the Free State authorities and deported to Ireland for internment.[35] These arrests paralysed the Volunteers in Britain for the remainder of the Civil War and prevented the mounting of a terrorist campaign.

What was the impact of these acts of terrorism? The most immediate effect, of course, was the resultant fatalities. Apart from Wilson, five people were killed in IRA attacks. William Ward, a civilian, suffered a fatal wound while attempting to assist the police in capturing IRA arsonists in Liverpool on 27 November 1920.[36] In April 1921, Vincent Fouvargue was executed in London as a spy.[37] Next month, Glasgow Volunteers shot dead a policeman (Robert Johnston) while attempting to rescue a Sligo comrade from police custody.[38] Two weeks later, Horace MacNeill was shot by a group of Volunteers in search of his son-in-law, a member of the RIC.[39] Thomas Lovelady, a clerk, was killed in a post office raid in June 1923 in what seems to have been an attempt by two IRA men to acquire money for the dependents of their imprisoned comrades in Ireland.[40] In addition, a fireman died in March 1921 when his engine overturned while returning from tackling an IRA arson attack on a farm.[41] Furthermore, a night-watchman named John Duffy committed suicide attributed to nervousness arising from an incident in February 1921, when he was held at gunpoint while his workplace was set alight.[42] The IRA itself suffered three fatalities as a result of its terrorist operations. John Morgan was killed at the Irish Club in Hulme, Manchester, on 2 April 1921, when a shoot-out occurred between Volunteers and police investigating arson attacks committed earlier that day.[43] The other fatalities were Dunne and O'Sullivan, executed in August 1922 for the assassination of Sir Henry Wilson.[44] Many Volunteers, civilians, and policemen also sustained injuries in terrorist incidents.

An indirect victim of the terrorist campaign in Britain was the IRA in Ireland, for attacks usually precipitated a police response that in turn interfered with gun-smuggling. In the aftermath of the Liverpool arson attacks on 27 November 1920, the police raided many houses of well-known Irish nationalists. With the arrest of Neil Kerr the elder, his son Tom, and Steve Lanigan, the Merseyside gun-running organization lost its leadership. Collins was much irritated by

the resultant suspension of activity, depriving the Volunteers across
the Irish Sea of much-needed armaments. After little more than
a week, however, Paddy Daly stepped into Neil Kerr's shoes and
munitions smuggling was resumed.[45] Increased police vigilance in
the wake of the Liverpool attacks also led to the arrest of two senior
Scottish gun-runners in Alloa. This contributed to the confusion
that engulfed gun-running operations north of the border in late
1920 and early 1921. The problem was compounded five months
later by police reaction to the shooting of a policeman during the
attempted rescue of Frank Carty from a prison van in Glasgow.[46]

It is difficult to assess the influence of IRA terrorism in Britain
in prompting the British government to negotiate the Truce of July
1921 or the Treaty that followed five months later. No British minister admitted that the campaign in Britain had been a factor. Seán Ó
Murthuile, secretary of the IRB's Supreme Council, believed that the
campaign 'had the effect of concentrating the average Englishman's
attention of what was being done in Ireland in his name'. He was
doubtful, however, if the public, thus enlightened, actually affected
the government's Irish policy.[47] Yet the terrorist threat to British
civilians, and the resultant need for tighter security to protect min-
isters, must have heightened ministerial awareness of the dangerous
implications of their Irish policy. As Paddy Daly later noted, the
campaign was at least 'a thorn in the side of the authorities'.[48] The
subsequent assassination of Sir Henry Wilson had an unmistakable
consequence for British policy and Irish history. Convinced that this
was the work of anti-Treaty republicans, the British government
pressurized the Provisional Government into dealing with the garrison holed up in the Four Courts.[49] Contrary to the intention of its
perpetrators, therefore, Wilson's assassination precipitated rather
than averting the outbreak of Civil War on 28 June 1922.

How did the IRA's terrorist campaign in Britain compare with
that in Ireland? Augusteijn argues that two factors were critical in
enabling the Volunteers in Ireland to wage bloody guerrilla warfare.
The first was the growing alienation of the community from the
forces of 'law and order', while the second was the separation of IRA
men from the restraining influence of that community. By removing
Volunteers from the influence of neighbours and friends, the crea-

tion of active service units or flying columns enabled them to overcome the social and psychological barriers that normally prohibited
the killing of policemen and soldiers.[50] The upsurge in the number
of RIC men killed by the IRA in Ireland coincided with the creation
of flying columns.[51]

While the IRA in Ireland had the support of a large alienated
populace and a network of flying columns, their comrades in Britain
had a much smaller support base and lacked flying columns. Did
the absence of flying columns in the British IRA account for its
failure to fight a terrorist campaign similar to that in Ireland? Did
the communities in which they resided constrain the Volunteers in
the type and intensity of operations they could mount? While this
was certainly the case in Ireland, where operations were sometimes
modified to avoid inconveniencing the populace, this was apparently not the case in Britain.[52] The sources at our disposal do not
indicate any attempts by friends or neighbours, whether British or
fellow-Irish, to inhibit the terrorist campaign. The only constraints
imposed were those set down by GHQ. In contrast to the IRA in
Ireland, therefore, the Volunteers in Britain seem to have operated
free from communal influences.

That this did not lead to an even more concerted campaign by the
IRA in Britain than in Ireland must be ascribed to their contrasting
rationales. For the Volunteers in Ireland, attacking policemen and
soldiers – the personification of foreign rule – was an end in itself.
The Volunteers in Britain, living in an alien environment and defi-
cient in membership and popular support, existed only to assist
the IRA in Ireland. For them to have engaged in similar attacks
on policemen and soldiers in Britain would have been foolhardy,
probably provoking mass arrests and leading to the collapse of the
republican movement. This, in turn, would have further disrupted
gun-running, the most important service provided by republicans in
Britain throughout the revolutionary period. Terror, therefore, was
a tool that the IRA in Britain could not afford to over-use.

NOTES

1. *The Observer*, 3 Apr. 1921.

2. Peter Hart, *The I.R.A. at War, 1916–1923* (Oxford 2003), pp. 141–77 (141).

3. Iain D. Patterson, 'The activities of Irish republican physical force organisations in Scotland, 1919–21', *Scottish Historical Review*, 72, no. 1 (1993), 39–59 (46).

4. Michael Collins to Art O'Brien, 6 June 1921, NAD, DE 2/330.

5. I would like to thank TCD and Limerick County Council for funding the research for the doctoral thesis on which this essay is based: Gerard Noonan, 'Irish physical-force republicanism in Britain, 1919–1923' (PH.D. thesis, TCD 2011).

6. John A. Pinkman, *In the Legion of the Vanguard*, ed. Francis E. Maguire (Dublin 1998), pp. 48–50.

7. Paddy Daly to Michael Collins, 9 Mar. 1921, UCDA, Richard Mulcahy Papers, P7/A/4.

8. Pinkman, *Legion*, pp. 48–54.

9. Paddy Daly to Michael Collins, 11 Mar. 1921, Mulcahy Papers, P7/A/4; *The Times*, 10, 11 Mar. 1921; CC, Cheshire to USS, HO, 20 Oct. 1922 and Ass. CC, Lancashire to USS, HO, 27 Oct. 1922, HO 144/4645.

10. Ernie O'Malley, *On Another Man's Wound* (Dublin 2002; 1st edn 1936), p. 188.

11. George Fitzgerald, MAD, BMH Papers, WS 684, p. 28.

12. Patrick O'Donoghue, WS 847, p. 11.

13. *Irish Volunteer*, 14, 21 Feb., 7, 28 Mar., 4, 18, 25 Apr., 2, 9, 16, 30 May, 6, 13, 20, 27 June, 4, 11, 18, 25 July, 1, 8, 15, 22, 29 Aug., 5, 12 Sept. 1914.

14. Frank Thornton, WS 510, pp. 1–10; Joe Good, *Enchanted by Dreams: The Journal of a Revolutionary*, ed. Maurice Good (Dingle 1996), pp. 13–17; Art Ó Bríain, 'Gaedhil thar sáile: some notes on the history of the Gaelic League of London', *Capuchin Annual*, 14 (1944), 126; Máirtín Seán Ó Catháin, 'A land beyond the sea: Irish and Scottish republicans in Dublin, 1916' in Ruan O'Donnell (ed.), *The Impact of the 1916 Rising: Among the Nations* (Dublin 2008), pp. 38, 45–6.

15. Noonan, 'Irish physical-force republicanism in Britain', ch. 2.

16. OC Britain to CS, 9 Sept. 1921, Mulcahy Papers, P7/A/24 [63–5]; John Carney to CS, 22 Feb. 1922, NLI, Sean O'Mahoney Papers, MS 24,474; S. Fullerton to Minister for Defence, 31 Aug., 6 Sept. 1922, MAD, Michael Collins Papers, A/06181.

17. Hart, 'Operations abroad', p. 177.

18. Noonan, 'Irish physical-force republicanism in Britain', ch. 3.